JONATHAN EDWARDS

The Jonathan Edwards Classic Studies Series

The Jonathan Edwards Center at Yale University is pleased to offer this volume, in grateful cooperation with Wipf & Stock Publishers, as part of its mission to encourage ongoing research into and readership of one of America's most original thinkers and one of its most significant historical and cultural figures. As much as the Edwards Center is devoted to presenting Edwards's own writings in a comprehensive and authoritative online format, we also see providing secondary resources as vital to supporting an ongoing understanding of Edwards's extensive and varied corpus, which can be accessed at http://edwards.yale.edu.

    Writings about Edwards's life, thought, and legacy continue to accumulate from authors representing a broad range of disciplines and agendas. Within the voluminous secondary literature, the Edwards Center recognizes the importance of insuring that certain key works—which sadly have gone out of print but yet remain in demand—are available for new generations coming to the study of Edwards and are recognized for their worth. These monographs represent some of the very best and most pioneering studies of Edwards, his times, and his influence, from scholars over the past half century and more. Indeed, these works not only greatly influenced the study of Edwards but American history in general. We hope these landmark studies, ranging from biography to intellectual and social history to philosophy and theology, continue to be sources of inquiry and inspiration for decades to come.

Harry S. Stout
Director
The Jonathan Edwards Center
Yale University

Jonathan Edwards Classic Studies Series

The Young Jonathan Edwards
by William Sparkes Morris
With a new foreword by Kenneth Minkema

Jonathan Edwards, Pastor
by Patricia Tracy
With a new preface by the author

Jonathan Edwards's Moral Thought and Its British Context
by Norman Fiering
With a new foreword by Oliver Crisp

Beauty and Sensibility in the Thought of Jonathan Edwards
by Roland A. Delattre
With a new foreword by Michael McClenahan

Religion and the American Mind
by Alan Heimert
With a new foreword by Andrew Delbanco

Samuel Hopkins and the New Divinity Movement
by Joseph A. Conforti
With a new foreword by Douglas Sweeney

Edwards on the Will: A Century of Anglican Theological Debate
by Allen C. Guelzo
With a new preface/acknowledgements by the author

Jonathan Edwards: The First Critical Biography, 1889
by Alexander V. G. Allen
With a new foreword by M. X. Lesser

Future volumes are forthcoming. For current updates see http://edwards.yale.edu.

JONATHAN EDWARDS

BY

ALEXANDER V. G. ALLEN, D. D.

PROFESSOR IN THE EPISCOPAL THEOLOGICAL SCHOOL, IN CAMBRIDGE, MASS.

WIPF & STOCK · Eugene, Oregon

Wipf and Stock Publishers
199 W 8th Ave, Suite 3
Eugene, OR 97401

Jonathan Edwards
The First Critical Biography, 1889
By Allen, Alexander V. G.
ISBN 13: 978-1-55635-716-9
ISBN 10: 1-55635-716-8
Publication date 11/9/2007
Previously published by Houghton Mifflin, 1889

Foreword to the 2007 Edition

At the unveiling of a memorial on the sesquicentennial of Jonathan Edwards's dismissal, Alexander Viets Griswold Allen (1841–1908) in "The Place of Edwards in History" spoke of "the deepest affinity" between Edwards and Dante—their idealized women and their idealized worlds; their intellectual, poetic imaginations; their banishments and exiles—such that *Divine and Supernatural Light, Distinguishing Marks*, and *Religious Affections* are likened in "spirit and purpose" to the *Divine Comedy*, not the *Institutes* of Calvin. Eleven years earlier, in the first book-length study of his thought—part of the American Religious Leaders series published by Houghton Mifflin and reprinted four times before 1900—Allen isolates Edwards's God-consciousness as the one "imperishable element" amid the "false premises" and "negative side" of his discarded theology, his dogged belief in the doctrines of divine sovereignty and original sin.

Though Allen insists that his study of the "father of modern Congregationalism" and the "greatest preacher of his age" is "not . . . devoid of sympathy," he characterizes Edwards's style as "thinking aloud," much as earlier critics had, but goes further, dismissing the speculative thought of his last phase—*Freedom of the Will, Original Sin, True Virtue*, and *End of Creation*—as an exercise "in confusion, if not failure" and his work on the Trinity, however modern it appears "weakened, if not neutralized" by his lack of interest in the humanity of Christ. Indeed, for Allen that is the central problem: "The great wrong which Edwards did, which haunts us as an evil dream throughout his writings, was to assert God at the expense of humanity."

That Allen was an ordained priest and, at the time, a professor of church history at the Episcopal Theological School in Cambridge for twenty years was enough apparently for some readers to find him ill-suited to deal fairly with Edwards since, as one held, he was "violently and even bitterly" opposed to his theology. To others, Allen seemed "too apologetic" and not critical enough of a theology that was "mistaken" and "a thing of the past." Such partisans hovered at the edges of the general response, most readers endorsing Allen's "stimulating and fascinating" book, "a foundation study in New England theology," fit to stand alongside his earlier books—*The Theological Renaissance of the Nineteenth Century* (1880) and *The Continuity of Christian Thought* (1884)—and in time, perhaps, his later ones—*Religious Progress* (1894), *The Message of Christ to Manhood* (1899), *Life and Letters of Phillips Brooks* (1901), *The Catholic Church and the Modern Sense of Nationality* (1904), and *Freedom in the Church* (1907). Anticipating Yale by more than half a century, an editorial in the *New York Times* for June 11, 1900, called for a new edition of the mystical and saintly Edwards, if only as "a matter of patriotism."

As was often the case at the close of the nineteenth century, the mystical Edwards was the valuable Edwards, and so he remained until well into the twentieth. His theology still a "blight upon posterity," Henry Bamford Parks forgoes the mystic Edwards of Allen for *Jonathan Edwards: The Fiery Puritan* (1930); two years later, Arthur Cushman McGiffert's study restores Edwards's "critical mysticism" though somewhat altered by his "modern-mindedness." By 1949, Perry Miller, in a presentation of the "drama of his ideas," renders an Edwards "intellectually the most modern man of his age," a speculative philosopher "infinitely more" than a theologian, a "major" artist rather, a psychologist and a poet in the native tradition. And now, at the turn of another century, with little poetry left in Edwards and even less mysticism, it may be useful, if not necessary, to turn again to Alexander V. G. Allen.

—M. X. Lesser
Northeastern University
November 2007

THE edition of Edwards' works to which references are made is known as the Worcester edition, in four volumes, published in New York in 1847. I have drawn freely from his Life by Dr. S. E. Dwight published in 1830. Valuable as this work is, it does not constitute an adequate biography. Much that would throw light upon Edwards' history is withheld from publication. It is greatly to be regretted also that there is no complete edition of his works. But in the method which I have followed I have not lacked for abundance of material. I have endeavored to reproduce Edwards from his books, making his treatises, in their chronological order, contribute to his portraiture as a man and as a theologian, a task which has not been heretofore attempted. I have thought that something more than a mere recountal of facts was demanded in order to justify the endeavor to rewrite his life. What we most desire to know is, what he thought and how he came to think as he did. The aim of my work is a critical one, with this inquiry always in view. Criticism, however, should be sympathetic to a certain extent with its object, or it will lack insight and appreciation. I have not found myself devoid of sympathy with one who has filled so large a place in the minds of the New England people. Edwards is always and everywhere interesting, whatever we may think of his theology. On literary and historical grounds alone, no one can fail to be impressed with his imposing figure as he moves through the wilds of the new world. The distance of time from that early period in our history lends its enchantment to the view, enhancing the sense of vastness and mystery which envelops him. Our great American historian, Mr. Bancroft, has justly remarked: "He that would know the workings of the New England mind in the middle of the last century and the throbbings of its heart, must give his days and nights to the study of Jonathan Edwards." He that would understand, it might be added, the significance of later New England thought, must make Edwards the first object of his study.

CAMBRIDGE, *March* 22, 1889.

CONTENTS.

FIRST PERIOD.

THE PARISH MINISTER, 1703–1735.

	PAGE
I. CHILDHOOD. — EARLY LIFE. — NOTES ON THE MIND	1
II. RESOLUTIONS. — DIARY. — CONVERSION	21
III. SETTLEMENT AT NORTHAMPTON. — MARRIAGE. — DOMESTIC LIFE	38
IV. EDWARDS AS A REFORMER. — SERMONS ON DEPENDENCE AND SPIRITUAL LIGHT. — SPECIAL AND COMMON GRACE	52
V. THE MORAL GOVERNMENT OF GOD. — FUTURE PUNISHMENT. — JUSTIFICATION BY FAITH	78
VI. EDWARDS AS A PREACHER. — HIS IMPRECATORY SERMONS	103

SECOND PERIOD.

THE GREAT AWAKENING, 1735–1750.

I. REVIVAL AT NORTHAMPTON. — NARRATIVE OF SURPRISING CONVERSIONS	133
II. THE GREAT AWAKENING. — DISTINGUISHING MARKS OF A WORK OF THE SPIRIT OF GOD	161
III. EVILS AND ABUSES OF THE GREAT AWAKENING. — THOUGHTS ON THE REVIVAL	177
IV. TREATISE ON THE RELIGIOUS AFFECTIONS	218
V. UNION IN PRAYER. — DAVID BRAINERD	232
VI. DISMISSAL FROM NORTHAMPTON. — QUALIFICATIONS FOR FULL COMMUNION	248

THIRD PERIOD.

THE PHILOSOPHICAL THEOLOGIAN, 1750–1758.

I. REMOVAL TO STOCKBRIDGE AS MISSIONARY TO THE INDIANS 273
II. THE FREEDOM OF THE WILL 281
III. DEFENCE OF THE DOCTRINE OF ORIGINAL SIN . 302
IV. TREATISE ON THE NATURE OF TRUE VIRTUE . 313
V. GOD'S LAST END IN THE CREATION . . . 327
VI. THE DOCTRINE OF THE TRINITY 338

CONCLUSION 377
BIBLIOGRAPHY 391
INDEX 395

CHRONOLOGICAL TABLE.

1631. None but church members admitted as freemen.
1633. Settlement of East Windsor.
1648. Cambridge Platform. Adoption of Westminster Confession.
1650. Descartes died.
1654. Settlement of Northampton.
1654. Approval of magistrates required in order to settle a minister.
1662. Synod at Boston adopted the Half-way Covenant.
1669–1758. Rev. Timothy Edwards.
1677. Spinoza died.
1679. Reformatory Synod in Boston.
1684. Withdrawal of the charters.
1685. Accession of James II.
1686. Sir Edmond Andros landed in Boston.
1688–1691. Witchcraft delusion.
1688. Accession of William and Mary.
1691. The new charter.
1692. Episcopalians, Baptists, and Quakers exempted from tax for support of Congregational churches in Massachusetts.
1701. Society for Propagation of the Gospel in Foreign Parts.
1701. Charter for college at Saybrook, afterwards Yale College.
1702–1714. Queen Anne.
1703. Jonathan Edwards born.
1703–1791. John Wesley.

CHRONOLOGICAL TABLE.

1705. Plea of Cotton Mather for increased efficiency of councils.
1706–1790. Benjamin Franklin.
1707–1709. Controversy on the Lord's Supper as a converting ordinance.
1708. Saybrook Platform in Connecticut.
1713. Order of Queen Anne establishing bishoprics in America.
1714–1727. George I.
1715. Malebranche died.
1716. Leibnitz died.
1719–1720. Edwards graduated from Yale College.
1722. Edwards licensed to preach.
1722. Secession of Congregational ministers in Connecticut to the Episcopal Church.
1724. Edwards a tutor at Yale.
1725. Proposed reformatory synod forbidden by the king.
1727. Edwards ordained at Northampton.
1726–1728. Berkeley at Newport.
1727–1760. George II.
1731. Edwards' sermon on Man's Dependence.
1734. Edwards' sermon on Spiritual Light.
1735. First revival at Northampton.
1735. Wesley sailed for Georgia.
1736. Bishop Butler's Analogy.
1736. Edwards' Narrative of Surprising Conversions.
1838. Date of Wesley's conversion.
1738. Whitefield in Georgia.
1738. Publication of Edwards' sermons on Justification, etc.
1739–1741. Whitefield's second visit to America.
1740. The Great Awakening.
1741. Edwards' sermon at Enfield.
1741. Publication of Edwards' Distinguishing Marks, etc.
1742. Edwards' Thoughts on the Revival.
1744–1748. Whitefield's third visit.
1744–1749. War with Indians and French, known as King George's War.

1746. Publication of Edwards on the Religious Affections.
1746. College of New Jersey founded, afterwards Princeton College.
1747. David Brainerd died.
1749. Troubles at Northampton.
1749. Publication of Edwards' Qualifications for Full Communion.
1750. Edwards' dismissal from Northampton.
1750. Decline of Half-way Covenant.
1751. Edwards removes to Stockbridge.
1752. Edwards' Reply to Williams.
1754. Publication of The Freedom of the Will.
1755. Treatises of Edwards written on Virtue and End of the Creation.
1757. Edwards called to Princeton.
1758. Publication of Edwards' treatise on Original Sin.
1758. Edwards died.

JONATHAN EDWARDS.

FIRST PERIOD.

THE PARISH MINISTER. 1703–1735.

I.

CHILDHOOD. — EARLY LIFE. — NOTES ON THE MIND.

JONATHAN EDWARDS was born October 5, 1703, in the town of East Windsor, Connecticut. His father's family is said to be Welsh in its origin. The earliest known ancestor was a clergyman of the Church of England, whose widow, having remarried, emigrated to this country with her son, William Edwards, about 1640. The son of William was Richard Edwards, of Hartford, Conn., a prosperous merchant, who also sustained a high religious character. His oldest son, Timothy, the father of Jonathan Edwards, was born in 1669, and graduated at Harvard College in 1691. He received the two degrees of bachelor and master of arts on the same day, — "an uncommon mark of respect paid to his extraordinary proficiency in learning." Having finished his preparatory theological studies, he was ordained "to the ministry of the Gospel" in the East Parish of Windsor in 1694. In the same year he was married to Esther Stoddard, a daughter of the celebrated Solomon Stoddard, minister of the church in Northampton.

Edwards' father was regarded as a man of more than usual scholarship and learning. In the absence of preparatory schools he was in the habit of fitting students for college, and had gained the reputation of a successful teacher. He gave to his daughters the same training with the young men who studied under his care; and if the latter went to college, the girls were sent to Boston to finish their education. For over sixty years Timothy Edwards maintained himself in good repute with his congregation. As a preacher, it is said that his people gave him the credit of learning and animation, while for his son Jonathan they reserved the epithet "profound." The father is spoken of as a man of "polished manners, particularly attentive to his dress and to propriety of exterior, never appearing in public but in the full dress of a clergyman." The details of domestic affairs he relegated to his wife, in order that he might occupy himself with his studies.

But to his mother Jonathan Edwards was chiefly indebted for his intellectual inheritance. She is said to have received a superior education in Boston. She is described as "tall, dignified, and commanding in appearance, affable and gentle in her manner, and regarded as surpassing her husband in native vigor of understanding." Remarkable judgment and prudence, extensive information, thorough knowledge of the Scriptures and of theology, singular conscientiousness and piety, — these are virtues attributed to the mother which reappear in the son. These also came as if by natural descent to a daughter of Solomon Stoddard. That she did not "join the church" until her son was twelve years old, is a circumstance which points to an intellectual independence which no amount of precedent or prestige could intimidate. In this mental characteristic the son resembled his mother.

Jonathan Edwards was the fifth child and the only son in a family of eleven children. He was educated with his sisters, the older daughters assisting the father in the superintendence of his studies. A few of his letters remain, written while he was a boy, but they disclose little of his character. He appears as docile and receptive, an affectionate and sensitive nature, responding quickly and very deeply to the influences of his childhood. He was interested in his studies, ambitious to excel, and particularly a keen observer of the mysteries of the outward world and eager to discern its laws. Everything points to him as a child of rare intellectual precocity. When not more than twelve years old he wrote a letter in a bantering style refuting the idea of the materiality of the soul. At about the same age he wrote an elaborate and instructive account of the habits of the field spider, based upon his own observation. He was not quite thirteen when he entered Yale College, then in an inchoate condition and not yet fixed in a permanent home. The course of instruction at this time must have been a broken and imperfect one. Such as it was, Edwards followed it faithfully, now at New Haven and then at Wethersfield, whither a part of the students emigrated in consequence of some disturbance in which he seems to have shared. A letter to his father from the rector of the college speaks of his "promising abilities and great advances in learning." He was not quite seventeen when he graduated, taking with his degree the highest honors the institution could offer.

One characteristic of Edwards as a student, which he retained through life, was the habit of writing as a means of mental culture. An inward necessity compelled him also to give expression to his thought. He began while in college to arrange his thoughts in orderly fashion, classifying his manuscripts or note-books under the titles of The Mind, Natural Science, The Scriptures, with a fourth collection called Miscellanies. Even at this early age, somewhere between the years of fourteen and seventeen, he was projecting a great treatise, which he proposed to publish. The Notes on the Mind and on Natural Science are to be regarded as the materials he was enthusiastically collecting for a work intended to embrace almost the entire scope of human learning. He carefully wrote out the rules which were to guide him in its composition. Thoughts were already stirring within him which he felt would awaken opposition. In his rules for guidance he appears as if preparing to besiege the fortress of public opinion, and must be cautious lest his attempt should end in defeat.

The intellectual impulse came from the philosophy of Locke, whose Essay on the Human Understanding Edwards read when he was but fourteen years old. The impression it left upon his mind was a deep and in some respects an abiding one. But even in his early adherence to the sensational philosophy he was still himself, independent, accepting or rejecting in accordance with an inward dictum which sprang from the depth of his being. Locke was after all rather the occasion than the inspiring cause of his intellectual activity. Had he read Descartes instead, he might have reached the same conclusion. Although Edwards came to his intellectual maturity before his religious experience had developed into what he called "conversion," yet his intellect was bound from the first to the idea of God. There is a peculiar charm in these early manuscripts written before his theology had received its final stamp. At times he seems as if almost losing himself in the realm of pure speculation. But the underlying motive in his Notes on the Mind or Natural Science is theological, not philosophical. The religious impulse may appear as fused with the intellectual activity, yet it is always there, and always the strongest element in his thought. Science and metaphysics do not interest him as ends in themselves, but as subordinated to a theological purpose. The God consciousness was the deepest substratum of his being, — his natural heritage from Puritan antecedents, coloring or qualifying every intellectual conviction he attained.

We turn, then, to these Notes on the Mind, in which the boy is seen revelling in the dawning sense of fresh creative power.[1] The point which he first proceeds to elaborate is entitled Excellency. Of this he writes: "There has nothing been more without a definition than excellency, although it be what we are more concerned with than anything else whatsoever. Yea, we are concerned with nothing else. But what is this excellency? Wherein is one thing excellent and another evil, one beautiful and another deformed?" In answering the inquiry he accepted the current

---

[1] It is impossible to give here a complete summary of these *Notes on the Mind*. It may be said of them in general that there is hardly a speculative principle in Edwards' later writings which they do not contain in its germinal form. They discuss the nature of the will and of freedom, abstract and innate ideas: there are passages which imply realism, and others a decided nominalism. They present a theory of causation resembling that of the late Mr. J. S. Mill, and anticipate Hume's law of the association of ideas. The *Notes on Natural Science*, if written as is supposed between the age of fourteen and sixteen, present Edwards as an intellectual prodigy which has no parallel. They indicate a marvellous insight into the gaps of knowledge, and an instinctive sense of how they are to be filled, which seems like prophetic divination. Cf. Dwight, *Life of Edwards*, p. 53; and pp. 702-761, where they are given in full.

statement that excellence consists in harmony, symmetry, or proportion. But he complains of this statement as affording no explanation. What he seeks to know is, why proportion is more excellent than disproportion, or why it gives greater pleasure to the mind. In the attempt to satisfy his mind on this point he was led to sound the depths of his youthful experience in order to reach some ultimate principle. He found this principle in the conviction that life in itself, simple existence, is the highest good, and therefore the foundation of moral excellence. He took his stand at the antipodes of pessimistic schemes or theories of the universe. He is at the furthest remove from the tired mood of Oriental dreamers, from the spirit of Buddhism with its primary postulate that existence is an evil. He represents the concentrated vitality and aggressiveness of the occidental peoples, — of the Anglo-Saxon race in particular, of which he was a consummate flower blossoming in a new world. The simple energy and potency of life is here deified, as it were, as if demanding in itself alone supreme adoration. He argues for the truth of this principle, from the possession of a deep inward conviction. He has striven in vain to conceive a state of nothingness. The very attempt to realize it in his mind throws him into confusion and convulsion. He speaks of *nothing* as "that which the sleeping rocks do dream of." The thought of the possible annihilation of that which has once existed fills him with horror. *Existence* then, in itself, must be the highest good, the greatest blessing.

From this principle he proceeds to deduce the conclusion that similarity, proportion, harmony, partake of the nature of excellence, since they are agreeable to that which has *existence*. These things are in accordance with the law implanted in our being. Beyond this statement it is not necessary to go. The simple gift of perception, with which intelligent being is endowed, is in itself a pleasure and a blessing, and perception is pleased in beholding harmony and proportion wherever he looks. All beings or existences appear to stand in certain relationships, and in the fulfilment of these relationships lies the fulness of a real life. Whatever contradicts harmony, or weakens or contradicts relationships, diminishes the fulness of *existence*, and approaches the state of *nothingness*, which is the greatest evil. To approve, then, of this primary law of one's being which demands the realization of harmony and proportion, is to recognize the principle of all excellence.

He carries the argument up to the divine existence. God is excellent simply because He exists, for "existence is that into which all excellence is to be resolved." Because God has an infinite amount or quantity of *existence*, He possesses in consequence an infinite excellence. The physical and the spiritual are here merged into one. In proportion to the dimensions of *existence* is the quantity of excellence. God, by the mere reason of His greatness, is the more excellent. "It is impossible that God should be otherwise than excellent, for He is the infinite, universal, and all-comprehending existence. . . . He is in Himself, if I may so say, an infinite quantity of existence." So vast and preponderating is His existence that when we speak of existence in general, it is enough to think of Him. "In comparison with Him, all others must be considered as nothing. . . . As to bodies, we have shown in another place that they have no proper being of their own. And as to spirits, they are the communications of the Great Original Spirit; and doubtless, in metaphysical strictness and propriety He is, and there is none else. . . . All excellence and beauty is derived from Him in the same manner as all being. And all other excellence is in strictness only a shadow of His."

The supreme law of existence is the law of love. While Deity is pleased with the perception of excellency as He witnesses existence in harmony with existence throughout the universe, yet the chief happiness of God lies in His love, or His consent to His own infinite existence. Herein lies the difference between the creature and the creator, that, if the creature would be in harmony with existence, he must above all things be in harmony with God, consenting to the law of the Divine existence, which is God's love for Himself. Love, therefore, is the highest excellency. The secret harmony between the various parts of the universe is only an image of mutual love. In God this essential principle operates from all eternity, as in the mutual love of the Father and the Son. In the Holy Spirit which binds together the Father and the Son is to be seen God's infinite beauty, or, in the writer's abstract expression, God's infinite consent to his own being, which is being in general. The love of God to the creation is the communication of Himself in his Spirit. If it seems as though this love of God to Himself carried too much the aspect of self-love, we must remember that " this love includes in it, or rather is the same as, a love to everything, as they are all communications of Himself." Under the influence of this principle the universe is transfigured as with the light of divine love.

" We are to conceive of the divine excellence as infinite general love, that which reaches all, proportionately with perfect purity and sweetness; yea, it includes the true love of all creatures, for that is His spirit, or, which is the same thing, His love. And if we take notice, when we are in the best frames meditating on the divine excellence, our ideal of that tranquillity and peace which seems to be overspread and cast abroad upon the whole earth and universe naturally dissolves itself into the idea of a general love and delight everywhere diffused." [1]

The answer to the inquiry as to the nature of excellence has been given at some length because

[1] Dwight, *Life*, etc., p. 701.

of its importance, and because it is apt to be overlooked in attempts to explain the genesis of Edwards' thought. Dr. Dwight, who edited the Notes on the Mind from the original manuscript, did not follow the order of time in which they were written, and has placed the treatment of excellence at the close of the treatise, although it is numbered One, and was therefore the first subject on which he committed his views to writing, and must have been uppermost in his mind. The reflections of the boy of sixteen must not be underrated as if they were immature, or as if they had afterwards disappeared from his consciousness. When, at the age of fifty, he wrote his dissertation on The Nature of True Virtue, he reproduced his early conviction with no substantial change. In later years, it is true, the genial outlook upon the universe which marked his youth is no longer maintained, and he may never have regained the beautiful vision which dawned upon the first opening of his mind. The devotion to a moral ideal had its dark side, which came into an exaggerated prominence during the time of his pastoral activity. But beneath the mutations of his mental history may still be traced the undercurrent of his youthful conviction that moral excellence must be grounded in God, must be identified with existence itself, in order that it may be seen as the only reality in a world of shadows.

In his treatment of excellence Edwards appears

as in agreement with Plato's conception of God as the idea of the good. There is also in his tone a still stronger reminder of Spinoza, — the doctrine of the one substance, of which the universe is the manifestation. In some respects also he approximates in these Notes on the Mind to the famous doctrine of Malebranche that we see all things in God; as when it is emphatically asserted that "the universe exists only in the mind of God." Truth is defined as the agreement of our ideas with *existence*, or, since God and existence are the same, as the agreement of our ideas with the ideas of God. Hence it may be said that God is truth itself. Of the inspiration which prophets had, it is remarked that it was in a sense intuitive. "The prophet, in the thing which he sees, has a clear view of its perfect agreement with the excellencies of the divine nature. All the Deity appears in the thing, and in everything pertaining to it. . . . He perceives as immediately that God is there as we perceive one another's presence when we are talking face to face."

With views like these of God, of existence, of truth, it is not surprising that Edwards believed that "corporeal things could exist no otherwise than mentally." Among the earliest statements in the Notes on the Mind, we read: "Our perceptions or ideas, that we passively receive by our bodies, are communicated to us immediately by God." Edwards may have reached this conclusion by combining his idea of God, as universal existence, with the principle derived from Locke that all ideas begin from external sensation. He emphatically affirms this principle when he says, "There never can be any idea, thought, or act of the mind unless the mind first received some ideas from sensation, or some other way equivalent wherein the mind is wholly passive in receiving them."[1] With Edwards' premises, the transition seems an easy one from the popular belief in the externality of the objects of our senses to a disbelief in the existence of matter. The question which he was asking himself was one which Locke had not answered, and had declared himself unable to answer, confessing it to be a mystery, — What is that substance, or thing in itself, concealed behind attributes and qualities, whose existence is revealed by perceptions of color or extension, but which cannot be resolved into these qualities? Is it " a something, we know not what "? Edwards refused to acquiesce in this confession of an impersonal and unknown something. "Men," he says, "are wont to content themselves by saying merely that it is something; but that something is *He* in whom all things consist." Sensations produced by external objects are thus at once resolved into ideas coming directly to the mind from God. All through the Notes on the Mind, phrases like these are recurring: "Bodies have no existence of their own." "All existence is mental; the existence of all things is ideal." "The brain exists

[1] Dwight, *Life*, etc., Appendix, p. 666.

only mentally, or in idea." "Instead of matter being the only proper substance, and more substantial than anything else because it is hard and solid, yet it is truly nothing at all, strictly and in itself considered." "The universe exists nowhere but in the divine mind." The popular conception of space is gross and misleading. "Space is necessary, eternal, infinite, and omnipresent. But I had as good speak plain. I have already said as much as that space is God." And to give a final summary of the whole question : —

"And indeed the secret lies here, — that which truly is the substance of all bodies is the infinitely exact and precise and perfectly stable Idea in God's mind, together with His stable will that the same shall gradually be communicated to us, and to other minds, according to certain fixed and exact established methods and laws; or, in somewhat different language, the infinitely exact and precise Divine Idea, together with an answerable, perfectly exact, precise, and stable will, with respect to correspondent communications to created minds and effects on their minds."

One cannot read this extraordinary production of Edwards' youth without noticing its numerous and striking coincidences with Berkeley's system of philosophic idealism. But when the question is raised whether he had read Berkeley, we become aware that a thick veil of obscurity rests upon these labors of his early years which we strive in vain to withdraw. In recent years there has grown up what may be regarded as a history of opinion on this difficult point. On the one hand it is maintained, that he had no acquaintance with the writings of Berkeley,[1] and that it is not necessary to suppose such an acquaintance in order to explain this reproduction, almost complete, of a philosophy which is identified with Berkeley's name.[2] On the other hand, those who hold that Edwards may have read Berkeley's works can bring no direct evidence to substantiate their opinion.[3] Berkeley's earlier writings, — the New Theory of Vision, the Principles of Human Knowledge, and the Dialogues, had been published by the year 1713. It is possible, therefore, that they may have reached this country before 1719, when Edwards graduated from Yale College. But we are assured on good authority that "there is no evidence that a copy of any

[1] This is the view of Dr. Dwight, in his careful *Life of Edwards*, p. 40.

[2] Professor Noah Porter, D. D., *A Discourse at Yale College on the 200th Birthday of Bishop Berkeley*, 1885. "Surrounded as it were by similar logical and spiritual impulses, Jonathan Edwards drew the same conclusions as Berkeley had done, from the same data in Locke's *Essays*, p. 71." So also Professor M. C. Tyler in *History of American Literature*, ii. p. 183: "The peculiar opinions which Edwards held in common with Berkeley were reached by him through an independent process of reasoning, and somewhat in the same way that they were reached by Berkeley."

[3] Professor Fraser, the biographer of Berkeley and editor of his complete works, first advanced the opinion that Edwards was indebted to Berkeley. Professor Fisher, of Yale College, also thinks it not improbable that copies of Berkeley's works had come into Edwards' hands, and found in him an eager and congenial disciple. Cf. *Dicussions in History and Philosophy*, p. 231.

of these works referred to was known at the college, and there is reason to believe that they were not then accessible."[1] We seem to come near finding the missing link in the fact that Dr. Samuel Johnson, afterwards President of King's College, New York, a personal friend of Berkeley and an ardent follower of his teaching, was a tutor at Yale College while Edwards was a student. But the conjecture that Edwards may have become acquainted with Berkeleyanism through Johnson fails us when it is put to the test. For Edwards was at Wethersfield while Johnson remained at New Haven, and was among those disaffected toward Johnson as a tutor.[2] Nor is there any evidence that Johnson was at this time acquainted with Berkeley's writings.[3] A recent writer has suggested another explanation, which deserves attention, — that the Notes on the Mind were written later than Dr. Dwight, the biographer of Ed-

[1] Professor Porter, *Historical Discourse*, etc., on Berkeley, p. 71.

[2] Professor Fisher, *Discussions*, etc., p. 231.

[3] Professor Porter remarks: "Dr. Johnson is said to have first become interested in Berkeley's idealism when he went to England in 1723 for episcopal ordination." *Discourse*, etc., p. 71. Dr. E. E. Beardsley, in his *Life of Johnson*, throws no light on the time when Johnson first became a disciple of Berkeley. But he thinks the Berkeleyan philosophy had been heard of at Yale so early as 1714, when Johnson graduated; — "Something had been heard of a new philosophy that was attracting attention in England; but the young men were cautioned against receiving it, and told that it would corrupt the pure religion of the country and bring in another system of divinity," p. 5.

wards, supposes.¹ The chief evidence on which Dr. Dwight relied to fix their date is the peculiarity of Edwards' handwriting, which in youth was round and legible, and at the age of twenty became angular and less distinct. But this is surely slender evidence on which to build an important conclusion. Only a careful reëditing of the manuscripts could determine this point. If the Notes on the Mind, begun while Edwards was in college, were continued for several years after he left college, this might give the desired time or opportunity to become acquainted with Berkeley's writings. There is evidence, indeed, that so late as 1725, when he had reached the age of twenty-two, his mind was still working in the direction toward which the reading of Locke had impelled

[1] Georges Lyon, *L'Idéalisme en Angleterre au XVIIIe siècle*, Paris, 1888, pp. 430, 431. M. Lyon also offers the suggestive hint that Edwards may have had some knowledge of Malebranche, either directly or through his English interpreters. Edwards' affinity with Malebranche is closer than with Berkeley. There is a divergence between Edwards and Berkeley on the important principle of causation, which shows that some motive was influential with the American youth which did not operate with Berkeley. Berkeley also denounces as absurd the statement to which Edwards assents, that space is God. Cf. *Principles of Human Knowledge*, London ed., 1820, i. p. 34. It is possible that Edwards may have had a knowledge of Malebranche, for two translations of the *Recherche de la Vérité* had been published in England so early as 1694. By 1704 had also appeared Norris' *Theory of an Ideal World*, in which Malebranche was worked up by an English mind. It would explain Edwards' transition from Locke if he had seen these works. M. Lyon's interesting and valuable work contains a fresh study of Edwards, and puts his philosophy in a clear light.

him, and was still undetermined whether to push the doctrine of Berkeley to a further conclusion. "The very thing I now want," he writes in his Journal for February 12, 1725, "to give me a clearer and more immediate view of the perfections and glory of God, is as clear a knowledge of the manner of God's exerting Himself with respect to spirit and mind as I have of His operations concerning matter and bodies." When Edwards wrote this sentence he was about ready to abandon philosophy, and turn to theology as the more congenial study. He gives no intimation of the conclusion he reached on this vital issue. But even then he must have inclined to regard the relation of God in each case as the same. Beyond that point his speculations did not go.

It seems on the whole a reasonable conclusion that the Notes on the Mind were, some of them at least, written later than is generally supposed. It is also easier and more natural to think that Edwards had some knowledge of Berkeley's writings. The reading of the Notes gives the impression that he is stepping into a heritage of thought rather than discovering principles for the first time. He seems to be more concerned also with the application of the new doctrine than with its demonstration or exposition. But if we adopt this opinion that Edwards was acquainted with Berkeley's thought, we have raised another and a grave difficulty. Why is he silent on the name of Berkeley, making no mention of him anywhere in his works? He paid an ample tribute to Locke, but if he had read Berkeley he must have known that there lay the greater indebtedness. He certainly could not have remained ignorant throughout his life of the nature of Berkeley's teaching, and how closely his youthful speculation had followed him. There is a difficulty and a mystery here upon which little or no light is thrown by Edwards' biographers. Surmise, suspicion, tentative hypotheses might be offered, but there is no space for their discussion. The manuscripts of Edwards, if carefully reëdited, might give the desired information. The soul of this marvellous boy went through great changes and perturbations of thought of which there is no published record.[1] At some moment he deliberately turned his back upon philosophy, when, if he had chosen to pursue it, it seems as if he could scarce have had his equal. He not only turned away from it, but he accustomed himself to speak of it in the underrating manner of the popular preacher. Perhaps philosophy had been to him as the scaffolding to the

---

[1] Frank as these early writings of Edwards may seem, they contain intimations of a reserved and even secretive temperament. He has recourse now and then to shorthand, in which he buried in oblivion his most intimate thought or feeling. He charges himself not to allow it to appear as if he were familiar with books or conversant with the learned world. He seems to feel that he has a secret teaching which will create opposition when revealed, and clash with the prejudices and fashion of the age. On one occasion, after writing in shorthand, he concludes with the remark, "Remember to act according to Proverbs xii. 23, — *A prudent man concealeth knowledge.*"

real structure, a thing to be removed from sight when it had served its purpose.

It may have been a reason why Edwards abandoned his project of publishing a treatise on the human mind that he felt it would be unwise, in a practical and cautious age, to unsettle the minds of men by remote speculations which only the few could appreciate, which to the majority must seem fantastic and absurd. In his Notes, after dwelling upon the statement that the brain exists only in idea, he confesses: "We have got so far beyond those things for which language was chiefly contrived that, unless we use extreme caution, we cannot speak, unless we speak unintelligibly, without literally contradicting ourselves." But he also comes to the satisfactory conclusion that, although the external world is immaterial and the universe exists nowhere but in the mind, "yet we may speak in the old way, and as properly and as truly as ever. . . . Although the place of bodies means only the possibility of mutual communications, and space is God, yet the language of Scripture is not improper which speaks of God as in heaven and we upon the earth, or of God's indwelling in the hearts of His people."

It may have been also that Edwards perceived deep incongruities and contradiction in the depth of his soul, which he felt himelf unable to reconcile. One ruling principle of his career as a practical theologian was the Augustinian idea of God as absolute and arbitrary will. But this conception finds only a faint expression in The Notes on the Mind, and indeed was not his conscious possession until he had experienced what is known as *conversion*. Before that crisis in his life, he conceives of God as Plato, or Spinoza, or Hegel had done, — the idea of the good, the one substance, the absolute thought unfolding itself or embodying itself in a visible and glorious order. And indeed these remained the poles of Edwards' thought throughout his life, — Spinozism on the one hand, Augustinianism on the other. Like Augustine, he abandoned philosophy for the absorbing devotion to Divine and arbitrary will, which better suited his practical career as a reformer, concerned mainly with the well-being of the churches. But the other element of his thought, though subordinated, was not annihilated. It appears in all his writings, — an element seemingly incongruous, and difficult to reconcile with his other teaching. It reappeared in his later years with something of the beauty which had fascinated the vision of his youth.

II.

RESOLUTIONS, DIARY, CONVERSION.

THE call of Edwards was not to metaphysical studies or to natural science, great as was the proficiency he showed in each. It was in the sphere of religion and the inner life of the spirit that his distinctive quality was most clearly revealed. To the life of the spirit he was anointed from his birth. Born and brought up in a typical Puritan household where religion was the very atmosphere and the church the leading interest in life, he did not react from the severity or narrowness of his training. His conversion may be said to begin with the dawn of consciousness, if it did not begin before his birth. From a very early period he showed susceptibility to religious impressions. He was accustomed as a child to go by himself to secret places in the woods for the purpose of prayer, and was wont to be greatly affected. His father's parish was the scene of occasional "attentions to religion," as they were called; and of these, while yet a boy, he speaks as if they involved the only realities of life. He was the subject of no sensuous religious influences such as might appeal to a childish imagination, — no dim religious light from windows filled with glorious color, no long-drawn aisles culminating in the mystery of the altar, no rich involutions of musical harmony, no accompaniment of the rolling organ, no inspiration from an imposing architecture. For some reason the plain meeting-house at East Windsor was unfinished in Edwards' boyhood. Not even seats were provided for the worshippers, who were driven to accommodate themselves on sills and sleepers. And yet never was a child imbibing deeper reverence for spiritual things. His soul revelled in the mystery of the Divine existence; and he grew into the knowledge of the majesty and the glory of God.

No exact date can be fixed for his conversion; even the time when he "joined the church" is unknown. But we know the years in which he was passing through the spiritual struggles out of which he was to emerge a man of God, recognizing the call of God and answering it with the entire devotion of his will. This period of conflict, of aspiration, of resolution, and of consecration follows upon his graduation from college in 1719 at the age of sixteen. For two years he remained at New Haven, in order, as was then the custom, to carry on his theological studies. He was then called to New York to take charge of a Presbyterian church newly organized, where he remained for eight months, preaching to the acceptance of the congregation and leaving them with reluctance. Returning to his father's house, he was soon after made a tutor in Yale College, an office which he held for two years (1724–1726), helping to overcome the shock to the college and the community caused by the secession of its rector Mr. Cutler, Mr. Johnson one of its tutors, and others to the Episcopal Church. He was, says Dr. Stiles, one of the *pillar tutors*, and the glory of the college at this critical period. His tutorial renown was great and excellent. He filled and sustained his office with great ability, dignity, and honor. "For the honor of literature these things ought not to be forgotten."

From 1720 to 1726, from the age of seventeen to the age of twenty-three, runs the period during which he wrote his Resolutions and the greater part of his religious Diary. These are no ordinary resolutions, and this is no common diary. It is, when we read them, as if we stood behind the veil witnessing the evolution of a great soul. Like Luther, he appears as in search for some high end, of whose nature he is not clearly conscious. But he will be content with nothing but the highest result which it is open to man to achieve, or for God of his grace to impart. Referring to this period of his life some twenty years later, he remarks, "I made seeking my salvation the main business of my life." What was it exactly for which he was in search? In some respects his experience is like that of all spiritual minds. And yet there are fine shades of distinction in these records of religious conflict which are worth discriminating. Luther labored for the assurance of divine forgiveness; Edwards, for the vision of the divine glory, for the assurance of his oneness in spirit with the ineffable holiness and majesty of God. We may trace in his experience the unmistakable marks of the mystic in every age, — union with God, absorption as it were into the inmost essence of the divine. He finds expression in the intense language of the Psalmist: "*My soul breaketh for the longing it hath; my soul waiteth for the Lord, more than they who watch for the morning.*"

The seeking and the waiting were at last rewarded. He was reading one day the words of Scripture, "Now unto the King eternal, immortal, invisible, the only wise God, be honor and glory forever, Amen," when there came to him for the first time a sort of inward, sweet delight in God and divine things. A sense of the divine glory was, as it were, diffused through him. He thought how happy he should be if he might be rapt up to God in heaven, and be, as it were, swallowed up in him forever. He began to have an inward, sweet sense of Christ and the work of redemption. The Book of Canticles attracted him as a fit expression for his mood. It seemed to him as if he were in a kind of vision, alone in the mountains or some solitary wilderness, conversing sweetly with Christ and wrapt and swallowed up in God. He told his father the things he was experiencing, and was affected by the discourse they had together. Walking once in a solitary place in his father's pasture, there came to him again a sweet sense of the conjunction of the majesty and the grace of God.

"After this my sense of divine things gradually increased and became more and more lively, and had more of that inward sweetness. The appearance of everything altered: there seemed to be, as it were, a calm, sweet cast or appearance of divine glory in almost everything. God's excellency, his wisdom, his purity and love, seemed to appear in everything, — in the sun, moon, and stars; in clouds and blue sky; in the grass, flowers, trees; in the water and all nature, which used greatly to fix my mind. I often used to sit and view the moon for continuance, and in the day spent much time in viewing the clouds and sky, to behold the sweet glory of God in these things; in the mean time singing forth, with a low voice, my contemplations of the Creator and Redeemer. . . . Before, I used to be uncommonly terrified with thunder, and to be struck with terror when I saw a thunder-storm arising; but now, on the contrary, it rejoiced me. I felt God, so to speak, at the first appearance of a thunder-storm; and used to take the opportunity, at such times, to fix myself in order to view the clouds and see the lightnings play, and hear the majestic and awful voice of God's thunder, which oftentimes was exceedingly entertaining, leading me to sweet contemplations of my great and glorious God. . . . I sometimes said to myself I do certainly know that I love holiness; it appeared to me that there was nothing in it but what was ravishingly lovely, the highest beauty and amiableness, — a divine beauty, far purer than anything upon earth. . . . The soul of a true Christian appeared like a little white flower as we see in the opening of the year; low and humble on the ground, opening its bosom to receive the pleasant beams of the sun's glory; rejoicing as it were in a calm rapture, diffusing around a sweet fragrancy; standing peacefully and lovingly in the midst of other flowers round about, all in like manner opening their bosoms to drink in the light of the sun."

This spiritual and mystic rapture does not end in words or in emotion. The first thing which he does is to write out Resolutions for the government of his conduct. He proceeds at once to sketch the conception of a perfect character. The moral ideal springs up spontaneously within him. The Resolutions express the essence of a virginal soul, — the desire for the divine image in the soul of man.

The germ of Edwards' theology is also apparent here, which, conceiving the will as predominant in God, conceives man also as an answering will, aiming to renounce itself in God; but it is a coming to the knowledge of God which evokes the process, which forces him to ask what are the actions, what the character, which alone correspond with the privilege of one who has been admitted into the inner shrine of the divine glory.

"On January 12, 1723, I made a solemn dedication of myself to God and wrote it down; giving up myself and all that I had to God, to be for the future in no respect my own; to act as one that had no right to himself in any respect; and solemnly vowed to take God for my whole portion and felicity, looking on nothing else as any part of my happiness, nor acting as if it were; and his law for the constant rule of my obedience, engaging to fight with all my might against the world, the flesh, and the devil, to the end of my life."

In accordance with this renunciation of self, Edwards resolves, in the first place, always to do whatever he thinks is most for the glory of God and his own good, without consideration of the time, whether now or never so many myriads of ages hence; no matter how great or how many the difficulties he meets with, to do his duty and what is most for the good of mankind in general. He is never to lose a moment of time, to live while he lives with all his might. He will do nothing out of revenge, nor suffer anger toward irrational beings, nor speak evil of any one unless to accomplish some real good. He must maintain the strictest temperance in eating and drinking, be faithful to every trust, do always what he can toward making or preserving peace, and in narrations never speak anything but pure and simple verity. He is to cultivate also a temper which is good and sweet and benevolent to all, quiet and peaceable, contented and easy, compassionate and generous, humble and meek, submissive and obliging, charitable and even, patient, moderate, forgiving, and sincere. In order to a completer victory over all evil in himself, he will take it for granted that no one is so evil as himself; he will identify himself with all other men, and act as if their evil was his own, as if he had committed the same sins and had the same infirmities, so that the knowledge of their failings will promote in him nothing but a sense of shame. It shall be a rule with him never to do anything which he should condemn as wrong in others. Whenever he does any conspicuously evil action, he determines to trace it back to its source, in order to more successfully overcoming it. Mingled with these resolutions are others of a more specific and local tone. He resolves never to utter anything that is sportive or a matter of laughter on the Lord's day: when he thinks of any theorem in divinity to be solved, immediately to do what he can toward solving it; to study the Scriptures constantly and frequently; not to allow the least sign of fretting or uneasiness at his father or mother, or to any one of the family.

He is constantly to examine himself as to his behavior at the end of every day, every week, every month, every year. All such things as weaken his sense of assurance of the divine favor he casts away. Moments when his sense of assurance is at its best, he will seize as opportunities for fresh consecration of himself.

As we linger over these Resolutions, which portray the ideal of human character and excellence as Edwards conceived it in his youth, we find him still influenced by the commoner notions of personal advantage and safety to be achieved hereafter. The sanctions of his deeds he looks for in another world; the test to which he subjects them is the hour and moment of death, when things are most clearly seen in their true relations. He will act in this world as he thinks he shall judge would have been best and most prudent when he comes into the future world; he will act in every respect as he thinks he should wish he had done if he should at last be damned. There is, too, the daring ambition of a youth conscious of great capacity, and thinking it not unfit that his ambition should spur him on in the race for spiritual excellence and reward. He has frequently heard persons in old age say how they would live if they were to live their lives over again. He resolves that he will live just as he can think he would wish he had done, supposing he were to live to old age. Nay, even "*on the supposition that there never was to be but one individual in the world, at any one time, in all respects of a right stamp, having Christianity always shining in its true lustre, and appearing excellent and lovely from whatever part and under whatever character viewed; resolved to act just as I would do if I strove with all my might to be that one who should live in my time."*

The Diary of Edwards, which covers the years when he was forming his resolutions, serves as a commentary on the difficulties he encountered in keeping his will true to the highest standard. There is the usual record of alternations between failures and successes, seasons of depression and of exaltation. The depressions and the failures are attributed to the withdrawal of the Spirit of God, as if his relation to the soul were not an organic one, but fitful and capricious. The Diary has certain personal touches, apart from their religious interest, which throw light on his character. His subtlety in making distinctions is apparent in what he says about revenge. On one occasion he accused himself of having felt a certain satisfaction in what he had done, because it might lead some persons to repent of their conduct. If he were satisfied with their repentance because they had a sense of their error, it would be right. But to have a satisfaction in their repentance because of the evil that is brought upon them would be revenge. He observes that "old men seldom have any advantage of new discoveries, because they are beside the way of thinking to which they have been so long used." Hence he resolves that he will not be affected by limitations of the lower nature, but "if ever he lives to years he will be impartial to hear the reasons of all pretended discoveries and receive them if rational, how long soever he may have been used to another way of thinking." None the less, in an entry for February 21, 1725, he seems to reflect upon the course of the clergy in Connecticut, whose secession to Episcopacy had made such a stir in the colony, as if their action had not been well considered, or as if it showed a lack of deference for authority and tradition. "If ever I am inclined to turn to the opinion of any other sect, resolved, beside the most deliberate consideration, earnest prayer, etc., privately to desire all the help that can be afforded me from some of the most judicious men in the country, together with the prayers of wise and holy men, however strongly persuaded I may seem to be that I am in the right."

The ascetic tendency which entered so largely into the composition of the New England character finds full expression in the early experience of Edwards. He esteems it as "an advantage that the duties of religion are difficult, and that many difficulties are sometimes to be gone through in the way of duty." At the age of twenty, he records his intention to live in continual mortification without ceasing, and even to weary himself thereby, and never to expect or desire any worldly ease or pleasure. He charges himself not to be uneasy about his state or condition, not to be envious or jealous when he sees that others are prosperous and honored and the world is smooth to them; rather to rejoice in all such things for others; while for himself, he is not to expect or desire these things, but to depend on affliction, and betake himself entirely to another sort of happiness. In his stoical desire for spiritual independence and completeness, he would strip himself of those things whose tenure is uncertain, so as not to be afflicted with fear of losing them, nor pleased and excited with the expectation of gaining them. The question arises, whether any delight or satisfaction should be allowed which ministers to any other than a religious end. At first he gives a tentative answer in the affirmative, for the reason that otherwise we should never rejoice at the sight of friends, or have any pleasure in our food, — a pleasure which contributes to the animal spirits and a good digestion. But the final answer is, never to allow any joy or sorrow but what helps religion. He complains of himself that he has become accustomed after working a great while to look forward to rest as if it were his due, and to expect to be released from labor after a certain time even if not really tired or weary. But if he did not expect ease, he should go on with the same vigor at his business without vacation times to rest. The suggestion comes to him that too vigorous application to religion may be prejudicial to health; but he will know this by his own experience before he abandons his aim. He believes that great mortifications and acts of self-denial bring him the greatest comfort. He applies his principle rigidly to his habits of eating. By sparingness of diet he shall gain time, and be able to think more clearly. These hints from his Diary point to the untiring worker of later years who did not know how to take rest, finding relief only in continuous labor.

Edwards did not suffer at this time from any disquieting self-consciousness as to the power of the human will to accomplish its highest resolves. There are allusions to the divine grace through which all human excellence is achieved, but these allusions have a commonplace reminder, as if they were said because they ought to be said. There is the recognition of a need of absolute dependence upon divine power, but he complains that he does not yet realize its need as he ought. "I find a want of dependence on God, to look to Him for success, and to have my eyes unto Him for His gracious disposal of the matter; for want of a sense of God's particular influence in ordering and directing all affairs, of whatever nature, however naturally or fortuitously they may seem to succeed." He had at one time felt repugnance to the principle of man's inability to accomplish any good work, for he records in his journal, under the date of March 6, 1722, that he has been regarding "the doctrines of election, free grace, our inability to do anything without the grace of God, and that holiness is entirely throughout the work of the Spirit of God, with greater pleasure than ever before."

Neither in the Resolutions nor in the Journal do we meet the deep, all-pervading sense of sin which we should naturally expect from one who afterwards made it so prominent in his theology. There are traces of the sense of sin and guilt in these records of early experience, but it is not the prominent feature: it is subordinate to the aspiration after an ideal, or to the methods by which the aspiration may be achieved. Forgiveness is not the word which becomes a key to unlock the secret of his spiritual history. There are some, like Luther, who begin their religious experience with the burden of a sinful conscience, — a burden which when it has disappeared, as at the foot of the cross, is gone never to return. And there are others, worshippers of an ideal, who attach themselves without reserve to God, thirsting for the righteousness which union with the divine demands. With these, the sense of sin may come later, growing out of a deeper love, out of the consciousness of failure to fulfil the standard of a perfect law. That such was Edwards' experience is intimated in a beautiful passage from his Treatise on the Religious Affections: —

"A true saint is like a little child in this respect: he never had any godly sorrow before he was born again, but since has it often in exercise; as a little child before it is born, and while it remains in darkness, never cries; but as soon as it sees the light of day it begins to cry, and thenceforward is often crying. Although Christ hath borne our griefs and carried our sorrows so that we are freed from the sorrow of punishment, and may now sweetly feed upon the comforts Christ hath purchased for us, yet that hinders not but that our feeding on these comforts should be attended with the sorrow of repentance, as of old the children of Israel were commanded evermore to feed upon the paschal lamb with bitter herbs. True saints are spoken of in Scripture, not only as those who have mourned for sin, but as those who do mourn, whose manner it is still to mourn: 'Blessed are they that mourn, for they shall be comforted.'"

There is another point in which the Diary is prophetic of work to be accomplished in the future. Several of the entries relate to the process which is called *conversion*. At this time neither the name, nor the process for which it stood, were as familiar as they have since become. In these allusions Edwards appears uncertain about his spiritual condition, because he is not clear as to what conversion requires. He determines that he will be constantly looking within, to the end that he may not be deceived as to whether he has a genuine interest in Christ. He makes it a point for future investigation to look most nicely and diligently into the opinions of our old divines concerning *conversion*. "The chief thing that now makes me in any measure question my good estate is my not having experienced conversion in those particular steps wherein the people of New England, and anciently the dissenters of old England, used to experience it. Wherefore have resolved never to leave off searching till I have satisfyingly found out the very bottom and foundation, the real reason why they used to be converted in those steps." All this is interesting in view of the fact that Edwards did more than any writer who preceded or followed him in determining the nature and the mode of conversion.

After years of concern about his inward state, yet so late as 1725 Edwards was still uncertain as to whether he had been converted. Nor in later life, as he reviewed these years of struggle and anxiety, was he able to describe with clearness the process through which he had passed. His conversion must be left, where he has left it, in mystery and obscurity. No mind, however subtle or introvertive, can trace the genesis of spiritual life, or analyze the steps by which the soul enters into union with God. But in Edwards' case, as in that of so many others, the process is confused and complicated by extraneous elements. An intellectual transition waited upon the spiritual process of which he gives no hint in his journal. He was tending away from the dreams of his youth, which reveal such extraordinary affiliations with Plato, with the Platonist fathers of the early church, or even with Spinoza, toward the Augustinian conception of God as unconditioned and arbitrary will. The change resulted in putting him in sympathy with the tenets of Calvinistic theology. He shows no appreciation of the significance of the transition, but he records the fact and its momentous consequences. " From my childhood up, my mind had been full of objections against the doctrine of God's sovereignty, in choosing whom He would to eternal life, and rejecting whom He pleased, leaving them eternally to perish and be everlastingly tormented in hell. It used to appear like a horrible doctrine to me." But the moment came to him when he rejected the natural, instinctive working of the conscience as carrying no sacred force. This inward repulsion might be only the carnal mood of the natural unconverted man; nay, even it might be a presumption in favor of the obnoxious tenet. Edwards no longer questioned the truth of the doctrine because it was repellent. What he aspired after was its reception with a willing and rejoicing mind. And somehow, he cannot tell exactly how, he finally attained this result.

" I remember the time very well when I seemed to be convinced and fully satisfied as to this sovereignty of God, and his justice in thus eternally disposing of men according to his sovereign pleasure; but never could give an account how or by what means I was thus convinced, not in the least imagining at the time, nor a long time after, that there was any extraordinary influence of God's spirit in it, but only that now I saw further, and my mind apprehended the justice and reasonableness of it. However, my mind rested in it, and it put an end to all these cavils and questionings. . . . God's absolute sovereignty and justice with respect to salvation is what my mind seems to rest assured of, as much as of anything that I see with my eyes; at least it is so at times. But I have often, since that first conviction, had quite another kind of sense of God's sovereignty than I had then. I have often had not only a conviction, but a delightful conviction. The doctrine has very often appeared exceedingly pleasant, bright, and sweet. But my first conviction was not so."

So Edwards entered into the heritage of his fathers and made the Puritan consciousness his own. There are traces of an inward rebellion which was suppressed. There is reason to believe that his success was not so complete as he fancied in eradicating his earlier thought. But the critical point of the transition is not explained. It is buried out of sight in silence and darkness.

III.

SETTLEMENT AT NORTHAMPTON. — MARRIAGE. — DOMESTIC LIFE.

On the 15th of February, 1727, Edwards was ordained at Northampton as the colleague of his grandfather, the Rev. Solomon Stoddard, then in his eighty-fourth year. The town of Northampton, a beautiful spot on the banks of the Connecticut, had been founded in 1654. The first minister was Mr. Eleazar Mather, a brother of the celebrated Increase Mather. After his early death came Mr. Stoddard, who held the pastorate from 1672 to 1729. He was one of the great men of early New England history. Edwards speaks of him as "a very great man, of strong powers of mind, of great grace, and a great authority, of a masterly countenance, speech, and behavior." Mr. Stoddard lived in the days when, as Hutchinson remarks, "the elders continued to be consulted in every affair of importance. The share they held in temporal affairs added to the weight they had acquired from their spiritual employments, and they were in high esteem." But for Mr. Stoddard there was felt something more than the usual respect and veneration. "The officers and leaders of Northampton," says Edwards, "imitated his manners, which were dogmatic, and thought it an excellency to be like him." Many of the people, he adds, esteemed all his sayings as oracles, and looked upon him "almost as a sort of deity." The Indians of the neighborhood, interpreting this admiration in their own way, spoke of Mr. Stoddard as "the Englishman's God."

It was not an easy task even for Edwards to follow such a pastor. Other circumstances increased the difficulty of the situation. The village of Northampton had grown rapidly in wealth and importance. Many of its inhabitants were marked by cultivation of mind, and refinement of manner. They were also characterized by a certain high-spiritedness which made them a turbulent people, not easy to control. They rejoiced in their reputation as a knowing people, and many of them having been promoted to places of public trust there had been much to feed their pride. There was also an unfortunate division among them: the court party, as it might be called, had wealth, land, and authority; while the country party, not so well endowed, was jealous of them, afraid of their having too much power in town and church. All this was not auspicious for the harmony of Edwards' pastorate. But we do not hear of these sinister aspects of the situation in the early years of his ministry. They were the dark possibilities of the future. On the other hand, from every point of view the settlement at Northampton seemed most fitting and desirable. The father and mother of the young minister had many friends in the parish, for whose sake he was welcomed. Mr. Stoddard must have felt a peculiar satisfaction in the new relationship, as if his own mantle would descend to his successor after his departure. The church at Northampton, although on the distant borders of the rising civilization, was a large and important one, being estimated as the strongest church in wealth and numbers outside of Boston. It was a suitable sphere for one who had already achieved some reputation as a scholar and preacher. Edwards contributed to the lustre of the town, while the congregation felt a justifiable pride in his powers.

He was at this time twenty-four years of age. In personal appearance he was tall, being upwards of six feet in height, with a slender form, and of great seriousness and gravity of manner. His face was of a feminine cast, implying at once a capacity for both sweetness and severity, — the Johannine type of countenance, we should say, just as his spirit is that of St. John, rather than that of Peter or of Paul. It is a face which bespeaks a delicate and nervous organization. The life which he laid out for himself, according to the ministerial standards of the day, was the life of a student, who would not allow his time to be frittered away in useless employments. He visited the people in cases only of necessity. Thirteen hours of study daily is said to have been his rule. His custom at first was to write two sermons every week, one of which was delivered on Sunday, the other at the weekly evening lecture. It is probable that he kept up the habit of writing his sermons in the early years of his ministry. His unpublished manuscripts show that he must have abandoned this practice, however, in later years, substituting plans or outlines carefully prepared. He was not, therefore, a mere reader of sermons, according to the general impression. On special occasions, his sermons were written in full. The tradition in regard to the sermon at Enfield makes it to have been read very closely from the manuscript. His manner in the pulpit is described as quiet exceedingly, with little or no gesture; a voice not loud, but distinct and penetrating. He could not have been called at any time a popular preacher in the ordinary sense; but he must have been very interesting to his congregation, — an interest which can still be felt in whatever he wrote. It is sometimes said of sermons like those of Whitefield, which now appear so dull as to be almost unreadable, that they depended for their power on the living speaker. Edwards' sermons also must have gained from his remarkable presence and personality. But, unlike most sermons, the fire of life and reality still burns in them.

From the first, Edwards was determined to do something more than the prescribed routine work of the pulpit. He sought, above all, a wider and more intimate knowledge of the Bible. To this end he kept a manuscript for notes on Scripture, which gradually became of large dimensions. He also followed out his resolution to be always solving difficult problems in divinity, his efforts in this line also going into manuscripts and notes. In his only diversion, his solitary rides and walks, he carried his thoughts with him, generally also pen and ink, having fixed beforehand the subject of his meditations. Returning from his rides he would bring with him various artificial remembrancers, such as small pieces of paper pinned to his coat, and on going to his study write out the reflections associated with them. His life was one of protracted, intense application, living by rule in regard to food, curtailing sleep, with little real recreation, and governed by the purpose, as we have already seen, of never indulging any weak desire for rest. He could not have carried a large library with him to Northampton. He read what he could get, borrowing some books, buying others, and knowing clearly just what books were necessary, if he could only get them. The connection of Northampton with Boston was a close one. Edwards managed to find out in some way what was going on in the world. He soon learned that the times were changing, even though the change went on more slowly in the remote and isolated province of the Massachusetts Bay.

We are studying the life of a Protestant theologian, the peer of his predecessors in any age of the church in intellectual power and acumen, as well as in a vast expanding influence. Let us turn then, as by a natural transition, to his marriage and his domestic life. If we were studying the lives of St. Augustine, or St. Jerome, or St. Bernard of Clairvaux, or St. Thomas of Aquin, we should think of them in their monastic cells denouncing the ties of human love and of the family relation, as unfit or even degrading for those who belong to the sacred order of the clergy. Of Edwards we must think as having wife and children, finding repose and consolation, and not only so, but inspiration and strength, in the bosom of his family. He, too, is a genuine ascetic at heart; but his asceticism, however it may have erred, is of a higher type than the ancient or mediæval forms. It is of the heroic cast which orders life with reference to the highest end. If he abstains from amusements, from excess of food, from many hours spent in sleep, it is not because he believes such abstinence scores so much to his merit, but because he has a work to do, and like his Master is sorely straitened until it be accomplished.

Hardly had Edwards become settled in his parish at Northampton when he bethought himself of a wife. Nor was there apparently any doubt in his mind as to where he should turn to find the heart which beat in sympathy with his own. While living in New Haven he had first heard of Sarah Pierrepont, then a young girl of thirteen years. Her ancestry was a distinguished one in colonial annals, as also in England, whence her paternal grandfather had emigrated to Roxbury, in Massachusetts. She was descended through her mother from the Rev. Thomas Hooker, called the father of the Connecticut churches, generally designated as the *great* Mr. Hooker, of whom it had been said that, if any man in his age came in the spirit of John the Baptist, Hooker was the man. Her father also was an eminent divine, connected with Yale College in various capacities of founder, trustee, and for a time professor of moral philosophy. Some connection with that production known as the *Saybrook Platform* is also ascribed to him. Sarah Pierrepont is spoken of as possessing a rare and lustrous beauty both of form and features. Her portrait, taken by an English painter, presents, says Dr. Dwight, "a form and features not often rivalled, with a peculiar loveliness of expression, the combined result of goodness and intelligence." Her beauty and attractiveness are alluded to by Dr. Hopkins, of Newport, who speaks of her, after she had passed the age of youth, as more than ordinarily beautiful. But her beauty, which throws a charm and softness over the severity of ancient Puritanism, was not all that recommended her in Edwards' eyes. She proved to be a woman of strong character, endowed with a natural religious enthusiasm, with a decidedly mystic bent to the piety that belonged to her from childhood. Her strongest attraction in the eyes of her future husband, when he first heard of her, was the natural ease with which she achieved and maintained so intimate a relationship with Deity. In this connection belongs the memorable passage written by Edwards at the age of twenty, while Sarah Pierrepont was thirteen, — a passage which Dr. Chalmers is said to have admired for its eloquence: —

"They say there is a young lady in New Haven who is beloved of that great Being who made and rules the world, and that there are certain seasons in which this great Being, in some way or other invisible, comes to her and fills her mind with exceeding sweet delight, and that she hardly cares for anything except to meditate on Him; that she expects after a while to be received up where He is, to be raised up out of the world and caught up into heaven; being assured that He loves her too well to let her remain at a distance from Him always. There she is to dwell with Him, and to be ravished with His love and delight forever. Therefore, if you present all the world before her, with the richest of its treasures, she disregards and cares not for it, and is unmindful of any pain or affliction. She has a strange sweetness in her mind, and singular purity in her affections; is most just and conscientious in all her conduct; and you could not persuade her to do anything wrong or sinful, if you would give her all the world, lest she should offend this great Being. She is of a wonderful calmness, and universal benevolence of mind; especially after this great God has manifested Himself to her mind. She will sometimes go about from place to place singing sweetly; and seems to be always full of joy and pleasure, and no one knows for what. She loves to be alone, walking in the fields and groves, and seems to have some one invisible always conversing with her."

Such was Sarah Pierrepont, to whom Edwards wrote from Northampton entreating her to a speedy marriage. His tone is as urgent as the heart of a maiden could desire. "Patience," he writes to her, "is commonly esteemed a virtue, but in this case I may almost regard it as a vice."[1] The marriage took place in 1727, only a few months after his ordination, the bride having attained the age of seventeen. Before turning to Edwards as the laborious pastor, involved in a long and fierce controversy, carrying the burden on his shoulders, as it were, of all the New England churches, one may be pardoned for lingering a moment on this scene at the opening of his career, when the young minister and his wife took up their residence in the

---

[1] Appleton's *Amer. Encyc.*, 1st ed., art. *Edwards*.

beautiful village of Northampton. As a minister's wife Mrs. Edwards fulfilled the somewhat exigent ideal which the ways of a Puritan minister demanded. She became the administrator of the household affairs, saving her husband from all unnecessary knowledge and annoyance. She studied economy as a religious duty, bearing in mind the words of Christ, *that nothing be lost.* " She paid," says Dr. Hopkins, "a becoming deference to her husband; she spared no pains in conforming to his inclinations, and rendering everything in the family agreeable and pleasant, accounting it her greatest glory, and that wherein she could best serve God and her generation, to be the means in this way of promoting his usefulness and happiness. And no person of discernment could be conversant in the family without observing and admiring the perfect harmony, the mutual love and esteem, that subsisted between them."[1] She had been " educated in the midst of polished life, familiar from childhood with the rules of decorum and good breeding, affable and easy in her manners, and governed by the feelings of liberality and benevolence."[2] As her husband's reputation grew throughout the colony, her name became everywhere associated with his, but also as of a person to be known and revered on her own account. It was said of her by a somewhat witty divine, that it was understood she had learned a shorter way to

[1] Hopkins' *Life of Edwards,* quoted in Dwight, p. 123.
[2] Dwight, p. 130.

heaven than her husband. There was nothing morbid or sad about her religion; she had no depressing experiences; her piety, like her character, was a joyous one, bringing with it light and gladness. She made the home at Northampton a centre of genial and attractive hospitality, till it became almost like a sanctuary to which multitudes resorted, as in the course of years Edwards came to be looked up to as a spiritual teacher and guide. The famous Whitefield, who spent several days at Northampton, has left his impressions of his visit in his diary, — a record, it is needless to say, which also throws light on his own character: —

"On the Sabbath felt wonderful satisfaction in being at the house of Mr. Edwards. He is a son himself and hath also a daughter of Abraham for his wife. A sweeter couple I have not seen. Their children were dressed, not in silks and satins, but plain, as becomes the children of those who in all things ought to be examples of Christian simplicity. She is a woman adorned with a meek and quiet spirit, and talked so feelingly and so solidly of the things of God, and seemed to be such an helpmeet to her husband, that she caused me to renew those prayers which for some months I have put up to God, that He would send me a daughter of Abraham to be my wife. I find upon many accounts it is my duty to marry. Lord, I desire to have no choice of my own. Thou knowest my circumstances."[1]

[1] Tracy, *The Great Awakening*, p. 99. "He had not yet learned, if he ever did," adds Mr. Tracy, "that God is not pleased to make 'sweet couples' out of persons who have no choice of their own."

As in most New England families of this period, the children were numerous, and Mrs. Edwards, in addition to her other duties, became responsible for their training and discipline. In this respect also she was admirable, seldom punishing, and in speaking using gentle and pleasant words. She addressed herself to the reason of the children, was in the habit of speaking but once, and was cheerfully obeyed. It was the children's manner to rise when their parents entered the room and remain standing until they were seated. Quarrelling and contention were unknown among them. She prayed regularly with them, bearing them also on her heart before God, and that even before they were born. She aimed to bring each young will into submission to the will of its parents, in order that it might afterwards become submissive to the will of God. She had also relations to sustain to the parish. Here, too, her influence was great, and the ideal of character which she aimed to embody in herself a high one. She not only made no trouble by indiscreet remarks, but set herself as an example in the regulation of the tongue. Such a woman was sure also to exert an attractive spell over her husband. What her influence was, and how largely it controlled his attitude, will be seen hereafter.

For two years after Edwards became his colleague, Mr. Stoddard continued to officiate half the day on Sundays. On February 11, 1729, he departed from his earthly labors. A peculiar interest attaches to him in consequence of his teaching in regard to the Lord's Supper. He thought the rite was far too greatly neglected in the Puritan churches. In advocating its importance he spoke of it as possessing a converting power. His views of the church approximated that conception of it, as an organic institution, which is found in Presbyterianism rather than in Congregationalism, which constitutes also a bond of kinship between the older Puritanism and the Anglican church, against which for other reasons it had revolted. Mr. Stoddard can be easily conceived in some other rôle than that of a Puritan minister. He held, it is true, the ordinary Calvinistic theology, but he held it with a difference which was his own. He was the author of several books, in which his soul shines still as that of a kindly, humane, and honest man, to whom life and its issues are very real, whose wisdom is drawn from experience and not from speculative discussion in the schools. He made prominent a doctrine which was afterwards disowned as mystical or irrational, — the imputation of Christ's righteousness as the ground of the sinner's hope and confidence.

It was fortunate for Edwards that he should have been associated in his early ministry with such a man. Though he finally rejected Mr. Stoddard's idea of the Lord's Supper as a converting ordinance, as well as his conception of the church, yet the influence of the elder pastor and his writings remained, a leaven of practical wisdom and of certain theological tendencies, which still distinguish Edwards from many of his followers. Before the death of Mr. Stoddard, there occurred at Northampton a season of unusual devotion to religion. Mr. Stoddard had become experienced in dealing with persons " under concern " about their salvation. A little work which he had written, called A Guide to Christ, etc., had been compiled for the help of young ministers. In it we may study the questions which the younger pastor was propounding to himself in his first years in the ministry. They illustrate the dark and sombre mood which marks the opening of the eighteenth century in New England. Among the questions proposed for solution are such as these: Whether God works a preparation in the soul before it goes to Christ in faith; whether men should be encouraged in the use of means toward their conversion; in what conversion consists; how God can be the author of it and yet man prepare himself for it; how decrees are compatible with human liberty; in what lies the unpardonable sin; whether a man is ever justified in thinking that he has sinned away the day of grace; whether the threatened punishments for sin are out of proportion to its guilt; whether God is under any obligation to hear and answer the prayers of those who are unconverted. With such sad, mysterious questionings as these, the mind of the New England people, or a large portion of them, continued for generations to be agitated.

IV.

EDWARDS, AS A REFORMER. — SERMONS ON DEPENDENCE AND SPIRITUAL LIGHT. — SPECIAL AND COMMON GRACE.

The condition of the churches in New England at the time when Edwards arose demands a few words of explanation as an introduction to his theology. It was a period of decline and of deterioration, of many attempts at reform which only ended in failure. The lamentations over the situation are heard from the time of the withdrawal of the charter in 1684, or the closing years of the reign of Charles II. They began as soon as it was evident that the unique and beautiful experiment of the Puritan fathers was over, when the theocracy which had inspired such heroism as the world had not seen before was hastening to its downfall. Such an event was a catastrophe of the direst kind in New England history. It seemed to falsify great hopes and aspirations. It was as if God had turned away from favoring an enterprise which had His glory in view as its sole object and justification. Sore perplexity and confusion befel the religious mind in proportion to the greatness of its venture of faith. In his History of Massachusetts, Hutchinson remarks that the moral decline or deterioration has been exaggerated. We need not demur to this statement from one who speaks with so much authority, with an almost contemporaneous knowledge of the time. But it is not, after all, a question of how great was the decline, but as to how the situation was regarded by the religious leaders who represent the feeling of the hour. In their view it was a time of such religious coldness and apathy as to call for the judgment of Heaven, if in some way the evil could not be averted by diligent reform. And indeed it was believed that the Divine judgment had already been visited upon the people for their deflection from the ways of their fathers. The feeling that God was incensed gave rise to a prevailing consciousness of a great wrong existent in the community which must needs be discovered, and atoned for by deep repentance. The sense of sin, to use the religious expression, became deeper and more pervading.

There are some things, some acts, which speak louder than words, louder than the decisions of synods or the writings of private individuals, and by these is more truly interpreted the real condition of the moment. The spread of the delusion about witchcraft, with its attendant horrors, was only possible at this dark hour, with its morbid superstitious fears. So far as it was believed that God, for some mysterious reason, had withdrawn His favor, so far also was it possible to believe that restraint was removed from the enmity of evil spirits, that devils were allowed to ravage the community at their will. The witchcraft delusion would have been impossible a generation earlier or later than its actual date in the closing years of the seventeenth century. It was the culmination of the fears and misgivings which had been long gathering momentum for some such tangible outbreak. And possibly also, as affording vent for the superstitious excitement, it may have been the turning point of a new era.

Whatever may have been the extent of the moral or religious decline which is so generally bemoaned in the years that followed the withdrawal of the charter from Massachusetts, no one can read the records of the time without being convinced that there was a decline, — that morals, religious fervor, interest in public worship, were not sustained at the same high pitch as in the best days of the theocracy. The religious faith or creed of Puritanism was also endangered by rival or hostile creeds, which were now free to be introduced and to grow as they could find supporters. The days of repression and persecution were over. There was surely enough material for reforming synods if only they could get at the root of the difficulty. The chief recommendation which all concur in making is the revival and more vigorous maintenance of the ancient discipline. But how could that, which had declined from no apparent reason but want of faith or interest, be revived again without some great motive to faith which did not yet appear? The situation would indeed have been a hopeless one, if it were not that the complaints and lamentations were in themselves the manifestation of a certain dissatisfaction and unrest, symbols of the birth, as it were, of some new ideal, heralds of a coming change. This change or reformation, when its advent was accomplished, must bear some proportion to the long and bitter pains and agonies which had preceded it.

In the confusion of the time, the ends to be achieved were not clearly seen. Now that they have been long since accomplished, it is easy to see the *rationale* of the process, and whither it was tending. First, it was necessary to reaffirm the principle of Puritanism in such an emphatic way as to reach, if possible, the reason and the conscience. In the second place, it was incumbent to readjust the relations of state and church which had become involved in so much confusion. The latter of these ends was the more important practical issue, although it was the theological principle which made the practical issue possible of attainment. The dissatisfaction of the time proceeded in great part from the condition of the churches, deprived of the sympathy or support of the state, and not having achieved the principle by which the church could exist and thrive through an independent life of its own. And further, the churches in New England had mutilated their peculiar constitution, diminishing its native vigor in order to adjust it to the relations with the state. The Half-way Covenant, the concession of the church in order to a more pliable connection with the state, was still in force after the state had been practically divorced from the church, — a continual source of weakness and depression. At this juncture Edwards arose to do his peculiar work. If it seem to any as if the story we are about to relate were a petty or a local one merely, without universal relations, it may be said that we stand here at the beginning of a new cycle in human history, in which Edwards is the leader, — a cycle whose scope and duration include the Church of Scotland, and ultimately the Church of England, as well as the church in America. Modern ecclesiastical history may be said to date from the impetus given by Edwards, so far as he reversed the teaching of Wycliffe, on which the relations of church and state had been based for four hundred years. The religious world as we see it to-day is still regulated by the principles which he was the first to enunciate in their fulness and vigor. To his theology we now turn, asking the interest of the reader in perusing a chapter of human thought, the like of which cannot be read elsewhere in history.

It was in the year 1731 that Edwards had the honor of being invited to appear as a preacher in the "public lecture" in the provincial town of Boston. The occasion was a representative one to the young minister from Northampton; we may take it for granted that his sermon also had a representative character, — that like an ancient prophet he felt called to deliver his burden. The subject of his sermon was the absolute dependence of man upon God, — its more exact heading, God glorified in Man's Dependence.[1] The sermon produced a profound impression. Its publication was not only demanded, but the ministers of Boston, with others, felt called upon to bear their testimony to Edwards' worth; — they had "quickly found him to be a workman that need not be ashamed, despite his youth; they thank the great Head of the church who has been pleased to raise up such men for the defence of evangelical truth; they express the hope that the college in the neighboring colony of Connecticut may be a fruitful mother of many such sons; and they congratulate the happy church at Northampton on whom Providence has bestowed so rich a gift."

This event was as significant in Edwards' life and in the history of New England theology as when Schleiermacher preached his discourse upon the same subject, which marks the date of the ecclesiastical reaction of the nineteenth century. Of Edwards, too, it might be said, as the great German preacher had then remarked of Spinoza, "that the Infinite was his beginning and his end; the universal his only and eternal love." The two sermons, however, have but little in common except the title. Edwards does not seek to show that an instinct of dependence is rooted in the soul, forming an essential element in the human consciousness, or that its development is important

---

[1] Works, vol. iv. p. 169, Worcester edition.

to a complete human culture. He looks at his subject from the divine point of view, not from the human. Human dependence is both true and desirable, because it tends to humiliate man and to promote the glory of God. But none the less was Edwards' sermon an epochal one. Those who listened to it must have felt that a great champion had appeared to defend the old discredited theology. The doctrine of human dependence which formed the main idea of the sermon was ordinary enough to a Puritan congregation, but the mode of Edwards' assertion of it was new. There is an emphasis of certainty, an intensity of tone, as though there were some invisible combatant to be overcome, — an excitement in the air as if some new issue had arisen. If we interpret the sermon, it was the preacher's challenge to the age, — to the fashionable Arminianism which was denying or ignoring the divine sovereignty, which was magnifying man at the expense of God, which was cheapening the gift of divine grace by extending it to all, instead of the few whom God had chosen.

At a time, then, when the prevailing Deism represented God as if a passive agent, governing the world by general laws and second causes, as well as far removed from the scene of human activity, Edwards presented Deity as immanent and efficient will. The stress of his conception is on God as will, rather than as idea or reason. The power which is displayed in every act or exercise of the human will which tends to overcome sin or strengthen right principle is nothing less than the power of God. The deliverance of man from evil is an act of immediate divine efficiency. It is not only from God, but the process of redemption is God. When it is said that those who are saved have their good in God, this means that they have a kind of participation in God. God puts his beauty upon them, — a sort of effusion of God is poured out upon the soul. It is not so much that the Spirit of God works good in the soul, but the good is in itself the Spirit of God, — the two are one and the same. The goodness and the righteousness in the world are therefore more than mere moral qualities or attributes: they are alive, as it were, in efficient Deity; they are the immanent God, and not the changing modes of human conduct.

Closely connected with this teaching about the divine efficiency is Edwards' assertion of the divine *sovereignty*. The word in itself is not obnoxious. In the earlier Calvinism, sovereignty had included the call or election of nations to some high struggle for liberty or moral advance. But the word as Edwards uses it becomes synonymous with the tenet of an individual election to life, or reprobation to death. In this form Edwards asserts it as the cardinal principle of his theology. He believes that he has biblical evidence in its support, for when he defines it he prefers to do so in words of Scripture; — the divine sovereignty means "that God has mercy on whom He will have mercy, and whom He will, He hardeneth." It also follows from the doctrine of sovereignty, as he conceives it, that God was under no obligation to do anything for man. That He vouchsafes to save men at all is an act on His part of pure gratuitous condescension. It is also of mere grace that the redemption is applied to some and not to all.

At this point we must pause for a moment to inquire into the process by which such a profound and speculative mind should have reached this conclusion. Unfortunately Edwards does not explain the process. The foundations of this cardinal principle in his theology seem to be sunk in an abysmal darkness, which he makes no attempt to sound. Between the time when as a youth he was writing his Notes on the Mind, and his appearance at the Boston lecture, there is a gap in his mental history, which must be filled out from a general knowledge of his thought. His early philosophy, as we have seen, was thoroughly Berkeleyan in its character. So far as the outer world is concerned, God was conceived as the universal substance underlying all external phenomena. It was God's immediate action on the mind, in accordance with His fixed and stable will, which gives to the mind the idea of an external world. Things in themselves have no existence but only in the mind of God. God is and there is none else. But does God's immediate efficiency apply also to the thoughts and exercises of the human soul?

Upon this point Edwards hesitated. He expresses himself to the effect that his thought needs to be as clear on God's relation to the mind as it is in regard to His relation to the outer world. Nowhere in his published works does he, however, take up the subject for a full discussion. But there can hardly be a doubt as to the conviction toward which he was tending as a youthful thinker, — the conviction which underlies his conception of sovereignty, and which affords the unfailing clue to his purpose. He must have believed that God's relation to the mind and will of man was in harmony with His relation to visible nature. In the invisible sphere of man's moral or intellectual existence, God was still the universal substance; it was He that alone existed and there is none else.

This very significant transition seems to have taken place in Edwards' mind as he contemplated the phenomena of the human will. Here his dependence upon Locke helped to lead him into a practical denial of the freedom of the human will. He thought it was sufficient freedom to concede to man, if he were conceived as having the power of acting in accordance with his inclination. He therefore denied to the human will any self-determining power — the power to the contrary according to which a man is free to revise his action. At a very early age he had come to the conclusion that God determines the will. He felt the more unhampered in making this conviction the ruling principle of his theology because he was at the same time convinced that man was still responsible for his own acts, even if they were done through him by another. The self-determination of the will was not essential to the quality of human acts. Praise and blame attached to the act in itself, and not to its origin in a will which possessed power to the contrary.

But when Edwards had reached this momentous conclusion he was in danger of making the world of human experience a mere lifeless machine, unless somewhere there did exist the power to the contrary, unless what he had denied to man he were to attribute in an increased degree to God. The materialism, the atheism, the religious indifference of the age, would be overcome most successfully by asserting the freedom of the will of God in the fullest sense, as including self-determination or the power to the contrary, so far as the issues of human life were concerned. The Divine will must not be hampered or thwarted by the chains of necessity. God must be conceived as having the ability to reverse His action. Hence followed Edwards' idea of sovereignty as by inexorable logic. If God chooses to redeem men from sin, He is under no necessity to do so. If He chooses to save one man rather than another, it was because He was pleased to do so of His arbitrary will. To represent Him as willing to save all alike would be to deny to Him a sphere where the freedom of His will can be displayed in the view of all. In no other way can the power to the contrary which inheres in the divine will be exhibited so manifestly, so unmistakably, as in *His having mercy on whom He will have mercy, while whom He will, He hardeneth.* The existence of evil in the world is a proof of the divine sovereignty. God was under no obligation to keep man from sinning. He decreed to permit the fall, and to order events to its accomplishment. By His decree, every individual of Adam's posterity was involved in his sin. In all this God was free and sovereign. "When men have fallen and become sinful, God in His sovereignty has a right to determine about their deliverance as He pleases, — whether He will redeem any or no, or redeem some and leave the others. If He chooses to redeem any, *His sovereignty is involved in His freedom* to take whom He pleases, and to leave whom He pleases to perish." [1]

With this doctrine of sovereignty Edwards threw down a challenge to the world of his time. We have seen how in his youth his soul had been filled with an unbounded enthusiasm as he took the idea of God as the only substance, the one universal Being. His spirit must have been turned with indignation when, entering his ministerial career, he looked abroad upon the low level of an age which talked and acted as if God were not in its thought; as he witnessed the spectacle of a religion which almost seemed as if it could dispense with God, so highly did it exalt the independent

[1] Sermon *On God's Sovereignty*, vol. iv. p. 549. Cf. also vol. iv. pp. 230, 231, 232, and 254.

faculties of human nature, which spoke of the sober performance of moral duty as if it were a substitute for the passionate devotion to a Being, with its moments of spiritual joy and elevation. The motive of his sermon on Dependence appears in its closing paragraph or application: "Those doctrines and schemes of divinity that are in any respect opposite to such an absolute and universal dependence on God derogate from His glory, and thwart the design of the contrivance for our redemption."

In asserting the divine sovereignty as necessarily involving the principle of predestination, Edwards had only done what under similar circumstances Augustine had also done in the ancient church, or Calvin in the age of the Reformation. But Edwards inclines to go beyond his predecessors. While the world to his view and theirs presents humanity as divided into two great classes of the elect and the non-elect, yet he was not content to consider the *non-elect* as left by God to their own devices. God does not merely pass over them, as if in negative fashion, leaving them to the operation of general laws which secure their destruction. The grace divine, which is only another name for immanent, efficient Deity, includes within the range of its activity the evil and the good alike. Wherever he looks, the world is, as it were, ablaze with the fires of omnipotent, energizing will. To the distinction between the elect and the non-elect corresponds another distinction between

God's special grace and His common grace. The first secures salvation; the other underlies the world of affairs, of every-day life, of moral duties, the world of society and human institutions. The common grace of God carries with it no saving efficacy; none the less it is essential to the ordering of the world, in order that God's special grace may have the freer course.

This distinction between *special* and *common* grace is so important in Edwards' theology that it deserves particular consideration; for it constitutes in some measure an original feature in his thought. It brings the whole world, and not merely a part of it, into the sphere of the Divine energizing. It also forced Edwards to revise the ordinary theological nomenclature of his time. To the sphere of God's special grace he confines the use of the word *supernatural*, while the realm of the *natural* includes the operations of his common grace. In ordinary use, the word supernatural meant the miraculous interposition of God, as contrasted with the course of ordinary life. But Edwards had risen above the necessity of attaching supreme importance to miracle as the highest evidence of God's activity in the world. In plain truth, he takes little or no interest in miracles. He makes them hold a subordinate place, as compared with the internal evidences of the truth of Christ's religion.[1] By *supernatural* he means the

[1] Cf. *Original Sin*, vol. ii. p. 477; also *Work of the Spirit of God*, vol. i. p. 557.

spiritual, as something above and distinct from the natural life of man. In this use of the term, he is in accord with Schleiermacher and Coleridge, who led the revolt of modern religious thought against the appeal to miracle as the final and highest evidence for Christian truth.

But the difference between Edwards and these modern theologians is also as striking as the agreement. In the realm of the natural he incloses so large a part of human life as to leave almost no place or opportunity for the spiritual or supernatural. The natural does not pass over into the spiritual through moral conflict or purpose; the law of the spiritual or supernatural is not presented as a gradual transmutation of the natural. The two are separated as by an infinite gulf. They are as distinct as light and darkness; the natural is the absence of light, as light ceases in a room when the candle is withdrawn. In the sphere of the natural life is included, as has been said, almost the whole scope of human activity. Even conscience, which has been called the voice of God in the soul, is not regarded by Edwards as belonging to the spiritual order. The moralities of common life, the duties and the virtues which human society involves or which constitute its bond of unity, the art and purpose of human government, the amenities and affections of the domestic circle, — these and most other things that can be thought or mentioned are placed by him on the inferior plane of the natural, higher in rank but in essential quality not different from the habits and instincts of the brute creation.

What, then, is this saving special grace, which seems to be in contrast with almost all that we know as good, which may be in opposition to all that we esteem most dear? Edwards may have felt that he had ruled out so much from the spiritual that a supreme effort was required of him to demonstrate the existence and the reality of the supernatural. He responds to the inquiry or the doubt in one of the most beautiful and most eloquent of his sermons. Its early date is significant as showing that his theology had matured into its final form during his first years at Northampton. Like his sermon on Dependence, its publication was called for, and it appeared in 1734, when Edwards had attained the age of thirty-one. The full title of the sermon as it stands in his Works is: A Divine and Supernatural Light immediately imparted to the Soul, shown to be both a Scriptural and Rational Doctrine. His text was the words of Christ to Peter: — "And Jesus answered and said unto him, Blessed art thou, Simon Barjona; for flesh and blood hath not revealed it unto thee, but my Father which is in heaven." The emphasis is Edwards' own when he says, — "What I would make the subject of the present discourse from these words is, that there is such a thing as a spiritual and divine light immediately imparted to the soul by God, of a different nature from any that is obtained by natural means."

A sermon so remarkable as this has not escaped the notice of those who have made any study of Edwards' theology. It resembles so closely the later transcendental thought of New England as almost to bridge the distance between Edwards and Emerson. A recent American critic, speaking from a literary point of view, has called attention to the word *sweetness* as being Edwards' characteristic word. But there is another word which recurs quite as often in his writings, and that, too, in the most important connections, — the word *light*. It is more than an illustration of his thought: light is a word that controls his thought. In comparing the essential quality of revelation to light, Edwards is widely separated from those who have conceived revelation mainly as law addressed to the conscience. We have here an element in his thought which he assumes without discussion as if unconscious of its deep significance — a relic, it may be, of his earlier attitude before he abandoned the pursuit of philosophy. In this respect he differs fundamentally from his predecessors in the Calvinistic churches, with whom the legal tendency is predominant.[1]

Closely related as Edwards' thought is to transcendental modes of speech, there is yet, however,

---

[1] Edwards' view of revelation gives to the reason an essentially religious function, making possible also free theological inquiry. His view is expanded by the late Bishop Ewing of Argyle in *Revelation Considered as Light*, — a work which, like Campbell *On the Atonement*, may be regarded as developing the Edwardian theology.

a great difference. He does not admit that the human reason has in itself a divine quality, or that it is a spark of the divine reason, forming a part of the divine image in man. There is nothing in human nature, as it exists since the fall, which has anything in common with the divine nature. It is only when the divine and supernatural light has been imparted that the reason is purified and quickened to behold the transcendent beauty and glory of God. Edwards assumes, as a first principle, that when God speaks to man His word must be very different from man's word. There is such an excellency and sublimity, such divine perfection, in the speech of God, that the words of the wisest of men must appear mean and base in comparison. The divine word is like a fire, and as a hammer that breaketh the rock in pieces. Into the meaning, the transcendent beauty and glory, the joy and sweetness, of the divine word, they penetrate directly and intuitively in whom a divine and supernatural light is shining. Reason does not give this light, though the light cannot come where reason does not exist. Scripture is powerless also to impart it, though it cannot shine where there is no knowledge of Scripture. It reveals no new truth which is not already in the Bible. In this way it differs from inspiration, which is the unique mode of conveying new truth to the world as by prophets or evangelists. And yet this divine and supernatural light is something higher and more to be valued than inspiration, or the power of prophecy or of miracle. Inspiration is a lower gift, for it is capable of being imparted to those who have no supernatural light, — a Balaam or a Saul. But this divine light is not the mere external power of God: it is of God's own inmost essence, it comes immediately and directly from Him; it is not the acting of God upon the soul from without, but a vital and personal force dwelling within the soul, as if henceforth an organic element in its life; it is the Spirit of God communicating Himself to man.

The effect of this divine and supernatural light is to give the soul an insight into the truth of the Christian revelation, revealing a view of things that are most exquisitely beautiful. Others who have it not may yet have an intelligent opinion about divine things, as a man may have some knowledge or opinion about sweet things who has not tasted them. But the taste of divine things, the realizing sense of what they are, belongs only to those whom God immediately enlightens. This light within them — Edwards will not call it the "inner light," for he has prejudices against Quakerism — may come to those to whom miracles would have no weight as evidence of the truth. The historical testimony of miracles must be weighed by those who have the necessary learning or leisure. But the divine light may come to children and to weak women, bringing with it its own evidence of divinity. "The evidence that they, who are spiritually enlightened, have of the truth of the things of religion, is a kind of intuitive and immediate evidence.[1] They believe the doctrines of God's word to be divine because they see divinity in them." This light within changes the nature of the soul, assimilating it to the divine nature. This light, and this light only, has its fruit in holiness of life.

But this divine and supernatural light must be considered from another point of view. As Edwards thought, it came to but a few, — the majority of the race were doomed to live without it. The first man had enjoyed its full possession at his creation. But when he sinned, by rebelling against the divine will, the supernatural light had been withdrawn; and since then, so far as it had been vouchsafed to man, it had been as individuals only, by a free and gracious act of the divine sovereignty. In all this, Edwards' teaching resembles the mediæval theology which had conceived the divine and supernatural light as not forming a necessary part of the constitution of man, but rather as the *donum supernaturale*, — something superadded to his constitution by which man is made capable of communion with God. While the supernatural element is essential to the perfec-

---

[1] In his *Notes on the Mind* Edwards had written of Inspiration: "The evidence of immediate inspiration that the prophets had, when they were immediately inspired by the Spirit of God with any truth, is an absolute sort of certainty; and the knowledge is in a sense intuitive, much in the same manner as faith, and spiritual knowledge of the truth of religion." — Dwight, *Life of Edwards*, p. 691.

tion and wellbeing of human nature, yet it is not essential to the constitution of human nature. One may have everything needful to his being man, and yet lack its possession.

It might be supposed at this point that the situation was not a desperate one. There is still left to man the large and noble sphere of the natural, — the world of political or social or domestic life. In this sphere there still remain lofty and unselfish ideals, tasking man's highest powers, calling forth patriotism and heroism, and all the manifestations of disinterested love. The divine and supernatural light may after all be but a delusion, and the natural life the only reality. Such, indeed, has been the inference drawn by the positivist or humanitarian schools. But such an inference was, from Edwards' point of view, not only remote but impossible. The withdrawal of the supernatural light from Adam and his descendants was a catastrophe in human history which the imagination can only imperfectly describe or conceive. It must be spoken of as "a fatal catastrophe, a turning of all things upside down, and the succession of a state of the most odious and dreadful confusion." It is a state of darkness, woful corruption, and ruin; nothing but flesh without the spirit; darkness, "as light ceases in a room when the candle is withdrawn." Others also have used similar comparisons. Human life without the guidance of divine light is like a ship without its rudder, drifting to its destruction. But the situation, as Edwards was forced to describe it, is worse than any such metaphor can portray. Because man is possessed of a will, and since the will, as Edwards conceives it, cannot exist in a state of indifference but is determined from without, and that not in its subordinate volitions only, but in its predominant choice, it follows that the human will now rages as violently against God as, under the influence of divine light, it cleaves vehemently to Him.

We reach here the negative aspects of Edwards' theology, — aspects the most appalling which can be found in any system of philosophical or religious thought. The explanation of this awful conception of humanity and its destiny is to be found again in his denial of the freedom of the human will. Others, too, in the history of the church, an Augustine or a Calvin, had made the same denial, but no one before Edwards had grounded the denial in a system of philosophy which called for consistent application, and certainly no one before Edwards had dared to face the consequences which the denial involved. If the will by its very nature existed in a determined state, and that not for God but against Him, then it followed that in the will of every natural man there was all manner of wickedness, the seeds of the greatest and blackest crimes, wickedness against man and against God. This wickedness is not merely a potential or possible thing: there is in every man, in virtue of his birth or creation, actual wickedness without measure or without number; wickedness perverse, incorrigible, and inflexible, that will not yield to threatenings or promises, to awakenings or encouragements, to judgments or mercies, to terror or to love. The natural man, even the little child, is as full of enmity against God as any viper or venomous beast is full of poison. Every man by nature has a heart like the heart of a devil. Men are by nature enemies to God, and would dethrone Him if they could.

A view like this was not reached by a study of the contents of the human consciousness: it was not the result of either experience or observation on a minute or an extended scale. It was an abstract conclusion, deduced from the abstract principle that the human will could not exist in a state of indifference or equilibrium; for indifference or indecision pointed to a self-determining power, and a self-determining power conceded to man was a practical atheism, since God was then left at the mercy of man, waiting to see which way his will would turn, and consequently unable to foresee or decree all things from eternity. But if the will of every man was determined from his birth, then a will determined to evil must be conceived and described as such. Edwards, however, seems to feel the difficulty implied in his abstract conclusion. He represents men as saying that they are conscious of no such enormity of wickedness, or that they are aware of no desire to dethrone God from the government of the universe. To this he replies by his theory of God's *common grace*, which is God's sovereignty over wicked men, as His *special grace* is His sovereignty over His favorite and dear children.[1]

The common grace of God operates in two ways, — either by assistance or restraint. According to the first of these ways, the divine will may stimulate the natural human powers to the performance of what they otherwise would be unable or unwilling to do. This assisting grace may carry a man so far in the direction of truth or order that the result may almost resemble the work of saving or special grace. The action of the natural conscience may be thus increased in all the grades of human endeavor, as in political, social, or family order, until God makes the world a habitable or endurable place for spiritual men. But it is primarily God's restraining grace which prevents the world from going rapidly to its destruction, as it would otherwise surely do. Thus in the present order the intensity of human wickedness is so repressed that men do not realize the depth of their enmity to God. For this reason also they remain ignorant of the malice that is in them, and seem to themselves better than they are. The Divine efficiency is supreme in the natural order as it is in the spiritual order. It extends to all human customs, training and education, home influences, the voice of conscience, the fears of evil, sensitiveness to reputation, temporal interests, the light of nature. By means of these and other checks, God restrains the working

[1] Cf. vol. iii. pp. 72, 135; vol. iv. p. 55.

of human evil until the dispensation closes and the restraint is no longer needed; or rather until the glory of the divine justice shall be better manifested by removing the restrictions which the divine economy now imposes.

To the eye of Edwards' imagination, as also to the eye of his reason, this world has become the scene of wellnigh universal tragedy. The situation is in some ways enhanced because of the prevailing unconsciousness of the tragedy which life involves. On the one hand is humanity, hating, resisting, defying God, aiming at His dethronement, ready to rejoice even in the thought of His extinction; on the other hand is God, exerting the might of omnipotence to hold humanity in check until the moment comes when He lets go His hold, and precipitates the quivering mass of angry, boiling hatred into the glowing fires of an endless hell. Edwards does not draw back as he contemplates the scene. He studies it in detail, aiming to make it more real to the imagination, portraying it in language which for its boldness has not been surpassed. One hardly dares follow him, as his imagination takes wing, with the desire to see the worst, and to convey some conception of what he sees. The idea of tragedy in the ancient world implied in the evolution of a blind and cruel fate, the dreams and nightmares of the middle ages, the pictures which Dante has drawn of souls in hell, the visions of Milton describing the consciousness of demons, — none of these surpass, perhaps they do not equal, the horror which one encounters in the sermons of Jonathan Edwards. For Edwards was a powerful preacher, addressing a congregation with the conviction that it was his duty to make them see and feel the truth of his conceptions. His language takes a personal form, urging the reality upon each individual conscience.

There may be an appeal in his tone, since there is for some a possible deliverance. But even of this deliverance it is an indispensable condition that men should acknowledge their hatred of God, their accumulated guilt, which has justly exposed them to the divine wrath. He imagines a man demurring to this charge of hatred, and denying that he has ever felt any desire to kill God. But if, says the preacher, the life of God were in your reach and you knew it, it would not be safe for an hour. Such thoughts as these would then arise in your heart: "I have the opportunity now to be set at liberty, and need henceforth have no fear of God's displeasure; He has never done justly by me; He has no claim on my forbearance; I can rid myself of Him without danger." No man knows his own heart who does not realize that such thoughts as these, and even others too horrible and dreadful to be mentioned, would rise within him if such an opportunity were presented.[1]

Or, again, he paints a solitary man standing out against the background of infinite power combined with infinite anger. "If you continue in

[1] *Sermons*, vol. iv. p. 48.

your enmity," he urges on such an one, "a little longer, there will be a mutual enmity between you and God to all eternity. It may not have reached this point as yet, but at any moment death may intervene, and then reconciliation is impossible forever. As you hate God, He will hate you forever. He will become a perfect enemy, with a perfect hatred, without any love, or pity, or mercy. He will be moved by no cries, by no entreaties of a mediator. But this enmity will be mutual; for after death your own enmity will have no restraint, but it will break out and rage without control. When you come to be a firebrand of hell, you will be all on a blaze with spite and malice toward God. Then you will appear as you are, a viper indeed, spitting poison at God, and venting your rage and malice in fearful blasphemies. And this not from any new corruption, but because God has withdrawn His restraining hand from the old corruption."

V.

THE MORAL GOVERNMENT OF GOD. — FUTURE PUNISHMENT. — JUSTIFICATION BY FAITH.

IN turning from the universal ruin in which humanity is involved, to the deliverance which God is working, we meet another ruling principle in Edwards' theology, — the doctrine of God as the moral governor of the world. This doctrine, like that of the divine sovereignty, was deeply imbedded in the Puritan consciousness. Closely as the two resemble each other, they are also sharply distinguished. The idea of God as a moral governor introduces the conception of law as regulating the divine procedure; while sovereignty implies the arbitrary will, the free choice to which none can dictate. Sovereignty implies freedom from law, while moral government implies subjection to law. Although these ideas are plainly contradictory to each other, yet it is this very contradiction which gave life to Calvinistic theology, necessitating as it did an inward conflict, raising issues which, within the limits of the Calvinistic churches, were never quite satisfactorily adjusted. The idea of God as a moral governor acts as a check upon the idea of His sovereignty, reducing to some extent the arbitrary display of power, forcing, as it were, the divine will to yield to the requirements of the divine justice. But where the line was to be drawn remained an open question. In proportion as sovereignty was urged and enforced would the idea of a moral government of the world be weakened. In the history of religion, the divine sovereignty, which is the earlier conception, appears as yielding to the growing conviction that God governs the world in accordance with law. Such had been the course of Jewish history. In Calvinism also, in proportion as this same truth was felt to be necessary, had the original severity of the system been mollified, till election and decrees had passed into a subordinate position and gave but little embarrassment.

The modification which Edwards was working in New England theology sprang partly from his vigorous reassertion of the doctrine of divine sovereignty at a period when this conviction was becoming a subordinate one in the religious mind. From Edwards' time the New England clergy were classed as old or moderate Calvinists on the one hand, and as new or consistent Calvinists, with reference mainly to this distinction. The increased severity of Edwards' theology, whether scientific or practical, was owing to the deeper emphasis he laid upon the arbitrary, unconditioned will of God. We may see the situation at a glance, when we remember that the ruin of the world is attributed to divine sovereignty, while the deliverance, so far as it goes, involves the necessity of an appeal to moral law.

But there were motives which forced Edwards to give prominence, as far as he was able, to the idea of God as a moral or constitutional governor of the world. While he never forgot that the doctrines he was maintaining must rest on Scripture for their authority, yet he also recognized the reason as a source of strength upon which he always felt at liberty to draw in their defence. The relation between reason and Scripture he never seems to have formally considered; but in most of his treatises, if we regard him as making the two practically coördinate, we shall do no great injustice to his thought. Like every mystic, like Anselm, whom he most resembles in his combination of mysticism with dialectics, he had an almost unbounded confidence in the powers of the human reason. It was also his fortune to live in an age in which the appeal was generally taken to the reason, whether by the friends or the foes of the received theology. But when it came to making an appeal to the reason in defence of his theological tenets, the divine sovereignty did not serve his purpose so well as the resort to the necessities of a divine moral government which could be expounded in accordance with the analogies of human order.

Among the theological tenets, which were beginning to be questioned so early as Edwards' time, may be included the doctrines of endless punishment, the Trinity, the atonement, justification by faith, or the imputation of Christ's righteousness as the ground of salvation. Upon these doctrines Edwards appears as meditating in his first years at Northampton. In their defence he rests mainly upon the ruling principle of God's moral governorship of the world. Another motive which inspires him in this defence is a desire to save the churches from the inroads of Arminianism. About the year 1734 that fatal error, as he regarded it, was disturbing the peace of New England. As a deeper seriousness appeared to be settling down upon the people, Arminianism was offering what seemed to him a shallow comfort to the soul. The excitement at this time must have been intense in the parish at Northampton and the surrounding country over the subtle progress of a doctrine which seemed to imply that there was no need for anxiety about the soul's deliverance from impending ruin; that religion consisted simply in devout observance of church ordinances, and the performance of the duties of life,— things which every one had the power to fulfil. It would seem as if families were divided upon this issue, as if a root of bitterness springing up was threatening serious trouble and confusion. It was under these circumstances that Edwards proposed to himself the task of defending the traditional faith. In giving a brief account of his position upon the disputed theological tenets, regard will be had chiefly to that which is most important and striking in his thought. Any complete résumé or analysis of his works bearing on these subjects is unnecessary, as it is, within the limits of this volume, impossible.

The doctrine of endless punishment Edwards regarded as so essential that if it were denied, the foundations, not only of Christian belief but of common morality, would be overthrown. He expresses amazement that the great Archbishop Tillotson, who has made such a figure among the new-fashioned divines, should have advanced an opinion calculated to weaken faith in such an important truth. If this doctrine were to be abandoned as untrue, there would be no evidence left that God is the moral governor of the universe. The conception which Edwards had formed of humanity, as deprived since its creation of any divine supernatural principle, made it impossible for him to hold that the law of God as a moral governor could be written within the heart to such an extent that the divine penalties against sin could be realized through the conscience in this present world. He makes no appeal to the human consciousness, wherein is contained, as if in miniature, the picture of God in his relation to all that is not God. Since the conscience of the natural man does not participate in divine supernatural light, what else could he hold than that this world is no theatre for the display of divine justice? The present is rather a confused, mysterious dispensation in which God is carrying on His strange work. It is in vain to point men to the traces of the divine moral government written in the order of human society. There is, to be sure, a certain artificial or external correspondence between the divine and the natural, — Edwards never failed to see this analogy, — but it does not go far enough or deep enough to become the basis of a belief in the moral government of the world by God. Everything here has been so involved in confusion and catastrophe by God's withdrawal from humanity, that it is to another world we must look for the evidence that God rules this world in the interest of eternal justice.

It is quite noticeable that, in his treatise on God's Moral Government, Edwards appears as having brooded over the scepticism of the Book of Ecclesiastes, — that his strongest arguments for the necessity of endless punishment should be drawn from the mixed conditions of human life therein described. There had been devout psalmists in the same dark era of Jewish history who had felt the same scepticism, but without drawing the same conclusions; who, when they went into the house of God, discerned how even in this world the reward is with the righteous. But Edwards writes: —

"For unless there be such a state (of future rewards and punishments) it will certainly follow that God in fact maintains no moral government over the world of mankind. For otherwise it is apparent that there is no such thing as rewarding or punishing mankind according to any visible rule, or, indeed, according to any order or method whatsoever. . . . Nothing is more manifest than that in this world there is no such thing as a regular equal disposing of rewards and punishments of men according to their moral estate. There is nothing in God's disposals towards men in this world to make His distributive justice and judicial equity manifest or visible, but all things are in the greatest confusion."[1]

One of Edwards' earlier sermons, which he esteemed as among the most effective he had ever

---

[1] *Of God's Moral Government*, i. 572. Edwards is oblivious to the fact that the sense of God as a moral governor had grown up among the Jewish people, not only without an appeal to a future state of rewards and punishments, but with no definite recognition even of the sanctions of a future life. It is interesting in this connection to recall the aphorisms of Emerson on this subject, such as: "No evil exists in society but has its check which coexists;" "Punishment not follows but accompanies crime;" "Base action makes you base, holy action hallows you." — Cabot *Life of Emerson*, vol. i. pp. 219, 332.

preached, is entitled The Justice of God in the Damnation of Sinners. To this sermon we turn for the argument with which he met the rising unbelief before it had as yet formulated its dogma that endless punishment was incompatible with either the justice or the mercy of God. A summary of his argument runs as follows. Every sin deserves punishment in proportion to its extent. If there be a sin infinitely heinous, it is justice which metes out to such a sin an infinite punishment. The degree of guilt involved in a sin is measured by our obligations to the contrary. The greater obligation we are under to love, or honor, or obey, so the greater is the sin when we refuse to render the love, the honor, or the obedience. Our obligation to these duties, in the case of any person, is in proportion to his loveliness, his honorableness, and his authority. In these things God excels all other beings; He is infinitely lovely, infinitely honorable, and of infinite authority. Therefore sin against God must be a crime infinitely heinous and demanding infinite punishment.[1]

[1] In the above statement lies the gist of Edwards' argument. But he goes on to remark that the justice is more clearly apparent when it is considered that sinful men are not only guilty in one particular but are full of sin, of principles and acts of sin, till their guilt is like a mountain grown up to heaven. In this connection occurs the famous passage in which is asserted the doctrine of total depravity. The method by which he reaches this conclusion is, as we have seen, an *à priori* or abstract method, following the maintenance of the abstract principle that the human will is from birth controlled by a predominant choice of evil. "They (sinful men) are totally corrupt in every part, in all their

This argument of Edwards, which has been often repeated, cannot be regarded as entirely satisfactory. But while the mind demurs to his statement, there is in it also a certain element of truth, which we recognize when presented in some other form. Had he said that all sin was under the eternal condemnation of God, no one could have objected. But when he identifies the sinful person with the sin, he goes beyond Scripture as also beyond reason. Then the objection is immediately raised that a person committing an infinite sin should at least be aware of its infinite enormity, committing the sin with the full consciousness of its guilt. But Edwards does not trouble himself with the utterance of the consciousness. The infinite sin may be committed unconsciously; indeed, it has been already committed by the unconscious child at its birth.

There is an objection, however, which he felt obliged to meet, — a common objection at the time to the prevailing Calvinism, — that the decrees of God have made sin necessary; that the corruption of human nature being unavoidable reduces the degree of its guilt. In meeting this objection he argues that men, in their relations with each other,

---

faculties and all the principles of their nature, their understandings, and their wills; and in all their dispositions and affections, their heads, their hearts, are totally depraved; all the members of their bodies are only instruments of sin; and all their senses, seeing, hearing, tasting, are only inlets and outlets of sin, channels of corruption." Cf. sermon on *The Justice of God*, etc., vol. iv. p. 230.

make no such allowances. They treat their fellowmen as if the necessity or certainty of their evil actions were compatible with full responsibility; they freely attribute to their fellows an original perverse disposition, as if this aggravated their guilt. Why, then, should the case be different with God? One can hardly believe that such an argument could be seriously urged. But the inherent weakness of his theology was here exposed, and he resorted to any expedient to meet the difficulty. He was forced to appeal to the divine sovereignty as a last refuge, when appeal to God's moral government was no longer possible. He is not sure that he understands all which the divine sovereignty implies; but of this he feels sure, that God in the exercise of His sovereign will may not only permit sin, but by permission may dispose and order it: for the only alternative is blind and undesigning chance.[1] At this point in his theology, upon which everything hinges, he takes refuge in darkness, not in light. What he needed, what he was sincerely striving after, was some formula which, while expressing the relationship of human sinfulness to the order and nature of things, should not impute to God complicity with or responsibility for its origin. But this he could not get so long as he denied the self-determining power of the human will. The desired formula may not yet have been reached; but in some respects this question of the ages is nearer a truer solution in pro-

[1] Sermon *On God', Justice*, etc., vol. iv. pp. 230, 231.

portion as its rightful place is conceded to humanity, and freedom of the will allowed to be its inalienable prerogative. It may ultimately appear that the possibility of sin eternally exists as the reverse or opposite implied in righteousness; that the doing of a righteous act involves the contemporaneous recognition of the sin and its condemnation. Thus sin may come into actual existence through the human will, which approves the wrong instead of the right; while the divine will and the divine righteousness make sin an object of eternal condemnation.[1] The difficulties of the subject are great. It is incumbent on us to recognize them when criticising a great thinker who was struggling in the toils. None the less is it necessary to insist that his failure was a momentous one, that if not his words, yet his thought points directly to God as the author of evil.

Under the principle of God's moral government, and not of his sovereignty, falls what is known in theology as the doctrine of atonement. From the point of view of sovereignty there would be no necessity for atonement. In Mohammedanism, where sovereignty is the supreme and sole theological principle, no need is felt for satisfying the divine justice. God may pardon whom He will, on whatever grounds His sovereign will may dictate. It had therefore constituted a great advance in Latin theology, as also an evidence of its immeas-

---

[1] Cf. Royce, *Religious Aspects of Philosophy*, p. 449, for an admirable statement of this point.

urable superiority to Mohammedanism, when Anselm for the first time, in a clear and emphatic manner, had asserted an inward necessity in the being of God that His justice should receive satisfaction for the affront which had been offered to it by human sinfulness. So deep was this necessity, as Anselm conceived it, that even the doctrines of the Trinity and of the Incarnation had been interpreted with reference to this end. God had become man in order that as God-man he might fulfil the requirements of the divine justice. It seems also to have been assumed by Anselm, though upon this point there may be some doubt, that punishment or suffering in some form constituted the inmost quality of the offering which satisfied the justice of God.

Such had been substantially the view which Calvin had received by tradition, but to which he had also accorded a vital place in his theology. As such it had prevailed in the Reformed or Puritan churches, and was now announced again with equal emphasis by Edwards. In his treatise, entitled Of Satisfaction for Sin, he repeats the premises of Anselm and draws the same conclusion. His mode of presenting the subject possesses no special significance in the way of originality of treatment, though it is characterized by the freshness and intensity of utterance which marks the independent thinker. And yet this small treatise on the atonement is among the most remarkable of Edwards' writings, as containing the germ of a departure from received views of the atonement, — a profound hint which had been overlooked for generations, until in our own age it gave birth to a thoughtful and spiritual discussion of the great theme, such as it had never before received in any age of the church.

Edwards lived at a time when the belief was beginning to prevail that God pardoned a sinner simply on condition of his repentance, — that therefore no necessity existed for such a costly propitiation of the divine justice as was involved in the sufferings and death of Christ. Edwards, of course, rejected such a view, on the ground that such repentance would be inadequate as a compensation for sin. But while rejecting it he admitted also that, if there could be an adequate repentance or sorrow, it would be an equivalent for an infinite punishment. It is requisite, so he argues, that God should punish sin with an infinite punishment, "unless there be something in some measure to balance this desert, — either some answerable repentance and sorrow for it, or other compensation."[1] It did not occur to him that Christ, instead of bearing the penalty of an infinite punishment, might be conceived as offering an infinite repentance and sorrow which would cover all human transgression. He made the extraordinary admission of the acceptability before God's justice of such a repentance, and then passed it by as if something irrelevant which demanded no further

---

[1] *Of Satisfaction for Sin*, vol. i. p. 583.

notice. But the idea, which flashed before him and disappeared, was like an open vision to Campbell, a theologian of Scotland, — the land where Edwards' influence has been felt as in no other country, — who, in his great work on the atonement, took up the theory of an adequate repentance accomplished by Christ, making it a means of emancipation from what had become to him not only a narrow but a false theology. As working out a thought which Edwards had originated and sanctioned, Campbell may perhaps be regarded as showing what manner of man Edwards himself might have been at a later day.[1]

But with Edwards, as we have seen, the mediæval, the feudal conception of Deity as an absolute sovereign, was a controlling principle from which he could not escape. God, he argues, is as capable of receiving satisfaction as He is of receiving injury. The injury done to the honor of His majesty calls loudly for reparation. Humanity had incurred a debt to God which must be paid to the uttermost farthing. Such a debt infinite in amount must be paid, if paid at all, by an infinite being.

---

[1] Dr. Campbell, in comparing Edwards with Owen, a distinguished theologian of the seventeenth century held in high repute especially among Independents, remarks: "Owen's clear intellect and Edwards' no less unquestionable power of distinct and discriminating thought, combined with a calmer and more weighty and more solemn tone of spirit," etc. Cf. *Nature of the Atonement*, p. 51. And again: "The pages of Edwards especially I have read with so solemn and deep an interest as listening to a great and holy man." p. 54.

Christ therefore bore the punishment of sin, suffering, in the place of the elect for whom He died, a penalty which was the equivalent of their endless misery. The satisfaction which Christ renders to the divine justice, while it consists in a deep and bitter sense of the horror and heinousness of sin, becomes to the imagination a more fearful thing because it is undergone apart from any alleviation of the divine love: God withdraws from Him in the agony upon the cross, leaving Him alone in the power of Satan, to realize all that the lost may suffer in hell.

The question, to whom are the benefits of Christ's atonement applicable, and how are they to be obtained, leads to the discussion of the doctrine of Justification by Faith. At a later stage in New England theology the controversy arose as to whether Christ died for all or only for the elect. Edwards assumes the latter conclusion, as if an axiom in theology. The elect among humanity, as he regards them, differ in so vital a manner from the non-elect that they almost constitute a different race, as if God were evolving out of the mass of human beings a certain higher order or grade of existence. The prominence assigned to election essentially modifies, therefore, the doctrine of justification. The *locus classicus* on this great doctrine, — "Therefore, being justified by faith, we have peace with God through Jesus Christ our Lord," is not the text of Edwards' discourse. He chooses rather a cognate passage in Paul's epistles, which brings out a somewhat different shade of meaning: — "But to him that worketh not, but believeth on Him that justifieth the ungodly, his faith is counted for righteousness." In Luther's conception, who first proclaimed the doctrine, it is the word *faith* which unseals the mystery of God's dealings with the human soul. Hence the profound inwardness of the German theology since Luther's time, which has sought to unfold the contents of the human consciousness, as if therein also were to be traced the natural workings of a divine spirit. But with Edwards it is not faith, as representing an inward process, on which the emphasis falls. The doctrine of justification is, in his view, but another confirmation of the principle announced in his Boston sermon, — the entire and absolute dependence of man upon God. It is not by him that worketh, but by God that justifieth the ungodly.

And still there is something significant in Edwards' devoting a treatise to Justification by Faith. It seems almost like a relic of an earlier theology, something intruded into an uncongenial sphere. The phrase itself was passing into disuse. Under the influence of what is known in philosophy as Nominalism, the principle of individualism was applied to redemption, and each man stood by himself and for himself in the process of salvation. The earlier conception of imputation, by which in virtue of a membership in Christ the merits and righteousness of the Head of the race may be claimed as their own by every member of His body, had begun to seem as unreasonable as it was obnoxious. Edwards was then reaffirming in the unsympathetic hearing of his generation the doctrines of realism, — the solidarity of all men in Adam, the first man, who is of the earth earthy; and the solidarity of the redeemed in Christ, the second man, who is the Lord from heaven. Against the popular tendency which held that each man must suffer his own punishment, or stand in the lot of his own righteousness at the end of the days, Edwards maintained that Christ had borne the punishment and achieved the righteousness, by which believers in Him were exempted from the endless fate which threatened them, and might claim His achievements as their title to eternal life.

So vital was this relationship to Christ, as Edwards conceived it, that it became with him an underlying truth, in the light of which Scripture must be interpreted. The Arminians urged that the Bible was full of passages or exhortations which implied that men were rewarded by God for the merit of their own virtue and obedience. *Every man shall receive his own reward according to his own labor. He who gives to drink a cup of cold water only in the name of a disciple shall in no wise lose his reward. Thou hast a few names even in Sardis which have not defiled their garments; and they shall walk with me in white because they are worthy.* To these instances,

IMPUTED RIGHTEOUSNESS. 95

and others like them, Edwards replies that beneath the obedience and the virtue lies the merit of Christ. This alone gives to human deeds their efficacy in the sight of God. "That little holiness and those feeble acts of love and grace receive an exceeding value in God's sight, because He beholds those who perform them as in Christ, and as it were members of one so infinitely worthy in His eyes." The obedience of the saints is as if the obedience of Christ; their sufferings fill up the measure of the sufferings of Christ.

Difficult or obscure as this teaching may appear, it has always had a representation in the church. It found an early expression in the profoundest of the ancient fathers, as when it was said that humanity had suffered and died in Christ, and with Him had risen again to a higher life. It was a teaching which had survived the Middle Ages, taking on, though it did, a perverted form in the belief that the merits of departed saints were capable of a transfer to the living, in view of some consideration offered to the treasury of the church. With Luther it had been revived in a purer form, and under the designation of *imputation* had been accepted in the churches of the Reformation without dissent. Edwards also held it, but with a certain emphasis of his own, which made it subserve at the same time the doctrine of the divine sovereignty, or of man's absolute dependence upon God. The following quotation illustrates in a characteristic way one leading motive in giving prominence to the doctrine: —

"Seeing we are such infinitely sinful and abominable creatures in God's sight, and by our infinite guilt have brought ourselves into such wretched and deplorable circumstances, and all our righteousnesses are nothing, and ten thousand times worse than nothing, if God looks upon them as they be in themselves, is it not immensely more worthy of the infinite majesty and glory of God to deliver and make happy such poor, filthy worms, such wretched vagabonds and captives, without any money or price of theirs, or any manner of expectation of any excellency or virtue in them, in any wise to recommend them? Will it not betray a foolish, exalting opinion of ourselves, and a mean one of God, to have a thought of offering anything of ours to recommend us to the favor of being brought from wallowing like filthy swine in the mire of our sins, and from the enmity and misery of devils in the lowest hell to the state of God's dear children, in the everlasting arms of His love, in heavenly glory; or to imagine that this is the constitution of God, that we should bring our filthy rags, and offer them to Him as the price of this." [1]

The doctrine of justification by faith gained nothing in attractiveness by its association with Edwards' conception of the divine sovereignty. But there were also other reasons which prevented him from seeing, as he might have done, the full force of the truth which he was advocating. He regards the relation of an elect humanity to Christ

[1] *Justification by Faith*, vol. iv. p. 131.

as an unique as well as vital one; but he does not attempt to define the relationship, or to seek for it an eternal basis in the very nature of man's relationship to God. There is a curious and somewhat indefinite allusion, in his treatise on Justification,[1] to those who dislike such expressions as "coming to Christ," or "receiving Christ," or being "in Christ." These persons are also alluded to as *disgusted* with the word "union" when applied to the intimate bond which exists between Christ and the soul; they regarded these expressions as obscure metaphors which might at one time have had some meaning, but as now no longer intelligible. Edwards treats these objectors with a certain amount of deference, as if anxious to say nothing which would alienate them still further, as if he would gain their consent to his argument by any reasonable concession to their prejudice. But what may be noted as singular, and as calling for an explanation, is the fact that he seems to be indifferent to the exact phraseology of the metaphors, which he admits them to be; he is willing to use other words if they are preferred; he will speak of a *relation* to Christ, instead of *union* with Him. He regards it as foreign to his purpose to determine regarding the *nature* of the union with Christ, and refuses to be dragged into controversy over it. One would have supposed that it was essential to his argument to determine this very thing, whether Christ stands in an eternal organic relationship to

[1] Vol. iv. pp. 70 ff.

the soul, and what the ground of this relationship is. It is not that Edwards does not believe in this relationship; on the contrary it is the comparison of the vine and the branches, or the marriage union between husband and wife, which sets forth to his mind the relation between Christ and his disciples. But why is he so cautious and so reserved at this critical juncture? He even quotes a passage from Archbishop Tillotson to the effect that the union between Christ and true Christians is a *vital* one, and not merely relative; and he remarks of Tillotson that he is " one of the greatest divines on the other side of the question in hand." The inference is, that if Tillotson held to a vital *union* and not a mere relation of some lesser kind, the idea cannot be altogether disgusting, or irrational, or dangerous.

The passage we are criticising is a curious one. Perhaps it is more: it may be prophetic in its very obscurity of the coming disruption in the New England churches; as if we stood at the remote sources of the schism, and were watching the beginnings of disaffection with the doctrine of the Trinity. If this supposition be right, then Edwards was silent at a time when he should have spoken. Whatever may have been the motive of his silence, or of his unusual moderation and deference towards those who oppose him, he cannot be suspected of any want of faith in the full deity of Christ. It is perhaps the most reasonable explanation, that he was silent because he saw no inward significance in that relationship between God and man by which Christ becomes necessarily the Head of a redeemed humanity. The doctrine of the Trinity, as he then held it, threw no light upon the creation as subsisting in Christ. He subordinated the Trinity and the Incarnation to the necessity of an atonement. It must have been at this stage of his mental progress, that he wrote: "The necessity of Christ's satisfaction to divine justice is, as it were, the centre and hinge of all doctrines of pure revelation. Other doctrines are of little importance comparatively except as they have respect to this."[1] And again, even the doctrine of the Trinity is held in abeyance to the divine sovereignty;—"It seems to have been very much on this account that it was requisite that the doctrine of the Trinity itself should be revealed to us; that, by a discovery of the concern of the several divine persons in the great affair of our salvation, we might the better understand and see how all our dependence in this affair is on God, and our sufficiency all in Him and not in ourselves."[2]

Passages like these, when taken also in connection with the general tendency of Edwards' thought, indicate that the Incarnation must depend, in the

---

[1] *Mysteries of Scripture*, vol. iii. p. 542. Cf. also *Work of Redemption*, where the Incarnation is subordinated to the Atonement: "He was born to that end that He might die; and therefore He did, as it were, begin to die as soon as He was born."—Vol. i. p. 412.

[2] *Justification by Faith*, vol. iv. pp. 130, 154.

last resort, on the divine sovereignty as its ground and justification. For sovereignty implies, as he construed it, that when man had sinned God was under no obligation to save him from the ruin which sin had wrought. If God should decide to save any at all, He was absolutely free to save whom He chose. It is only those whom God elects to whom Christ stands related in the intimate bond of union symbolized by the figure of the vine and the branches. There was, therefore, no eternal necessity for the Incarnation in the nature of things. It is reduced to a contingent event depending on the arbitrary will of God. Hence Edwards felt restrained when the question arose as to the nature and ground of that *union* with Christ, which many had come to dislike as indicating some mystical, obscure relationship no longer possessing any significance to the eye of faith or reason. He did not feel called upon, when treating of justification by faith, to carry the process back to its final origin in an arbitrary will. Elsewhere, as when treating of God's sovereignty, or of the origin of sin, he pushes the argument to its extreme conclusion. But there was something in the doctrine of justification by faith which pointed in another direction, away from a sovereign or arbitrary will to some eternal, divine constitution of things, of which the divine will was the executive expression. As St. Paul had presented the great doctrine after emerging from Judaism, it included an organic relationship of every soul to Christ;

there was a certain divine root in every man's being which, when discerned by faith, made it possible for him to believe that, however active or dominant the power of sin within him, yet his whole nature was not identified with sin; that in his true self as constituted in Christ, there was a righteousness which he might claim as his own, though he had not yet achieved it. This led him to exclaim: "If, then, I do that which I would not, it is no more I that do it, but sin that dwelleth in me." And again he declares that the true life within him was not only lived by faith in the Son of God, but that the divine Son, was actually living in him.

Edwards' treatise on Justification is most interesting, because it discloses his mind as strongly attracted to such an attitude, and yet prevented from discerning its full significance by his doctrine of sovereign election. In his conception of human nature every man is completely identified with evil, until divine grace arbitrarily restores a supernatural gift which was lost at the fall. So long as he was held in bondage to these doctrines, it was hardly possible that he should rise to the acknowledgment of an eternal necessity for the Incarnation. Had he attempted to reach such a conclusion from his own premises, it would have been incumbent on him to represent the fall of man as if it were a step forward and upward in the history of human development. A tendency, indeed, to this mode of speaking finds expression in a sermon entitled The Wisdom Displayed in Salvation. Here it is practically alleged that the situation is a higher one in consequence of the fall than it could otherwise have been. The relish of good is also greater by the knowledge man now has of evil. These contraries of good and evil heighten the sense of one another. If man had not fallen he would have had all his happiness of God by his own righteousness, while now he may claim to stand in the righteousness of Christ. And still further, the union between God and man is a closer one; there is a more intimate intercourse and relationship.[1] Thoughts like these are not incongruous with the conclusion which some have drawn, that God decreed the introduction of sin into the world as the means of a higher development. While Edwards does not draw this conclusion, and might have rejected it as unsatisfactory or untrue, yet his desire to magnify the Augustinian doctrine of original sin leads him nearer than he is aware to the interpretation of the fall as upward and not downward; or to the language of a mediæval mystic, Hugo St. Victor, who apostrophized the sin of Adam as *felix culpa*.

There had been those in the ancient church who had discerned the significance which the manifestation of God in the flesh must have, apart from its relation to sin, as the keystone of the creation and the crown of humanity. Even in the Middle Ages an occasional protest may be heard to the same

---

[1] Cf. *Wisdom of God*, etc., vol. iv. pp. 154, 155.

effect, — that Christ is the completion of the creation, fulfilling an eternal purpose, and not merely an afterthought, with a purely remedial mission. But Edwards is not in the number of these. Christ, according to his assertion, comes into relation with humanity in consequence of the fall. Had there been no sin, there would have been no necessity for an incarnation. Because of this limited, narrow view of the relationship of Christ to humanity, Edwards was powerless to stem the tide of Arminian aggression. Standing as he did where the ways began to divide, he could not present Christ as the Son of God in whom the sonship of men inheres by an eternal constitution. But on this subject a change came over his thought in his later years, too late to modify his theology, but yet significant still as expressing the latent spirit and aim of the man.

VI.

EDWARDS AS A PREACHER. — HIS IMPRECATORY SERMONS.

AMONG the sermons of Edwards there are a few to which attention may be directed as supplementing the general statement of his theology. Edwards made no distinction between a scientific and a practical theology. His sermons are heavily freighted with the results of his speculative thought. Of his life work it may be said that, instead of endeavoring to create a scientific theology which might be recast or interpreted by sacred rhetoric into a practical, effective form, he was occupied with the effort to give a scientific cast to what was originally a practical or regulative theology. One of the peculiar characteristics which marked his preaching grew out of a tendency to make the prevailing theology consistent with itself by a thorough enforcement of the principle in which it had originated, or which constituted its reason or justification. In this respect he did not go so far as some of his successors. A certain mental sanity kept him from pushing his principles to any absurd or fantastic conclusion. None the less relentless was he in their application, until life and its multifarious interests were interpreted by the light of an abstract idea.

But despite the defects of his method, or the severity which is the predominant tone of his preaching, there is shown also at times a marvellous tenderness. He had the power of inspired appeal and exhortation. Refinement, dignity, and strength, and always and everywhere a fresh and intense interest in his theme, make his sermons not only readable, but still forcible and impressive, as if the preacher were even yet standing in our midst. The deeper one goes into the spirit of the hour or studies its issues, the more it becomes apparent that he had a mission to his age. The exposition of this prophetic burden is reserved for the second period of his life. But this consciousness of a mission is shown from the first in a supreme confidence which marks his utterance; an authoritative certainty of manner, as of one speaking from direct insight or by divine authority. Above the preacher, above the thinker, there towered also the majestic purity of the man, entirely sincere and devoted, — a character that seems wellnigh flawless; so that in his own age he was, if possible, more deeply revered as a Christian man than as the dauntless, unwearied champion of the Puritan theology. It is not attempted here to give a complete picture of Edwards as a preacher. A few points only are selected for illustration which are closely related to his theology, or serve to explain the working of his mind.

The intellectual element, which has been a marked characteristic of the religion of New England people, appears as their most legitimate heritage when we read a sermon of Edwards on the Importance of the Knowledge of Divine Truth.[1] The sermon fitly opens the volume of his works which is devoted to his more elaborate discourses. No ancient Gnostic could have urged more strongly the importance of a speculative knowledge of theology. The necessity for pure knowledge is enforced almost in the spirit of Socrates or Plato, or as in the writings of the ancient fathers who had been influenced by Greek philosophy, as if, without specu-

---

[1] The date of the sermon is given as 1739. With it may be compared a short essay or paper on *The Mysteries of Scripture*, vol. iii. p. 537.

lative knowledge, obedience or salvation were impossible. A knowledge of the things of divinity is absolutely necessary. Without speculative knowledge we can have no practical or spiritual knowledge. What are called the means of grace, such as preaching or the sacraments, can have no force or validity except by conveying knowledge. The Bible is essentially a book of instructions, which can be of no profit except as it conveys knowledge to the mind. "He that doth not understand can receive no faith nor any other grace." Even love demands knowledge as its foundation, for an object cannot be loved which is unknown.

Edwards does not write thus without a special motive. He is resisting his old enemies the Arminians, "fashionable divines of the age," who are decrying a speculative knowledge of Christian truth as unimportant compared with the practice of Christian duty. He has found, as he thinks, the secret of their indifference to theology in their conception of virtue as consisting in benevolence towards men, and not rather in love towards God. To know God, then, becomes the highest, the most pressing, of all obligations. He recommends the pursuit of the knowledge of God to his hearers by every variety of argument and appeal. He is tempted to depreciate philosophy, as he thinks of the transcendent claims of divinity. Let the philosophers differ among themselves as they may, it makes little difference to the Christian which may be in the right. But he warns his hearers not to apply this principle to theology. Divine truth is not a matter for ministers only, who may dispute among themselves as they can. It is of infinite importance to the common people to know what kind of a being God is, all that relates to His essence or His attributes; the doctrines also which relate to Christ, His incarnation, His mediation and satisfaction; the doctrine of justification, or the application of redemption in effectual calling.

To this end he pleads with his hearers to make diligent and laborious study of the Bible. It is not a cursory reading which will ever lead to thorough knowledge. Let them not be content with what they hear from the preacher or may gain in conversation, but search the Scriptures for themselves, using the same diligence with which men are wont to dig in mines of gold and silver. The incentives to this pursuit of divinity grow upon the preacher as his mind dwells upon the theme. It will be a noble way of improving the time; it will help people to a knowledge of their duty; it will enable them to defend the doctrines of religion when attacked by their adversaries. Incidentally we get a glimpse of the social life which Edwards is anxious to improve. If the people will only attend to this great study, they will find something profitable with which to employ themselves during the long winter evenings,— something besides going about from house to house spending the hours in unprofitable conversation, with no other object than to amuse themselves or wear away the time. Some diversion is doubtless lawful; but it is wrong to spend so many long evenings in sitting and talking and chatting in one another's chimney-corners; there is danger of foolish and sinful conversation, of venting their jealousies and evil surmises against their neighbors. He recommends them to procure and diligently use other books than the Bible, which will stimulate their minds as well as further the same great purpose. He has noticed in his pastoral calls among the people that they have a few books, indeed, which now and then on Sabbath days they read; but they have had them so long and read them so often that they are weary of them, and it is now become a dull story, a mere task to read them. He remarks that there are many excellent books extant which would afford them pleasant and profitable entertainment in their leisure hours. He laments that, through their unwillingness to be at a little expense, they do not furnish themselves with helps of this nature. For the rest, let conversation with others be improved to the same end. But the preacher is too wise not to see dangers and abuses in the course which he is recommending. In concluding he warns his hearers to avoid ostentation, and not study divinity for the sake of applause, or merely to enable them to dispute with their neighbors. Let them look to God, realizing their ignorance in His sight and the need of divine illumination. And finally, if they will only practise according to what knowledge they have, they will be on the way to further knowledge. This the Psalmist approves: *I understand more than the ancients because I keep thy precepts.* This also Christ affirms: *If any man will do His will, he shall know of the doctrine.*

It is a remarkable feature of Edwards' preaching which calls for explanation or comment, that though he is a philosophical necessitarian, denying the freedom of the will in its ordinary acceptation, yet his sermons abound in appeal and in pathetic exhortations, as if the will had the power of choosing between the motives of self or God. It has, indeed, been often remarked in regard to one of his notable sermons with the title, Pressing into the Kingdom of God, that it is thoroughly inconsistent with his doctrine of the certainty or necessity of human actions. In this sermon he insists on the use of *means* as indispensably necessary to those who are seeking for reconciliation with God. He brings to bear upon the will all conceivable motives to an immediate decision, as if at any moment it might exert its self-determining power. To press into the kingdom of God is represented as involving strength of desire, firmness of resolution, greatness of endeavor, engagedness and earnestness directly concerned with this special business.

That there is here an emphatic contradiction requires no proof. What is more to the purpose is to show, if possible, why Edwards himself did not feel the contradiction, — why he should not have been embarrassed when making an appeal to the will. There is a hint in his earliest writings which may throw some light on this obscure mental process. After having demonstrated that the world has no external reality but exists only in the mind of God, he remarks that we must continue to speak in the old way about things, because of the necessities springing from the defects of human language. We may infer, then, that though he does not believe in the freedom of the will he sees no impropriety in using the customary language. This also is the method of Scripture and of the common usage of life. Here, too, language has assumed its final shape, and cannot be bent to conformity with any speculative principle.

Other reasons may be assigned which throw light upon this fundamental inconsistency. While Edwards believed that human actions are but links in the chain of necessity, that God determines the will or that the will is governed by motives instead of possessing the power to choose between motives or to create a motive to itself, yet he also held that the will might be called free, inasmuch as freedom consists in the power of a man to act according to his inclination. He therefore seems to have felt that his admission that the will was free in the sense in which he defined freedom, warranted him in using the vocabulary of those who, like the Arminians, conceived of freedom in a widely different, in a real and vaster sense. It is a singular case of delusion, of bondage to the mere jugglery of words. The Edwardian notion of freedom stands as a hollow, grinning ghost, or as a mere *deus ex machina* ready to relieve the theological situation when the stress became unendurable.

But it is one of the subtle revenges which the reality inflicts upon a thinker who is seeking to evade it, that it creeps into his thought and moulds it unconsciously, even against his will. Bishop Butler gave expression to this recondite truth when he said, "Things are what they are, and the consequences of them will be what they will be." The emphasis which Edwards laid upon the will as the principal factor in man as well as in God, gave prominence to the will in matters of religion or of common life; and things being what they are, the consequences of them were what they always must be. Edwards was in reality making a powerful appeal to the will, and the human will responded in prolonged and mighty efforts to secure the great ends of life as Edwards was presenting them. The conscious self-direction of the will became the characteristic of New England Puritanism, constituting strength and nobility of character, standing out also in sharp contrast to the milder methods which affirm the principle of an unconscious growth as the law of the religious life. Some such qualification of the working of Edwards' theology is demanded if we care to understand and do justice to New England history. Not that Edwards escaped the consequences of his denial of a fundamental truth. It will be shown, directly, how his error followed him. But before we turn to this unfortunate and even calamitous result of an evil theory, we may present him as making his appeal in pathetic and affectionate language, urging men to seek an interest in Christ and to hasten to escape from impending danger.

The effect of Edwards' preaching, then, upon the minds of many who listened to him, was reduced to an urgent, absorbing appeal to the will. Some, it is true, may have been paralyzed by the fearful motives which he invoked, so frightened by the horrors of the dangers described, as to weaken the capacity for action. Some of an intellectual cast of mind may have been entangled by snags from which they could not get free, eddying about in an uncertain, aimless way. But there were those also who, in this process of spiritual evolution, felt goaded to greater and sublimer efforts in proportion as the horror of the situation was impressed upon their imagination. These, in accordance with the preacher's exhortation, struggled with desperate determination until they took the kingdom of God by violence. Those who succeeded were from one point of view an illustration of the selection of the fittest. Instead of being demoralized, they were incited to more vigorous effort, as they considered the extreme necessity of the case, the imminent danger of eternal destruction, the shortness of the time, the uncertainty of the opportunity, the difficulties to be encountered, the possibility of overcoming, the exceeding excellence of the reward. The preacher advises those who have undertaken to make the conquest of God's kingdom to keep their eye fixed upon the plain issue of the struggle, and not to fight shadows by the way. It will be a mistake and weaken them in the conflict if they are questioning about God's secret decrees, searching for signs by which they may read God's mind before its accomplishment. Let them cease to be distressed with fears that they are not elected, or have committed the unpardonable sin, or that for them the day of grace is over. When men complain that strong desires and thorough earnestness are not theirs to command, it is answered that God ordinarily works by means; that it is in their power to attend on the ordinances of religion and to strive against the corruption of their hearts, their dulness, and the other difficulties in their way. Earnestness of mind will follow earnestness of endeavor; and if there be painful striving, it will not be long before earnestness and desire will take possession of the soul.

All this may sound commonplace and familiar. And yet we are walking here in a field which is strown with the perplexities of a bygone age. There is one objection in particular, which the preacher strives to meet, which has a remote air, as if it never could have been real or genuine. Some, he remarks, may object that if they are earnest and take a great deal of pains they shall be in danger of trusting to what they do, and thus come to depend on a righteousness of their own. In this objection Calvinism is seen as the opposite extreme to Romanism, which makes religion consist so largely in outward works. If the Romanist feared that he should not do enough to secure salvation, the Calvinist is fearful lest he shall do too much, and thus come to depend upon his doing. Edwards disposes of the objection with no great difficulty, denying that there is any danger corresponding to such a fear. Instead of its being true that the more they do the more they will depend on their doing, the reverse is true, — the less will they be likely to rest in their doing, and the sooner will they see the vanity of all their works. But the objection really went deeper than Edwards perceived. It grew out of the inmost mood of the Calvinistic theology. Not only so, but not long after Edwards' time there arose the sect of the Sandemanians, who asserted as their fundamental principle the deadliness of all doings, the necessity for inactivity in order to let God do His work in the soul. Sandeman, the best representative of the sect, was a highly educated man, a Scotchman, earnest and intense as Edwards himself. He had drawn an inference which gave New England Calvinists an uneasy consciousness in the generation that followed Edwards. It was fortunate for Edwards that he lived before Sandeman appeared.[1]

But even in Edwards' most affecting appeals there still lurks the sense of the divine sovereignty,

[1] Cf. Sandeman, *Theron and Aspasia*, in which his thesis is worked out with skill and with considerable grace of style.

which orders even salvation in accordance with arbitrary will. He urges his hearers to sacrifice everything in this work of pressing into the kingdom of God, to forget the things behind, to labor for a heart to go on and to hold out to the end. But he also cautions them: "Remember that if ever God bestows His mercy on you, He will use His sovereign pleasure about the time when. He will bestow it on some in a little time, and on others not till they have sought it long. If other persons are soon enlightened and comforted, while you long remain in darkness, there is no other way but for you to wait: God will act arbitrarily in this matter, and you cannot help it. You must even be content to wait, in a way of laborious and earnest striving, till His time comes." But even so there is no certainty of the result. "If you stop striving and sit still, you surely die; if you go forward you *may* live." God has not bound Himself to anything that a person does while destitute of faith and out of Christ, no matter how hard or how long he may strive; but there is a great *probability* that those who hearken to this counsel, who press onward and persevere, will at length by violence take the kingdom of heaven.

The effects of Edwards' denial of the freedom of the will may be traced in a group of sermons to which it is now necessary to turn, painful though the necessity be. They may be called his imprecatory sermons. Out of the forty sermons included in the fourth volume of his works, they form a large proportion, being eight in number. They are written out in full, — an indication that they were the deliberate utterance of the preacher. It has been said, by way of extenuation for their severity, not to say cruelty, that they were delivered under peculiar circumstances. Attention has also been called to the hardness and cruelty of the age, which, if not justifying their vehemence, created a different standard of speech, in accordance with which they should be judged rather than by the gentler, more sentimental standard of a later time. It is quite possible, too, that they were demanded by the prevailing taste, that they were relished and admired by those who listened to them. It was a remark of the last century, that in matters of religion men take pleasure in being terrified, and admire the preacher who can rouse the most dark and awful feelings. But in this respect, even in the last century, there must have been a limit to human endurance.

When all allowances have been made that should be made, these sermons still possess an unique character in homiletic literature. They are marked by a vehemence not only unrestrained, but which seemed to be justified or demanded by the fundamental principles of the preacher's theology. Why should Edwards, of all other men, have taught in such an extreme form the doctrine of endless punishment, — a form unsurpassed, if not unequalled, in the whole range of Christian literature? The explanation must be sought, not in his character, not altogether in the conditions of the time, but in his theoretical denial of the freedom of the will. It has not been by accident that he has been chiefly known and is still chiefly remembered by his elaborate work on the Will. Even if we could not see clearly the connection, we might suspect there was some relation between what was obnoxious in his preaching and what was irrational in his theology. But the connection is not remote or obscure.

It was the result of Edwards' attitude on the subject of the will that he was forced to conceive the will as constituting the most essential or distinctive quality of humanity; and as the will of every man who is born into the world is fixed and determined toward evil, there was nothing to hinder him, there was indeed every motive to force him, into the identification of every individual man with unqualified and infinite wickedness. Men have not only a tendency to sin, but their very nature is identical with sin. Every man is born with a predominant choice for evil, which controls all lesser volitions and vitiates every act of his life. There is no border land which the will may cross from a state of indifference or indecision to one of conscious purpose; no twilight of the soul in which its forces gather undiscerned for some great resolution. There is no divine root of goodness in human nature which may be depended on to resist the evil tendency. Those who are determined toward evil are wholly evil, corrupt in every part of their being, totally corrupt in all their faculties and dispositions and affections; all their senses being mere inlets and outlets of sin, channels of corruption.

If sin, then, were already cursed by God, why should not the preacher be free to curse what God had cursed? Why should he be more restrained when speaking of sinful men than when speaking of sin in the abstract? Even the little child, notwithstanding its innocence and winning ways, was but the incarnation of evil, unmitigated and undiluted. How much worse were mature men, with whom the predominant choice of evil had been exemplified in almost countless acts of sin! This was Edwards' conviction, and he believed it his duty to proclaim it in a fearless and unmistakable way. It was a mistaken kindness to speak softly or indifferently. And besides, in view of Arminian laxity, there were special reasons for giving prominence to his convictions. The incipient tendency toward a denial of the doctrine of endless punishment was an urgent motive for its more emphatic proclamation. Devotion to God, if not to man, required that the divine justice in the punishment of the sinner should be maintained at whatever cost to the natural affections. If the sinner were wholly evil, so that the deepest root of his being was grafted in sin, then the sinner deserved to be denounced in such language as men reserve for that which excites their strongest and most righteous indignation. In the performance of his task Edwards was facilitated by the autocracy freely accorded to the Puritan clergy in an earlier stage of New England history, which, although it had begun to decline, had not by any means disappeared.

One of the strongest of these imprecatory sermons, whose argument is condensed in its title, Wicked Men Useful in their Destruction Only, illustrates a peculiar phase of Edwards' thought. It has often been noticed that a certain pantheistic tendency attaches to the extreme forms of the doctrine of divine sovereignty. There are various types and phases of pantheism, as there are of monotheism. To that form of the belief which attempts the deification of nature, or of all that is, Edwards had no direct leaning. Nor to the Buddhistic temper, which treats the world of outward things as an illusion destined to cease, had he any inclination. In the shape, also, which pantheism sometimes assumes, that final annihilation waits upon all which does not realize absorption into God, there was something which to Edwards was repulsive. To his mind, the outward world was real only as being the expression of the stable will of God. Annihilation is impossible because he entertains a profound reverence for being or existence, so that he who is once possessed of will, and whose will is determined by God, is born to exist forever. But this evil will, whether in men or angels, though it seems to act in defiance of God, is no dualistic factor in the universe: it still serves the one divine will quite as really as if devoted to the righteous service of God. All men alike, whether sinners or saints, are useful in the divine economy. "There can be but two ways in which man can be useful, either in *acting* or in being *acted upon* and *disposed* of."[1] The latter constitutes the usefulness of the wicked. They are the material upon which the divine justice operates. Without their existence, God's justice would have remained inactive, as a potency without opportunity for exercise or manifestation. God may be said to need the wicked in order to the activity of His justice, as much as the righteous in order to the display of His love. When men objected that they were useful to their fellows in the various walks of life, that they were not wholly bad, since they aimed to live for one another, for their friends, their neighbors, or the public weal, — nay, that they might even be of service to the church by the promotion of civil order, — to such pleas Edwards replied, that so long as men did not perform these duties designedly, with a conscious direction of the will toward God, they were not useful as men or as rational creatures, but useful only as irrational things are useful, as the timber and stone of which a house is built. However great their service, it was of no more value in God's eyes than the actions of the brute creation. Their only real usefulness lay in being reserved as vessels of dishonor, through which God glorified His majesty.

[1] Vol. iv. p. 301.

In order to overcome the indifferent mood in which people might listen to the preaching of endless punishment, Edwards expatiates at length upon its nature; he shows how intolerable it will be, how it is without remedy or relaxation or mitigation, how it is as unavoidable as it will be intolerable. Every evasion or loophole of escape, every fond imagination of a possible release, is shown to be futile and vain. No individual, thinking himself so obscure as to be beneath notice, may hope to elude attention, or to crawl into heaven unobserved: neither annihilation nor restoration after ages of suffering are equivalent substitutes for the punishment of an infinite sin, which calls for infinite penalty. The fertility of Edwards' mind is displayed in the supply of images with which he presses home upon his hearers his awful theme. His imagination attempts to measure the significance of the word *eternal*. The thought of these terrific sermons reaches its climax when the saints in glory are represented as callous to the sufferings of the lost. For there is one last hope, one last refuge to which sinful humanity is driven to cling, when confronting the desperate situation. If God be, as He is said to be, without pity, as He executes eternal judgment on His foes; if it be that His heart is full of burning anger against those who have defied Him, so that the possibility of appealing to His love is forever closed, may it not be that those who have the good fortune to be saved, the parents, the friends, the lovers of their kind, will still retain something of their common humanity, — the natural compassion or sympathy which will reduce their own pleasure in heaven when they witness the agony of souls in hell? To this pathetic hope, which in the lowest extremity still trusts in humanity when there is no basis for trust in God, Edwards replies by affirming in substance that the humanity of the saints is absorbed or annihilated in God. They, too, will look upon the scene without flinching; their serenity will not only be undisturbed, but their happiness will be the deeper because of the contrast afforded by this ever-present spectacle of woe. "There will be no remaining difficulties about the justice of God, about the absolute decrees of God, or anything pertaining to the dispensations of God towards men. Divine justice in the destruction of the wicked will then appear as light without darkness, and will shine as the sun without the clouds." Those who are saved will then be thinking, not of man, but of God, how God is glorifying His justice on the vessels of dishonor, or glorifying His grace on the vessels of mercy. Even fathers and mothers will then rejoice and praise God as they witness eternal justice poured out upon their own offspring. If this seems strange or impossible, it must be remembered that the circumstances of our nature will then be changed. What is virtue here will be no virtue there. Now virtue shows itself by natural affection, but natural affection is no virtue of the saints in glory. However the saints in heaven may have loved the damned while here, especially those who were near and dear to them in this world, they will have no love to them hereafter. Virtue will then be exercised in some other and higher manner.[1]

It is not that God and the saints will be unable to realize the sufferings of the lost. Although the saints look upon the smoke of their torments and the raging of the fires of their burning afar off, they will yet measure the misery and the agony more truly than any of us do here. "God also is everywhere present with His all-seeing eye. He is in heaven and in hell, and in and through every part of His creation. He is where every devil is, and where every damned soul is; He is present by His power and by His essence. He not only knows as well as those in heaven who see at a distance, but he knows as perfectly as those who feel the misery. He seeth into the inmost recesses of the hearts of those miserable spirits, for He upholds them in being."[2] While the joy which the saints feel, as they contemplate the sufferings of the lost, springs partly from their devotion to God's glory and their desire to see His justice vindicated, yet it also springs from the deeper realization of their own happiness. They are lost in adoring wonder at the mystery of the love which elected and redeemed them. The sight of hell torments will exalt the happiness of the saints forever. They will prize their own blessedness and God's love the more when they see the doleful condition

---

[1] Vol. iv. pp. 291, 294.   [2] Vol. iv. p. 291.

of the damned, and how dreadful it is to suffer the anger of God. It will give the saints a deeper sense of the distinguishing love of God, who has made so great a difference between themselves and others, who are now lost, but who were no worse than themselves and have deserved no worse of God. When they shall behold all this, how will heaven ring with their praises; with what love and ecstasy will they sing the song of the redeemed![1]

The preacher does not hesitate to avow his belief that the great majority of mankind have been lost. To this conclusion he was driven by observation and experience, by theoretic considerations, by the enforcement of a high ideal. Again and again he reiterates the statement that out of the great mass of mankind only a few will be saved. "The bigger part of men who have died heretofore have gone to hell." The whole heathen world is hopelessly doomed. In the Christian world the prospect is little better for large masses of men under the dominion of idolatry and superstition. The majority of each passing generation is lost. In every congregation there are many whose damnation is sure.[2]

Edwards defended his manner of preaching, on the ground that, if these things were true, it was only kindness to a congregation to present them,

---

[1] Cf. vol. iv. p. 307; also ch. iii. of *Miscell. Observations*, vol. iv. p. 612.

[2] Cf. vol. i. pp. 78, 537; vol. ii. p. 499; vol. iii. pp. 448, 449; vol. iv. pp. 316, 386, 583.

and that, too, in what he calls the "liveliest" manner. When ministers preach of hell in a cold manner, though they may say in words that it is infinitely terrible, they contradict themselves. The main work of ministers is to preach the gospel. A minister would miss it very much if he should insist too much on the terrors of the law and neglect the gospel; but yet the law is very much to be insisted on, and the preaching of the gospel is like to be in vain without it.[1] But no one can read these imprecatory sermons without feeling that the preacher goes beyond the requirements of duty or of rhetoric. There enters into them a personal tone, as if he spoke in the divine name to curse the enemies of God. He is almost over-zealous for the honor of the Lord of Hosts. He reflects the spirit of the old dispensation, — *Shall not I hate them, O Lord, that hate Thee, and rise up against them that rise up against Thee? Yea, I hate them right sore, as if they were mine enemies.* "You have often seen a spider or some other noisome insect when thrown into the midst of a fierce fire, and have seen how immediately it yields to the force of the flames: there is no long struggle, no fighting against the fire, no strength exerted to oppose the heat, or to fly from it, but it immediately stretches forth itself and yields; and the fire takes possession of it, and at once it becomes full of fire and is burned into a bright coal. Here is a little image of what you will be the subjects of in hell."[2] And

---

[1] Cf. *Marks of the Work of the Spirit*, etc., vol. i. p. 538.
[2] Vol. iv. p. 264.

again he seems to lose patience, to grow provoked, because men still resist his intense earnestness of appeal. He closes a sermon with these words: "You who now hear of hell and the wrath of the great God, and sit here in these seats so easy and quiet and go away so careless, — by and by you will shake and tremble, and cry out and shriek, and gnash your teeth, and will be thoroughly convinced of the vast weight and importance of these great things which you now despise. You will not then need to hear sermons in order to make you sensible."[1]

But if it be painful to read these sermons of Edwards, what must it have been to have heard them! The traditions still linger in New England of the effect they produced. One man has recorded that, as he listened to him when discoursing of the day of judgment, he fully anticipated that the dreadful day would begin when the sermon should come to an end! He was the greatest preacher of his age. It is only at rare intervals that a man endowed with such a power appears. His effectiveness did not lie in voice and gesture. He was accustomed to lean, it is said, upon one arm, fastening his eyes upon some distant point in the meeting-house. But beneath the quiet manner were the fires of a volcano. His gravity of character, his profundity of spiritual insight, his intense realism as if the ideal were the only real, his burning devotion, his vivid imagination, his master-

[1] Vol. iv. p. 265.

ful will, — these entered into his sermons. He was almost too great a man to let loose upon other men in their ordinary condition. He was like some organ of vast capacity whose strongest stops or combinations should never have been drawn. The account has been left to us of the impression he produced in the little village of Enfield, in Connecticut, where he went to preach one Sunday morning in the month of July, 1741. The congregation had assembled in its usual mood, with no special interest or expectation. The effect of the sermon was as if some supernatural apparition had frightened the people beyond control. They were convulsed in tears of agony and distress. Amid their tears and outcries the preacher pauses, bidding them to be quiet in order that he may be heard.[1] This was the sermon which, if New England has forgiven, it has never been able to forget. Its title was, — Sinners in the Hands of an Angry God. The text was a weird passage from the book of Deuteronomy, — *Their foot shall slide in due time.* The wicked are here represented as, equally with the righteous, a manifestation of the one living, eternal will. They illustrate an attri-

---

[1] Cf. Trumbull's *History of Connecticut*, vol. ii. p. 145. According to another account, Edwards preached this same sermon on an occasion when he was called to take the place of Whitefield, who had failed to appear when a multitude were gathered to hear him. Although unknown to most of his audience in person, and with the disappointment of the assembly to overcome, he produced an effect which Whitefield could not have surpassed. Cf. Rev. J. W. Alexander, *Centen. Discourse of New Jersey College.*

bute of the divine nature. The justice of God is visible in their continuance in life: it will only be more visible hereafter. God now holds them in this life as long as it suits His purpose; He holds them on the slippery declining ground, on the edge of a pit where they could not stand alone without His help. They are already under a sentence of condemnation. When God lets go they will drop. God does not keep them from sliding to their fate because he has any consideration for them. He is even more angry with many of those now living, "yea, doubtless with many that are now in this congregation," than He is with many of those who are in hell. For these the wrath of God is burning, the pit is prepared, the fire is ready, the furnace is hot, the flames do rage and glow. The devils are waiting and watching for them, like lions restrained that are greedy for their prey. "The unconverted are now walking over the pit of hell on a rotten covering, and there are innumerable places in this covering so weak that they will not bear their weight, and these places are not seen." These do not realize what will be their fate. Though they know that the majority of men are lost, they flatter themselves with a prospect of peace and safety. They do not realize that the wrath of God against them is like great waters dammed up for the present, but rising higher and higher; that "God holds them over the pit of hell much as one holds a spider or some loathsome insect over the fire; that they are ten thousand times more abominable in

His eyes than a venomous serpent is in ours." And there is no reason to be given why those sitting in the presence of the preacher have not dropped into hell since they rose in the morning, or since they have been sitting there in God's house, but God's mere arbitrary will, — the uncovenanted, unobliged forbearance of an incensed God. In some of his sermons, Edwards warned his hearers not to abuse his preaching to their discouragement. But in this discourse there is no qualification; it is one constant strain of imprecation against sinful humanity from beginning to close. And the sermon ends with the words: —

"If we knew that there was one person and but one, in the whole congregation, that was to be the subject of this misery, what an awful thing it would be to think of! If we knew who it was, what an awful sight would it be to see such a person! How might all the rest of the congregation lift up a lamentable and bitter cry over him! But, alas! instead of one, how many it is likely will remember this discourse in hell! And it would be a wonder if some that are now present should not be in hell in a very short time, before this year is out. And it would be no wonder if some persons that now sit here in some seats of this meeting-house, in health and quiet and secure, *should be there before to-morrow morning.*"

The Personal Narrative of Edwards, which covers the earlier years of his ministry, discloses the preacher as endeavoring, by meditation and an ever-deepening experience, to make real to himself the doctrines he was preaching to others. He records that the gospel seemed to him like the richest treasure. Even seeing the name of Christ causes his heart to burn within him. He often recalls the affecting and delightful text, *A man shall be as an hiding-place from the wind and a covert from the tempest.* He likes to think of himself as a child taking hold of Christ, to be led by Him through the wilderness. Once, as he rode out into the woods in the year 1737, and alighted in a retired place, he had a view of Christ, as a mediator, of His sweet grace and love and condescension, a view wherein the person of Christ appeared of such transcendent excellence, as great even above the heavens, that he was overcome, and remained for an hour in a flood of tears and weeping aloud. The holiness of God appeared to him as the most lovely of His attributes. He had learned also to delight in His sovereignty, in His showing mercy to whom He would show mercy. It was a pleasure to ask of Him this sovereign mercy. But these religious raptures were also accompanied by affecting views of his own sinfulness and vileness. The sense of his wickedness and the badness of his heart was stronger after his conversion than before. His wickedness seemed to surpass that of all others. No language was too strong for the purposes of self-condemnation. His heart seemed to him like an abyss infinitely deeper than hell. He constantly longed for a broken heart and to lie low before God. He could not bear to think of being no more humble than other Christians. "Others speak of their longing to be 'humbled to the dust;' that may be a proper expression for them, but I always think of myself, that I ought, and it is an expression that has long been natural for me to use in prayer, 'to lie infinitely low before God.'" If he preached to others the necessity of dependence upon God's grace and strength, of standing only in the righteousness of Christ, and of adoring the sovereignty which presides over the universe, it was not as mere tenets of a sound doctrine. He had come for himself to have this sense of absolute dependence; he abhorred his own righteousness; the thought of any goodness in himself was detestable to him. Once more, in 1739, he was overcome and burst forth into loud weeping as he thought how meet and suitable it was that God should govern the world, ordering all things according to His own pleasure.

It is suggestive to note that these high experiences are always recorded as coming to him when he is alone with nature, as when he rides through retired and lonely roads, or, leaving his horse, plunges into the still depths of the forest. This sympathy with nature had shown itself when he was a child, leading him into solitary places in the woods in order to communion with God in prayer. In his youth also he had displayed a marvellous aptitude for reading the secrets of the external world. Though he had abandoned the study of

[1] Dwight, *Life of Edwards*, p. 133.

natural science when he turned to theology, his days were still bound together by natural piety. In the contrast also which nature offered with its unconscious life, where there is no continuous strain and effort of anxious purpose, he could find comfort and relief, — a closer communion with God than when scrutinizing the workings of the intense and concentrated will.

SECOND PERIOD.

THE GREAT AWAKENING. 1735-1750.

I.

REVIVAL AT NORTHAMPTON. — NARRATIVE OF SURPRISING CONVERSIONS.

THE preaching of Edwards, of which illustrations have been given, could at no time have been listened to with indifference. If on the one hand it may have provoked intense resistance, on the other hand, when received as true, it must have been followed by some extraordinary attestation of its power, or, in the current phraseology, have been remarkably blessed. The time had now come for that great ecclesiastical reaction or revival, whichever we may term it, for which synods had been laboring, though ineffectually, for nearly fifty years. The lamentations of clergy and laity over the low estate of the church, the aspirations for a church restored to its pristine earnestness, as in the early days of New England history, — these were prophetic of the event which now came to pass under the inspiration of Edwards' influence. To him belongs the credit of initiating a movement which, beginning at Northampton, was to spread over New

England and throughout the colonies in America,— which was to penetrate into Scotland and England, stimulating and giving form to ideas which were already fermenting in the mind of Wesley.[1]

The impulse of the Great Awakening was a theological conviction which first took shape in Edwards' mind, — a belief in the immediate action of the Divine Spirit upon the human soul. When Edwards as a youth was meditating upon the divine immanence as constituting the reality of the outward world, he was preparing himself for his distinctive task. At some later stage of his history (the exact moment is unknown, as the process is undescribed), he took a step which carried him beyond Berkeley by applying the Berkeleyan principle to the human mind. God was then seen to be holding as direct and immediate a relationship to the soul as he held to the external world. This principle became the foundation of Edwards' doctrine of conversion.

---

[1] 'In her *Life of Wesley*, p. 196, Miss Wedgwood remarks: "A great awakening to the interests of eternity, as they would then be called, had already taken place in America, an account of which, written by Jonathan Edwards, under whose preaching it had originated, was read by Wesley during a walk from London to Oxford (1738). 'Surely this is the Lord's doing, and it is marvellous in our eyes,' he writes in his journal after the perusal. Nothing equal to the sudden and general emotion described by Edwards had as yet occurred in his own country, and he doubtless was led to desire earnestly that England might not lag behind America in the path of grace." Three months after this date occurs the first instance of "bodily effects" under Wesley's preaching.

But the origin of the principle may be traced still further back until we come to the peculiar ideas which Calvin had stamped upon the churches owning allegiance to his authority. While Calvin had separated God and man to such an extent as to make almost impossible a communication between the divine and the human, he had endeavored to compensate for this deficiency in his theology by attaching greater importance to the office and work of the Holy Spirit. Luther had connected God and man through the medium of devout feeling, so that the word of God in Scripture became the reflex of human experience. Calvin regarded Scripture as an arbitrary and external revelation of the divine will. In order to bring the mind to a recognition of the truth of Scripture, he presupposed an activity of the Holy Spirit, which bore testimony in the heart to the truth of the written Word. This element in Calvin's teaching does not appear at once as directly operative in the theology of the Reformed churches. It first became an effective principle, not in the Presbyterian communions of Scotland or England, but in the more extreme form of Calvinism known as Independency. And it was not in England, but in the Puritan churches of the New England theocracy, that the custom first became a general one, of requiring a statement of the experience wrought by the Holy Spirit within the soul, as a condition of church membership. In so doing the Puritans of New England had introduced a theological as well as a practical idea, which, however obnoxious it may have been in its workings, was none the less of profound significance for the future of religion and theology. It was destined to spread to England, and to revive the spirit of Presbyterianism; it was to be the means of bringing the Calvinistic theology into line with the inwardness of German theology. It was this doctrine which was taken up by Edwards, and was combined with his speculative principles of the immediacy of the divine action, whether in the external world or in the sphere of human thought and feeling.

It was therefore no accidental circumstance that the first great instance of what are called revivals should have been witnessed in America and not in England. The idea of revivals is the gift of American to foreign Calvinism. Methodism also appears as indebted to Puritanism chiefly for this leading characteristic of its system of religious culture. When the Puritan churches arose from their depression, whether in England or America, they found the principle of their restoration in a seed of life after their own kind, which had long remained dormant, but which was first quickened into vital power in the mind of Edwards. It is for this reason, among others, that he deserves recognition as a theologian who has sensibly affected the interests of scientific and of practical theology. That he had not entirely measured the significance of the principle, or that it was still accompanied by some imperfection in its statement; that it needed to be supplemented with other truth in order to its clearer and more consistent presentation, — this will be apparent as we follow him in his progress through the issues created by the Great Awakening. But yet he stands supreme among Protestant theologians, at least in the Reformed churches, for firm adherence to the principle despite all obstacles and discouragements. We must go back to the mystics of the Middle Ages, or to the fathers of the ancient church, to find a predecessor for Edwards who apprehended and urged this truth with equal power. It is true that Fox and Barclay among the Quakers had taught the same essential doctrine. If Edwards surpasses them, it is because he grounds his conviction upon a philosophical basis, and expounds it in more scientific manner. But while his doctrine is that of the "inner light," it assumes a different form. From one point of view more effective because associated with his thought of God as energizing will, it suffers by its restriction to the elect, instead of being the prerogative of a common humanity.

There had been movements marked by religious fervor, here and there among the churches, for many years before Edwards appeared. So far as they received a name, they were spoken of as occasions of increased attention to religion. They had been known in East Windsor under the ministry of Edwards' father. Mr. Stoddard counted five of them during his ministry at Northampton, comparing them to seasons of harvest. Small as they may have been, they were the harbingers of the great agency which was to create an independent life in the churches. The country could not therefore have been taken wholly by surprise when the extraordinary movement began at Northampton which fastened upon that remote town the interest of the provinces. The event has been described by Edwards, in his Narrative of Surprising Conversions, with local touches that bring the scene vividly before us. The Narrative reads as if it were intended to be a philosophical account of what had occurred, and not a mere enthusiastic report with a design to enkindle enthusiasm in the reader. It was written at the request of one of the Boston clergy, and was not long in finding its way into Scotland and England. The importance of the Narrative justifies some detailed account of its contents.

The people of Northampton, as Edwards thinks it necessary to remark, were not in any respect different from other people in the province. They were as sober, orderly, and good sort of people as in any part of New England. But the town had its peculiarities, its advantages and disadvantages. The "families dwelling more compactly together than in any town of such a bigness in those parts of the country" was a reason why its corruptions and its reformations were more swiftly propagated. The isolation of the town in a corner of the country had served as a barrier against vice as well as error and variety of opinion. It was also Edwards' opinion, at least at this time, that the people were chiefly remarkable for religion and for attainments in Christian experience, circumstances which were chiefly owing to the influence of his grandfather and predecessor. But shortly after Mr. Stoddard's death in 1729 there came a time of extraordinary dulness in religion. Licentiousness now began and continued for some years to prevail. The youth of the town became "addicted to night-walking and frequenting the tavern;" the lewd practices of some exceedingly corrupted others. "It was their manner very frequently to get together in conventions of both sexes for mirth and jollity, which they called frolicks; and they would spend the greater part of the night in them, without any regard to order in the families which they belonged to; and indeed family government did much fail in the town. It was become very customary with many of our young people to be indecent in their carriage at meeting, which doubtless would not have prevailed to such a degree had it not been that my grandfather, through his great age (though he retained his powers surprisingly to the last), was not so able to observe them." A spirit of contention also existed between two parties in the town which created jealousy and opposition in public affairs. A custom which then prevailed made the evening which preceded the Sabbath a part of holy time; and it was a source of evil that the young people had fallen into the habit of devoting the evening after the Sabbath as a time for mirth and company-keeping,—a practice adapted to dissipate any good influence produced by the public lecture.

Such is the substance of Edwards' preface to his Narrative. Its object may have been to show that nothing in the human environment of the church at Northampton could be adduced as explaining the extraordinary movement which was now to take place; that on the contrary it was the work of God alone. But given the circumstances above described, — a town predisposed to religion by all its antecedents; a moment in its history when no great external interest preoccupied the minds of the people; an isolated town, far from the centre of activity, in which the want of healthy amusements or excitement to give food to the imagination had a tendency to breed as a substitute the more vulgar forms of immorality; and add to these, Edwards' force as a preacher, his unique personality which intensified the effect of his preaching, as if by some unexplained magnetic power, — in the light of this conjuncture of favoring circumstances, it is not strange that the religious awakening of New England should have begun at Northampton. These things are not mentioned in order to deny or to depreciate the divineness of the work which Edwards is describing. But it is none the less necessary to bear them in mind. Had Edwards made allowance for them, his judgment on the incidents of the movement would have been less open to criticism.

It was so early as the year 1733 that signs of a change began to appear among the younger part of the people, in consequence of which the pastor was able to break up the habit of company-keeping after the public lecture on Sunday. Instead of this custom, the practice was introduced of spending the Sunday evenings in social religion, the people dividing themselves into several companies for the purpose. At this time Edwards began preaching the sermons already mentioned on justification by faith, the justice of God in the damnation of sinners, the excellency of Christ, the duty of pressing into the kingdom of God. All accounts agree in ascribing to these sermons a prominent place among the causes which promoted the revival. How highly the people regarded these particular sermons is shown, as Edwards remarks, by a willingness to incur the expense of their publication at a time when the erection of a new meeting-house was already making a heavy demand upon their finances. One reason for this interest was the fear which had begun to spread that God might withdraw from the land, or that it would be given over to strange doctrine. To the prevalence of this fear, it is needless to say that Edwards had contributed.

And now many began to be moved and much affected. A young woman who had been one of the greatest "company-keepers" in the whole town became "serious, giving evidence of a heart truly broken and sanctified." Presently upon this a great and universal concern about religion and the eternal world became universal throughout the town, among persons of all degrees and all ages.

"It was in the latter part of December (1734) that the spirit of God began extraordinarily to set in, and wonderfully to work amongst us." And now all other talk but about spiritual and eternal things was soon thrown by. Conversation upon all occasions turned on these things, so much so that worldly affairs were treated as of very little consequence. Business was followed, but without any special disposition for it; indeed, there was danger that temporal affairs would be neglected in the interest of religion. The main thing with all of every sort was to get into the kingdom of heaven, or to flee from the wrath to come. There was scarcely a single person in the town, either old or young, that was left unconcerned about the things of the eternal world. Meetings were appointed in private houses, and were wont to be greatly thronged.

"The work of God as it was carried on, and the number of true saints multiplied, soon made a glorious alteration in the town; so that in the spring and summer, anno 1735, the town seemed to be full of the presence of God: it was never so full of love, nor so full of joy, and yet so full of distress, as it was then. There were remarkable tokens of God's presence in almost every house. It was a time of joy in families on the account of salvation's being brought unto them, parents rejoicing over their children as being new-born, and husbands over their wives, and wives over their husbands. *The goings of God were then seen in His sanctuary, God's day was a delight, and His tabernacles were amiable.*

Our public assemblies were then beautiful; the congregation was alive in God's service, every one earnestly intent on the public worship, every hearer eager to drink in the words of the minister as they came from his mouth: the assembly in general were from time to time in tears while the word was preached; some weeping with sorrow and distress, others with joy and love, others with pity and concern for the souls of their neighbors. Our public praises were then greatly enlivened; God was then served in our psalmody in some measure in the beauty of holiness. It has been observable, that there has been scarce any part of divine worship wherein good men amongst us have had grace so drawn forth, and their hearts so lifted up in the ways of God, as in singing His praises: our congregation excelled all that ever I knew in the external part of the duty before, the men generally carrying regularly and well three parts of music and the women a part by themselves; but now they were evidently wont to sing with unusual elevation of heart and voice, which made the duty pleasant indeed."

The chief interest of the Narrative is the picture it presents of Edwards himself, eagerly studying every phase of the movement, in order to the verification of his theology. He carefully collates and examines the experiences of those affected, as if he were following the actual traces left by a Divine Spirit. He was quick to notice all that confirmed the working hypothesis with which he came to his task, and yet not incapable of seeing things for which he could find no formula. He also notes a rich variety of experience where others have labored for a special type. But there is a tendency, even with him, to put a forced interpretation upon what he witnesses, in order that it may accord with a preconceived theory. He does not realize that the experiences he observes may be in some measure but the echo to his own teaching. Believing that his teaching has been the exact reproduction of revealed truth, the process among the people appeared to him as if wholly divine. It seemed to him an exceptional moment in human history, as when a rift in the clouds enables an observer to gaze directly upon phenomena otherwise concealed from his view. He may not have so expressed himself, but in reality he is seeking to ground his theology in the human consciousness. What we call psychology was to him an unknown science, and yet no modern psychologist could have laid more stress upon the importance of observing the different phases of human experience. In this study, his conception of inspiration or revelation enabled him to move with perfect freedom. The same spirit which clarified the vision of apostles or prophets was now illuminating the minds of the common people with a divine supernatural light.

The first point upon which Edwards dwells, in describing the manner in which persons are wrought upon, is what may be called the tragic element in the process. Salvation consists in a great deliverance. The first stage of awakened consciousness is the realization of an awful danger and the importance of speedy escape. This stage of fear and anxiety may vary in degree of duration or intensity, but no one is described as attaining peace without some degree of inward trouble. With some the sense of divine displeasure and of the danger of damnation was so great that they could not sleep, or they awakened with heaviness and distress still abiding on their spirits. These apprehensions of misery and danger for the most part increased the nearer they approached deliverance. A melancholy distemper at times mixed with these genuine fears. With these cases Edwards remarks that it is difficult to deal. Everything that is said to them they turn the wrong way, or to their own disadvantage: there is nothing that the Devil seems to make so great a handle of as a melancholy humor. But apart from such cases, there are instances noted of persons whose sense of danger and misery has been so great that a little more would have destroyed them. Others were brought to the borders of despair, and it looked to them black as midnight just before the day dawned within their souls. In some, however, the terrors were not so sharp when near comfort as before: their convictions have rather led them to see their own universal depravity and their deadness in sin. With others, again, the awakening process appeared like a great struggle with some hostile power, as of a serpent disturbed or enraged. These have experienced heart-risings against God, murmurings at His ways, and envy toward those who are thought to have been converted. In dealing with them it was much insisted on that they were in danger of quenching the Spirit, or of committing the sin against the Holy Ghost.

The second stage in this process of an awakening soul was the realization of an absolute dependence on sovereign power and grace, and also the universal need of a divine mediator. To these results the legal strivings, the fears, the anxieties, appeared to tend as if by a necessary law. What Edwards meant by the divine sovereignty we have already seen, and also how he had set forth the necessity for a divine mediation. As he surveyed the field of the Spirit's operation, he saw that many who were struggling for peace with God found great difficulty in its attainment, while some never achieved the desired result. He has enumerated the difficulties encountered with a minuteness which it is not necessary to follow. We get a confused picture in which the consciousness of sin in the sight of God leads the sufferer in various ways to seek relief. Persons in this condition wander in a kind of labyrinth, and some wander ten times as long as others before they gain the outlet. Some did not have great terrors, but had a very quick work. Some were under trouble but a few days, others for months and years. The one conclusion to which it is necessary that somehow all must come is the discovery of the justice of God. Those who reach this conclusion express themselves in such ways as this, — that God would

SPIRITUAL METAMORPHOSIS.   147

be just if He were to bestow mercy on every person in the town, and damn themselves to all eternity. So great has been their sinfulness that they feel that if they were to seek and take the utmost pains all their lives, God might justly cast them into hell. All their labors, prayers, and tears can make no atonement for sin. The sense of sinfulness also finds diversified expression: with some it is particular sins that appear vile and loathsome, with others it is the acknowledgment of a general sinful condition. But to all must come the revelation of the divine justice. On the eve of this great discovery there is restlessness, and struggle, and tumult; as soon as the conviction is reached, there follows an unexpected quietness and composure. It seems to fascinate Edwards' mind as he witnesses this strange metamorphosis from a child of earth and hell to one of the children of God. When a person thinks it is all over with him as he makes this discovery of divine justice, he is actually on the verge of being born again. There is a weird sense of satisfaction even in confessing the divine justice. Some have appeared to revel in it, to have had such a deep feeling of the excellency of God's justice, and such indignation against themselves, that they have spoken of their willingness to be damned. Edwards' comment on this mood indicates no sympathy with it. He thinks they cannot have had clear and distinct ideas of damnation, nor does any word in the Bible require such self-denial as this. What they really mean to say is, that salvation seems too good for them; so great has been their sin, that it seems to them inconsistent with the glory of God's majesty that they should be saved.

There were many, however, who could not arrive at this or any similar state of mind, despite their struggles and tears. What was the message which Edwards proclaimed to these and others who continued for years in a state of distress or agony? It does not occur to him that there may be even a larger breadth and variety in God's method of dealing with souls than he is capable of discerning. Although he saw more than many of his contemporaries, he still suffers under a limitation of his vision. He knows nothing of a gradual maturing of the will under a divine education. There is no such thing with him as a quiet, unconscious growth into the kingdom of heaven. For every one is reserved the same tragical process before salvation can be obtained. And the bitterness of the tragedy lies in the uncertainty of the result, as also in the absence of divine sympathy, until success has been achieved. No one can be sure that the divine love is extended to him in his effort to reach out after God. Edwards is certain that to have preached such a doctrine would have been disastrous. It would have put an end to the awakenings; it would have established strife and contention with God because He accepted some or rejected others; it would have blocked the way to that humiliation before the sovereign will, which is assumed to be the first step in the process of salvation. We have met with this difficulty before in Edwards' theology, and it is constantly recurring. His doctrine of divine sovereignty was built upon the doctrine of election, and the doctrine of election made it impossible that God should love any but His elect. Hence the only encouragement which could be held out in the storm of the soul's conflict was the abstract principle of the mercy of God in Christ, or the probability of success to those who had strength to hold out until the delayed relief should come.

When the legal distress had done its work, there came a calm to the soul, with special and delightful manifestations of the grace of God. This period of what Edwards calls "gracious discoveries" also varies in different persons. Many continue a long time in a course of gracious exercises and experiences before they know themselves to be converted. But his observations lead him to conclude that those who have had great terrors are more apt to enter suddenly into light and comfort. It is in this stage that wise direction is most needed. It is impossible here to follow Edwards, as he specifies the different states of religious consciousness in which the subsidence of anxiety leaves the soul. He enumerates many distinct varieties, all of which he regards as genuine, remarking that God is further from confining Himself to certain steps and a particular method than it may be some do imagine. These fleeting phases of spiritual experience are all very real to Edwards' view, more real than any similar number of varieties of species in the animal or vegetable kingdom. The one common element that runs through them all is relationship by feeling or emotion to an infinite Person. He would never have defined religion, as some have done, to be morality quickened by enthusiasm. Morality is there by a stringent necessity, but it is rather taken for granted than placed in the foreground.

Edwards is specially desirous that his converts should express some conscious relationship to Christ, as well as to God. If his teaching regarding justification by faith were true, Christ must of necessity reveal Himself in every soul. On this point his satisfaction was not always complete. A certain deistic tone marks the experience of some. "It must needs be confessed that Christ is not always distinctly and explicitly thought of in the first sensible act of grace." But turning over in his mind the confessions of such as these, he finds that they imply the Christ, though His name be not mentioned.

This period of gracious strivings and discoveries is a confused and mixed period, — a period when souls are coming to the birth, when the blind are first beginning to see, and, their spiritual senses not being trained, they may see men as trees walking. It is a period when resolutions are formed, and holy longings after God and Christ are nourished. It is now possible to admit a direct and supernatural guidance, which draws forth the powers of the soul, — the dawning of a bright day when the soul, turning its face toward the sun, opens out as flowers open their leaves under kind and genial influences.

In his capacity as a spiritual director Edwards strove to be prudent, though in after years he saw that he had made mistakes, and lamented his want of experience. He was criticised at this time for pronouncing too positively upon people's condition, — for giving or withholding certificates of conversion. It was surely a task full of peril, from which any one might shrink, to pronounce judgment upon one's fellows, — to assure some that they had entered into the life that is supernatural, or decide that the experience of others did not warrant a favorable conclusion. But at this time Edwards did not shrink from a task which seemed to him to lie in the way of duty. After he had seen the mischief of rash and premature judgments, he would have been content to lay down principles, allowing to the judgment of charity the largest possible scope. As it was, he took a more comprehensive view than others in his age, vastly more comprehensive than was the fashion when revivals had been reduced to a part of the ecclesiastical machinery. He warned his people against being deceived in their own case, or the case of others; he insisted that sincerity of life was better evidence than the manifestation of words. He admits that it is not necessary or possible for all to be aware of the exact moment when the mysterious change passed over them. He pointed out the difference he had observed in those who gave indubitable evidence of having successfully met the great crisis. With some, converting light was a glorious brightness suddenly shining; with others, it was like the slow dawning of the day. But in all cases it seemed to him "necessary to suppose that there was an immediate influence of the Spirit of God." One of the means by which the Spirit often worked was in bringing texts of Scripture to the mind. He would not call it an immediate revelation without the action of the memory; but yet there was in it an immediate and extraordinary influence of the Spirit in leading the thoughts to passages of the Bible, or exciting them in the memory. Another illustration of the Spirit's working was in giving a direct insight into the truth of the great things of religion, an insight more convincing than the reading of many volumes of argument would produce. Those who had witnessed this action of the Spirit had seen, tasted, and felt the divinity and the glory of Christian truth; they might not be able to satisfy an inquirer with their reasons for believing, while yet they have intuitively beheld and immediately felt its reality. And it was a mistake into which many fell, that, because the illumination was in and through the reason, and so in accordance with their natural faculties, that therefore it had only a human origin.

There was another result of the Spirit's action upon which Edwards much insists, — the spiritual delights and joys which follow upon conversion. This had been at times his own experience. Without some measure of this joy and ecstasy, it seems as though he would have mistrusted the genuineness of the Spirit's work. Since God is a supremely happy Being, the soul united to Him must necessarily share in the divine blessedness. Hence those who are converted express themselves to this effect, speaking of the excellency of that pleasure and delight of soul which they now enjoy; how it is far more than sufficient to repay them for all the agony through which they have passed; how far it exceeds all earthly pleasures, making them seem mean and worthless in comparison.

"The light and comfort which some of them enjoy gives a new relish to their common blessings, and causes all things about them to appear as it were beautiful and sweet and pleasant to them; all things abroad, the sun, moon, and stars, the clouds and sky, the heavens and earth, appear as it were with a cast of divine glory and sweetness. The sweetest joy that these good people amongst us express, though it include in it a delightful sense of the safety of their own state, and that they are now out of danger of hell, yet frequently, in times of their highest spiritual entertainment, this seems not to be the chief object of their fixed thought and meditation. The supreme attention of their minds is to the glorious excellences of God in Christ. . . . The joy that many of them speak is that to which none is to be paralleled; is that which they find when they are lowest in the dust, emptied most of themselves, and as it were annihilating themselves before God, when they are nothing and God is all." [1]

In a time of such intense and almost universal excitement as that which pervaded the town of Northampton in 1734-35, it was to have been expected that there should be phenomena of a physical kind, — a consequence indeed of the religious excitement, but having no essential religious character. There was much less of this kind of nervous manifestation in this first revival at Northampton than in the Great Awakening which followed five years later. This may have been owing in part to the prudence of Edwards, and to the fact that he kept the control of the movement as far as possible in his own hands. But under these favorable circumstances there were some things of a character to discredit the movement. Many persons, as Edwards remarks, had a mean idea of the great work from what they heard of "impressions made on the imagination." These impressions consisted of lively pictures of hell, as of some dreadful furnace; or visions of Christ as a person with glorious majesty and a sweet and gracious aspect; or of Christ upon the cross with the blood running from his wounds. Edwards doubts if those who had these vivid impressions supposed that any objective character corresponded with them; he thinks that such impressions were natural enough, and what was to have been expected from human nature un-

[1] *Narrative*, etc., vol. iii. p. 255.

der such exceptional circumstances. He was diligent in teaching persons the difference between what was spiritual and what was imaginary, cautioning them to lay no stress on any external things. But he also admits that there have been some few instances of impressions on persons' imaginations that have seemed mysterious to him, and which he has been at a loss to explain, uncertain whether they may not have involved some objective reality. But the subject is merely alluded to, at this time, in a casual way. We may also dismiss it here, recurring to it again, when it had assumed greater prominence and had become a matter of controversy.

It has been already remarked that morality as such does not at first occupy a prominent place in Edwards' description of the effects of the revival. He is chiefly concerned with the emotional moods which are aroused by coming into an immediate as well as endearing relation with God. As has also been pointed out when treating of his theology, morality is included in the sphere of common grace, — the grace which may come to all, but which does not bring salvation. Nowhere in his works does Edwards enter into an exposition of the moral law, as enjoined in the second table of the decalogue. He is occupied almost exclusively with the duty towards God. But while morality finds no place in Edwards' systematic theology, except as the declaration of God's will revealed in Scripture, yet in practice there is no lack of emphasis upon the moral duties of life. Edwards would not have been a Puritan had he shown indifference to the moral law, by which society is held together, by obedience to which comes self-respect and earthly prosperity. But he did not discuss ethical precepts, or reason about their validity. He took them for granted, as if at least so much must be required in order to the attainment of a higher ideal.

A beautiful and impressive illustration of the high importance attached to the common duties of life is to be found in the Covenant which Edwards drew up, and which the people of Northampton subscribed. Though it belongs to a later stage of the revival, when its necessity was more stringently felt, its introduction here may not be inappropriate. There is a reminder in it of a similar covenant which Pliny, the Roman governor, describes as forming a part of the worship of God in the primitive Christian assemblies. Because of God's great goodness and His gracious presence in the town of Northampton during the late spiritual revival, — so runs in substance the preamble to the covenant, — the people present themselves before the Lord, to renounce their evil ways and to put away their abominations from before His eyes. They solemnly promise and vow before the Lord, in all their concerns with their neighbor, to have a strict regard to rules of honesty, justice, and uprightness; not to overreach or defraud him in any matter, or, either wilfully or through want of care, to injure him in any of his honest possessions or rights; and to have a tender respect, not only to their own interest, but to his; and particularly never to give him cause of offence by wilfully or negligently forbearing to pay their just debts; wherever they may be conscious of having in the past wronged their neighbor in his outward estate, never to rest till they have made that restitution which the rules of moral equity require. They promise to avoid all backbiting, evil-speaking, and slandering, as also everything that feeds a spirit of bitterness or ill-will or secret grudge; not to ridicule a neighbor's failings, or needlessly insist on his faults; to do nothing in a spirit of revenge. And further, they will not allow their private interest or honor, or the desire for victory against a contrary party, to lead them into any course of which their consciences would reproach them as hurtful to religion or the interests of Christ's kingdom; and particularly, in public affairs, not to allow the interests of party or the desire of worldly ambition to lead them counter to the interest of true religion. Those who are young promise to allow themselves in no diversions or pastimes, meetings or companies, which would hinder a devout spirit engaged in religion, to avoid everything that tends to lasciviousness, and which they believe will not be approved by the infinitely pure and holy eye of God. They finally consecrate themselves to perform with great watchfulness the duties entailed by family relationships, whether parents and children, husbands and wives, brothers and sisters, masters, mistresses, and servants.[1]

Among the results of this extraordinary dispensation, as Edwards calls it, was the large addition to the ranks of the church, raising the number of communicants to about six hundred and twenty. The unusual spectacle was presented of persons thronging into the church, nearly one hundred being received at one time and sixty at another, whose explicit profession of Christianity was very affecting to the congregation. Of these, Edwards remarks significantly, that he had sufficient evidence of their conversion, though it was not the custom at Northampton, as it was in some churches in the country, to make a credible relation of their inward experience the ground of admission to the Lord's Supper. In the space of six months the number of those converted was upwards of three hundred, of whom as many as one half were men. This also seemed to Edwards a remarkable fact, inasmuch as he remembered to have heard Mr. Stoddard say that in his time many more women were converted than men. He was also struck with the large number of children who professed what he regarded as a genuine experience. Among them was a child of four years, whose case seemed to him so wonderful that he has related it at length, thinking that otherwise it would be incredible; and incredible it does appear, despite the detail of his statement.

[1] Dwight, *Life of Edwards*, pp. 166–168.

The excitement of the movement began to decline in the spring of the year 1735. "In the latter part of May it began to be very sensible that the Spirit of God was gradually withdrawing from us, and after this time Satan seemed to be more let loose and raged in a dreadful manner." The first instance which illustrated his malignity was the case of a gentleman of high standing in the town, who fell into melancholia, and in this condition committed suicide. The people of Northampton were extraordinarily affected by this event, being as it were struck with astonishment. "After this, multitudes in this and other towns seemed to have it strongly suggested to them and pressed upon them to do as this person had done. And many that seemed to be under no melancholy, some pious persons that had no special darkness or doubts about the goodness of their state, nor were under any special trouble or concern of mind about anything spiritual or temporal, yet had it urged upon them, as if somebody had spoken to them, '*Cut your own throat! now is a good opportunity. Now! now!*' So that they were obliged to fight with all their might to resist it, and yet no reason suggested to them why they should do it."

We may be thankful to Edwards for the frankness with which he describes the evil symptoms attending the movement in its decline. They indicate the exhaustion of the nervous system after the prolonged tension of the struggle or tragedy through which the people had been passing. A morbid state had been induced where men are seen treading the ground which borders on insanity, where irrational suggestions and blind impulses threaten the supremacy of the will. But this frank avowal of the evils accompanying an excitement which was largely physical in its nature should not be abused to the spiritual discredit of the movement. Society was in the throes of a new birth. A step forward was to be taken which was to change the face of the social as well as the religious order. In such moments abnormal elements are sure to be found, mingling with, even appearing to grow out of, what is sound and true. It is quite possible that Edwards' extraordinary personality, combined with his "terrific" preaching, should be held responsible in some measure for these morbid tendencies. But to attribute them to this cause alone is to lose the deeper significance of the fact, that similar phenomena have always attended those epochs when humanity is seen striving in some unusual way to realize the spiritual as distinct from and above the natural. Indeed, as we think of the sources from which great principles have so often taken their rise, or recall the disfigurements connected with revolutions that have advanced the truth, we are tempted to repeat the cry, Can any good come out of Nazareth? But in all this we are anticipating a controversy which the opponents of the revival waged against its friends and leaders.

II.

THE GREAT AWAKENING. — DISTINGUISHING MARKS OF A WORK OF THE SPIRIT OF GOD.

FROM the first, Edwards had regarded the revival at Northampton as the forerunner of some greater work. What had gone on under his vision seemed so exceptional in its character as to point toward the accomplishment of some vast organic change. If the movement had seemed to decline, it was in appearance only. In its apparent subsidence it was like a fire that was slumbering. At last the smouldering embers broke forth in a great conflagration.

It is not necessary to describe at length what has received the name of the Great Awakening. The account given of the first revival at Northampton will suffice to show its substantial character in the one hundred and fifty towns or more into which it extended. Edwards has left a brief account of its rise in his own parish in a letter to a Boston correspondent.[1] In some respects it differed from the first movement, more particularly in the matter of "bodily effects," such as faintings, outcries, and convulsions, which now became a common occur-

---

[1] Cf. Dwight, *Life of Edwards*, pp. 160, ff. For a description of the movement as a whole, cf. Tracy, *The Great Awakening; a History of the Revival of Religion in the time of Edwards and Whitefield*, Boston, 1842, — a work of great interest and value.

rence, disturbing the order of public worship. The irrational purpose which aimed to bring young children under the influence of religious excitement was also more pronounced, nor does Edwards feel its incongruity. But what is chiefly important to note is, that the magnitude of the event was an adequate setting for the greatness of mind and character which Edwards now reveals. He stands forth as the originator, the director, the champion, of the movement. As such he was recognized at home and abroad. The deep response of religious sentiment originally evoked by his preaching called forth all his powers for its direction or defence. To the works which he now put forth in rapid succession we must turn our attention. They constitute the most important literature of the revival. Most of them were republished in Scotland or England. They have an air as if of supreme mastery of the situation. The reply to the enemies or critics of the movement is marked by the eloquence springing from the consciousness of a great cause. While his style is never free from cumbrous sentences and awkward involutions, there are passages continually occurring which remind one of the masters of modern English.

The first in this series of apologetic treatises is entitled The Distinguishing Marks of a Work of the Spirit of God. It was an expanded sermon, which had been delivered in 1741 at New Haven, from the text, " Beloved, believe not every spirit; but try the spirits whether they are of God: because many false prophets are gone out into the world." In this treatise Edwards appears as committing himself unreservedly to the divine origin and the divine character of the revival. It is true that so early as 1741 the worst features of the movement had not been developed. But evil tendencies were at work, which those saw most clearly who had no sympathy with the movement, or who disowned the idea that it was divine. If it seems to any like a derogation from the greatness of Edwards that he should have been entirely carried away by a movement which involved so many irrational if not superstitious elements, where the puerile, the extravagant, and the false were so largely mingled with what was true, yet in this respect he is not an exception, but illustrates directly the rule in accordance with which men have risen to greatness in the church. "It is the higher order of minds," as a recent writer has remarked, "those endowed with the fire and sensibility of genius, whom religion seizes with an attractive force, and carries away with a bewildering enthusiasm." So also in the ancient church, the most eminent of the fathers, Athanasius and Basil, Jerome and Augustine, had been identified with the evils and the superstitions of monasticism, as it swept like a wave over the church of the fourth and fifth centuries. Those who were in opposition in both cases were men of an inferior stamp, except in a certain mediocrity of common sense. But it will appear before we close our study of the movement that Edwards was also going through a process of growth, of intellectual and spiritual purification, so that when the movement was over he is not standing exactly where he stood when it began.

In his treatise on the Distinguishing Marks by which a work of the Spirit of God is to be known or tested, Edwards dwells at first in a general way on the principles at issue in any movement which claims to be of God. He meets in a negative fashion the various objections which have been or may be urged. Nothing, he argues, can be contended against any religious movement from the fact that it is unusual or extraordinary. God is spoken of in Scripture as doing a strange work. There is reason to believe also, from prophecies in the Bible, that His greatest, most extraordinary work would take place in the latter ages of the world. Nor can any one conclude anything against such a work from "bodily effects," such as tears, groans, outcries, convulsions, or the failure of strength. Indeed it is only natural, in view of the close relation of body and spirit, that such things should be. So also in Scripture the jailer fell down before Paul and Silas in distress and trembling. The Psalmist exclaimed, under convictions of conscience and a sense of the guilt of sin: "When I kept silence my bones waxed old through my roaring all the day long; for day and night Thy hand was heavy on me." The disciples in the storm on the lake cried out for fear. The spouse in the Canticles is overpowered with the love of Christ, and speaks of herself as sick with love. Again, it is no argument against *the work* that it occasions a great deal of noise about religion. So it was also in the apostles' days, when they were charged with turning the world upside down. The vivid picturings of the imagination, which many disliked, Edwards does not find unreasonable. "Such is our nature that we cannot think of things invisible without a degree of imagination." He is even inclined to maintain a principle which may become the ground of the crudest anthropomorphism, — the necessity of an image in the mind in order to realize the spiritual and invisible. If the imagination is the gift of God, he thinks it may be expected that He will make use of it for divine purposes, especially in those who are ignorant and must be dealt with as babes. It is not strange or unnatural that those upon whom the Spirit of God is working should go into ecstasy and have visions, as though they were rapt up into heaven and saw glorious sights. Such instances he himself has known. Some may interpret them wrongly, or lay too much weight upon them, but nevertheless they may be wrought by the Spirit of God, however indirect or incidental His operation. And again, if some thought lightly of the revival because it seemed to be propagated by the contagion of example, Edwards contends that the word of God may operate through example and make it effectual. A work may be from God also, and yet its subjects may be guilty of great imprudences and irregularities. Errors in judgment and delusions of Satan may be intermixed with what is divine. It was so also in the apostles' days, as in the church at Corinth. And even if some who seem to have been wrought upon fall away into gross errors or scandalous practices, this is no argument that a work is not of God. Some of the opponents of the revival had attributed the movement to the preaching of the terrors of law and of endless punishment. This also Edwards defends as a legitimate method, indeed the only honorable method, of procedure. If these things were true, they could not be preached too strongly.

As to the positive features of a work of God, they are such as these: the awakening of the conscience to a sense of sin and need of a Saviour; the confirmation of men in the belief in Jesus as the Son of God; the increased importance attached to the truths of the Bible, and its more frequent use. To turn men from darkness to light, to impart a spirit of divine love or Christian humiliation, — these are things which the evil spirit would not do, nor could he if he would.

But the interest of this treatise does not lie in this general consideration of the subject. Whatever Edwards wrote had always some very definite bearing, some concrete relation to the issues of the time. It is when we come to the last section of his book, which is headed "Practical Inferences," that we touch the vital questions to which the revival had given birth. The first of these is the "bodily effects," the outcries, faintings, and convulsions, which caused many sensible men to look upon the movement as of purely human origin, or as having its rise in diseased or abnormal conditions of mind or body. Upon this point Edwards' voice has no uncertain sound. He appeals to his large experience as the ground of his conviction that the "bodily effects" are wrought incidentally by the Spirit of God, and are evidence of His unusual presence and power in the congregation. He has no desire to check this feature of the revival. It is no mark of confusion, but rather the sign of a higher order which God is evolving. These uncommon appearances have been manifested by those who have been in great distress from an apprehension of their sin and misery; or else by those who have been overcome with a sweet sense of the greatness, wonderfulness, and excellency of divine things. In very few cases has there been any appearance of feigning or affecting such manifestations, and in very many cases it would have been utterly impossible to suppress them.

"Not but that I think the persons thus extraordinarily moved should endeavor to refrain from such outward manifestations, what they well can, and should refrain to their utmost at the time of their solemn worship. But if God is pleased to convince the consciences of persons, so that they cannot avoid great outward manifestations, even to interrupting and breaking off those public means they were attending, I do not think this is confusion or an unhappy interruption, any more than if a company should meet on the field to pray for rain and should be broken off from their exercise by a plentiful shower. Would to God that all the public assemblies in the land were broken off from their public exercises with such confusion as this the next Sabbath day! We need not be sorry for breaking the order of means by obtaining the end to which that order is directed. He who is going to fetch a treasure need not be sorry that he is stopped by meeting the treasure in the midst of his journey."

Edwards gives an intimation, however, in passing, to the effect that he does not suppose that the degree of the Spirit's influence is to be determined by the degree of effect on men's bodies; or that those are always the best experiences which show the greatest influence on the body. The caution was needed, but he does not enlarge upon it. He is at present preoccupied with another purpose,— to affirm strongly that this work is of God, despite all its extravagances; or else we may as well throw by our Bibles and give up revealed religion altogether. The imprudences, irregularities, and the mixture of delusion are things to be expected and taken for granted. "As in the first creation, God did not make a complete world at once, but there was a great deal of imperfection, darkness, and mixture of chaos and confusion, after God first said, 'Let there be light,' before the whole stood forth in perfect form." So in the deliverance of the chosen people from Egypt the false wonders were for a time mixed up with the true. When the sons of God came to present themselves before the Lord, Satan came also among them. When daylight first appears after a night of darkness, we must expect to have darkness mixed with light for a while before the perfect day and the sun in his strength. The fruits of the earth are green before they are ripe, and come to their perfection gradually; and so, Christ tells us, is the kingdom of God. The errors that have attended the work are the less to be wondered at because it is mainly young persons who have been the subjects of the work. And further, the situation has been so extraordinary that even ministers have not always known how to conduct themselves. But, on the whole, judging from his own experience at Northampton, there has been less of enthusiastic wildness and extravagance than in the earlier revival of 1735. He closes his book with a pathetic charge to those who are indifferent to the work, and then offers some suggestions to its friends.

To the first of these classes he speaks with that unique power of direct appeal which made him the foremost preacher of his day. So intense is his conviction that Jehovah has bowed the heavens and come down, and appeared wonderfully in the land, that those opposed to him must have almost wanted to feel, despite their reason, that they were in the wrong. Those silent ministers who stood by, waiting to see what would come out of the movement, he accused of standing in the way of God. He assures those who are offended by stumbling-blocks, that these rocks of offence are likely to increase rather than diminish; and *Blessed is he whosoever is not offended in me.* He is afraid that these prudent persons, who stand at a distance and look on, will miss the most precious opportunity of obtaining light and grace which God ever gave in New England. He warns those who speak contemptuously of these things to beware lest they commit the unpardonable sin. But whether they resist or not, God will have His way in the long run, and make all men know that the great Jehovah has actually been in New England.

To the friends of *the work* he finally appeals, urging them to avoid as far as possible all occasion of reproach. He thinks that some of them have erred in giving too much heed to *impulses* and *strong impressions* on their minds, as if they were signs from heaven revealing to them the will of God. The disposition to attach value to these impulses and impressions he attributes in some measure to a wrong conception which many entertain, that in the approaching happy days of the church the extraordinary gifts of the apostolic age will be restored. While Edwards admitted and justified the "bodily effects," he stood like a rock in resisting this tendency, which many exhibited, to concede value or reality to impulses and impressions. Whitefield, it is well known, magnified the importance of these impulses; he sought for them in prayer, and professed to be guided by them. When he visited Northampton in 1740, Edwards took occasion, both in private and in company with others, to remonstrate with him for giving too much heed to these things. It was Edwards' opinion that Whitefield, though he received his remonstrance kindly, did not from that time regard him as an intimate and confidential friend, as he might otherwise have done.[1]

It may seem like an inconsistency in Edwards to have admitted the "bodily effects" while denying the validity of impulses. But there is something also to be said in his behalf. The subject will be resumed in a later chapter, when Edwards' attitude will appear more clearly. But in regard to impressions on the mind which revealed the will of God, his reasoning was clear and powerful. Not only so, but his eloquence in resisting them rises to its greatest height. All that was most profound and distinctive in his theology lay beneath his repugnance to what seemed to him as unspiritual as it was irrational. The extraordinary gifts of the Spirit, such as marked the apostolic

---

[1] Cf. Dwight, *Life of Edwards*, p. 147. The practice of the brothers Charles and John Wesley in this respect differed from that of Whitefield. But they differed also from each other in regard to "bodily effects." John Wesley approved them. It is said that Charles, however, on one occasion notified his congregation that any one who was convulsed should be carried out, and this notice insured perfect quiet. But both Charles and John were agreed in accepting the Moravian method of solving doubts as to some course of action by opening the Bible at hazard and regarding the passage on which the eye first alighted as a revelation of God's will in the matter. Cf. Wedgwood, *Life of Wesley*, p. 193; Southey, *Life of Wesley*, vol. i. p. 216.

age, even the inspiration of prophets and evangelists, these are of a different nature from, as well as inferior to, those gracious influences of the Spirit which mark the Christian calling. "God communicates His own nature to the soul, in saving grace in the heart, more than in all miraculous gifts." Salvation is promised to the possession of divine grace, but not of inspiration. A man may have these extraordinary gifts and yet be abominable to God. Spiritual life in the soul is given by God only to his favorites and dear children, while inspiration may be thrown out, as it were, to dogs and swine, — a Balaam, Saul, and Judas. Many wicked men at the day of judgment will plead that they have prophesied, and cast out devils, and done many wonderful works. "The greatest privilege of prophets and apostles was not their being inspired and working miracles, but their eminent holiness. The grace that was in their hearts was a thousand times more their dignity and honor than their miraculous gifts. . . . The apostle Paul abounded in visions, revelations, and miraculous gifts, above all the apostles; but yet he esteems all things but loss for the excellency of the spiritual knowledge of Christ. . . . To have grace in the heart is a higher privilege than the blessed virgin herself had in having the body of the second person in the Trinity conceived in her womb by the power of the Highest overshadowing her. 'And it came to pass, as He spake these things, a certain woman of the company lift up her voice and said unto

Him, Blessed is the womb that bare Thee, and the paps which Thou hast sucked! But He said, Yea, rather blessed are they that hear the word of God and keep it.'" It is the influence of the Holy Spirit, or divine charity in the heart, which is the greatest privilege and glory of the highest archangel in heaven; this is the thing by which the creature has fellowship with the Father and the Son, and becomes partaker of the divine nature in its beauty and happiness.

"The glory of the approaching happy state of the church does not at all require these extraordinary gifts. As that state of the church will be the nearest of any to its perfect state in heaven, so I believe it will be like it in this, that all extraordinary gifts shall have ceased and vanished away. . . . The apostle speaks of these gifts of inspiration as childish things in comparison of the influence of the Spirit in divine love; things given to the church only to support it in its minority, . . . which should vanish away when the church came to a state of manhood. Therefore I do not expect a restoration of these miraculous gifts in the approaching glorious times of the church, nor do I desire it. It appears to me that it would add nothing to the glory of those times, but rather diminish from it. For my part, I had rather enjoy the sweet influences of the Spirit, showing Christ's spiritual, divine beauty, infinite grace, and dying love, drawing forth the holy exercises of faith, divine love, sweet complacence, and humble joy in God one quarter of an hour, than to have prophetical visions and revelations the whole year." [1]

---

[1] *Distinguishing Marks*, etc., vol. i. pp. 556, 558.

In the light of these words, what Edwards thought about the "bodily affections" grows clearer. While he held that such things were incidental merely to the communication of the divine grace, yet it may be that he clung to them the more strongly in proportion as his idealism threatened to snap the bond which connects the spiritual with its physical embodiment. But it is in these passages above quoted that we have his deepest conviction, his most characteristic thought. And these forcible and beautiful utterances, asserting the superiority of the spiritual as if ineffably higher than all mechanical gifts or outward signs or manifestations of power, have important and far-reaching relations. They may be taken as marking an epoch in the history of religious progress. Their spirit has passed into the theology of New England, forming, as it were, a bulwark against mediæval religion with its tendency to deify the material and the outward, or to sanction the worship of the body rather than the spirit of Christ. They have become the charter of religious idealism as contrasted with religious materialism. They stand out in sharp contrast also with reactionary religious movements in our own day, notably that led by Edward Irving, whose object was to restore to the modern church the gifts of the apostolic age, such as prophesyings, speaking with tongues, or miraculous cures of disease, as if these were the highest reaches of faith, the evidences most needed or desired in order to attest the vitality and certitude of Christian belief.

One inference from his attitude on this subject Edwards immediately proceeded to draw. Itinerant preachers were then beginning to travel about the country, proclaiming that human learning was not necessary to the work of the ministry. The phrase, "lowly preaching," was coming into vogue as compared with the ministrations of an educated clergy. Against the itinerants, who decried theological culture and depended upon inspiration, Edwards urged his hearers not to despise human learning. But he does not stop to argue the point. It was too manifest to be denied, that God might make great use of human learning. And if so, then study, the means by which it was to be acquired, should not be neglected. "Though having the heart full of the powerful influences of the Spirit of God may at some times enable persons to speak profitably, yet this will not warrant us to cast ourselves down from the pinnacle of the temple, depending upon it that the angel of the Lord will bear us up, and keep us from dashing our foot against a stone, when there is another way to go down, though it be not so quick." He also urged that *method* in sermons should not be neglected, since it tends greatly to help the understanding and memory. And another thing he would beg the dear children of God more fully to consider is, how far and upon what grounds they are warranted by Scripture in passing judgment upon other professing Christians as hypocrites, and ignorant of real religion. It is God alone who knoweth the hearts of the children of men. To his own master every man standeth or falleth. Judge nothing before the time, until the Lord cometh. Let tares and wheat grow together till the harvest. They greatly err who take upon themselves to determine who are sincere and who are not. His own experience has taught him that the heart of man is more unsearchable than he had once supposed. "I am less charitable and less uncharitable than once I was. I find more things in wicked men that may counterfeit and make a fair show of piety; and more ways that the remaining corruption of the godly may make them appear like carnal men than once I knew of." And finally he admits that it would be wise to consider that excellent rule of prudence which Christ has left us, *not to put a piece of new cloth into an old garment.* In former years, he thinks there was too great confinement within one stated method and form of procedure, which had a tendency to cause religion to degenerate into formality. And now whatever has the appearance of great innovation may shock and surprise the minds of people, setting them to talking and disputing, perplexing many with doubts and scruples, and so hinder the progress of religion. That which is much beside the common practice, unless it be a thing in its own nature of considerable importance, had better be avoided. Let them follow the example of St. Paul, who made it a rule to become all things to all men, that he might by all means save some.

III.

EVILS AND ABUSES OF THE GREAT AWAKENING. — "THOUGHTS ON THE REVIVAL."

THE Distinguishing Marks had been written in 1741, before the Awakening had reached its greatest headway as a movement, before it had engendered the abuses which were destroying not only the peace, but threatened the very life, of the New England churches. In 1742 it became evident that something must be done to guide and control the movement if it were not to issue in religious anarchy. In ecclesiastical parlance, it was "an unhappy time" for the churches during the years from 1742 to 1745. So grievous were the evils that some have thought the subsequent slumber of the American churches for nearly seventy years may have been owing to the reaction which they produced. These evils sprang from the extravagant assertion or misapplication of the principle for which Edwards stood as the foremost champion. The doctrine of the immediate contact of the Holy Spirit with the human heart — a principle in whose defence he never wavered — was the source, or to speak more correctly the occasion, from whence came the confusion, the divisions and separations, the superstitions, which disfigured a movement which he believed to be divine. What Luther had feared, when he first heard of the teachings of the

Zwickau prophets, had actually come to pass in the New England churches. What the early Puritans themselves had dreaded as the necessary outcome of Quaker preaching was now resulting from the influential utterance of similar views by one the most honored in their own ranks.

It is better not to obscure the issue by seeking some other cause for the confusion. Edwards himself recognized that this principle of the immediate divine influence not only gave birth to the disorder, but was likely to result in still greater disorder before the work was over. But, unlike Luther, Edwards refused to abandon the principle, though he was becoming keenly alive to the mischief which its misapprehension was working. In the presence of the Zwickau prophets, Luther denied the truth of the immediacy of the divine action, falling back upon the Word and the Sacraments as the external channels of the divine communication. Edwards adhered to his conviction, and labored to purify it from abuse and misinterpretation.

The history of these years, from 1742 to 1745, may be studied elsewhere.[1] It is only as Edwards is concerned that we propose to follow it. But a general summary of the situation may be given, in order to a clearer appreciation of his work as a religious teacher and reformer. One of the most embarrassing features of the revival, with which the clergy were called to deal, was the disturbances

[1] Cf. Tracy, *Great Awakening*, pp. 286, ff.

in the congregations on Sunday caused by the "bodily effects," — the faintings and fallings, the weeping and shouting, the trances, the convulsions. This was bad enough. But a worse effect followed from the popular idea that these things were the best evidence of the Spirit's presence and power. Religious experiences came to be tested by the "bodily effects." There was a rivalry among the people as to who should display the most striking manifestations. Even at Northampton, among a people of whom Edwards was proud as having had an excellent training under Mr. Stoddard in spiritual things, and who were noted for their large and varied experiences, as well as by their wisdom and sobriety, even here the delusion extended. People came from abroad who had seen displays of power to which Northampton had hitherto been a stranger; and the work, which had before been comparatively pure, now degenerated into this unspiritual rivalry. The revival had issued everywhere in a sharp distinction between the converted and the unconverted. Those who believed themselves converted were not only puffed up with pride, but undertook to judge the condition of others in the light of their own experience. This practice was most fruitful in bitter results. The converted drew off from the unconverted, avoiding those who were regarded as still in darkness, and addressing each other as brother or sister. Itinerant lay preachers, as well as itinerants among the clergy, now appeared on the scene to add to the disorder.

They were uneducated in many instances, trusting to impulses and impressions, which they held to be the direct result of the voice of the Spirit within them; they appealed to the feelings of those already excited by irrational and noisy exhorting; and, worst of all, they undertook to pronounce upon the spiritual condition of the pastors of the various churches in the towns which they visited. It is mainly to Whitefield that this principle of confusion must be attributed. He had allowed himself to intrude into parishes, to condemn their ministers as unconverted, and had in many cases advised the people to separate from their ministry. It is only proper to add that Whitefield saw his errors and acknowledged them, but not before he had been the author of a great mischief. The report was bruited about that he intended to bring over young men from England to take the place of unconverted ministers.[1] Separatist congregations

[1] This report gave rise to a prolonged personal controversy between Edwards and Rev. Mr. Clap, rector of Yale College. It seems that Whitefield had told Edwards that he intended to bring over from England into New Jersey and Pennsylvania a number of young men to be ordained by the two Mr. Tennents. This was in 1740. Some time afterwards, when the excitement over Whitefield's course in New England was at its height, Edwards happened to be riding on horseback to Boston in company with Rector Clap, to whom he imparted this information of Whitefield's former intention in regard to New Jersey, and added, perhaps incautiously, that he supposed him to have a similar intention in regard to New England. On the strength of this conversation, Rector Clap declared publicly, that Edwards had informed him that Whitefield had told Edwards that he intended to bring over young men from England, etc., to supply the places

were springing up all over New England, based upon the ancient Montanist principle that it was the will of God to have a pure church, in which the converted should be separated from the unconverted. All the errors of the revival were embodied in these separatist congregations, — reliance upon impressions as guides to conduct, and to the knowledge of their own and each other's conditions; disowning of the ministers and churches of the land as lacking the attestation of the Spirit; approval of lay exhorting as having the only evidence of a divine presence.[1]

Those opposed to the revival now put forth a vigorous opposition. The colleges at Cambridge and New Haven pronounced against the movement, and did much to stay the disorder by the influence of prescriptive authority. The opposition was led by Dr. Chauncy, of the First Church in Boston, in bold and able treatises,[2] in which he condemned the

of the New England clergy. Such a report, of course, was fuel to the excitement. Edwards denied the veracity of Rector Clap's statement. Many letters passed between the two, in which the Rector of Yale College was finally worsted. The controversy has no value beyond illustrating the tenacity with which Edwards hung on to an opponent until he had silenced him. The correspondence was published, and may be found in the library of the Massachusetts Historical Society.

[1] Cf. Tracy, etc., p. 317, for the Confession of Faith of one of these separatist churches at Mansfield.

[2] In 1743 Chauncy published a reply to Edwards' *Distinguishing Marks*, etc., under the title, *The Late Religious Commotions in New England Considered*. He seems to have been fond of issuing his works anonymously. In this case he signs himself "A lover of truth and peace." Edwards makes no allusion to him by name in his works written in defence of the revival.

whole movement as a delusion, — the bodily effects as evidence of human weakness rather than divine power; and denounced the intrusions into quiet villages, and the separations from the established order, as the greatest evil with which New England could be visited. Religion, with him and those who agreed with him, consisted in responding to the divine will by a simple life of obedience to the moral precepts of the gospel. Emotions and high experiences he rejected, along with impulses and impressions, as having a common origin in a debased abnormal condition. The Arminians, and their sympathizers among the old Calvinists who did not follow with Edwards, appear as the conservative power in the churches, resisting changes which were dissolving the ancient Puritan order. The General Convention of Congregational Ministers in the Province of Massachusetts Bay put forth in 1743 their testimony "against errors in doctrine and disorders in practice which have of late obtained in various parts of the land." In Connecticut the evils of the time were met by an effort to enforce the principles of the Saybrook Platform, in which Congregationalism availed itself of Presbyterian discipline as a better method of resisting disorder than the principle of the independence of the local congregation.

It is characteristic of Edwards that, in rising to the emergency, he does not fall back upon external authority, or any adventitious methods which might serve a temporary convenience. He grapples with the principle at issue, making his appeal to the pure reason. Hitherto his writings had been addressed in the first instance to a congregation from the pulpit. In his Thoughts upon the Revival in New England he speaks to all the clergy and people in the provinces of the new world. No high ecclesiastical official, no successor of Augustine in the chair of Canterbury, not even Gregory the Great when he spoke with authority to Western Christendom, reproving and exhorting as by divine right, — none of these surpassed Edwards when he rose in the consciousness of his strength, clothed with the majesty of what he held for vital and eternal truth, to instruct and to warn the people of New England as to their duty in a great crisis. His leading aim is to show what are the things which should be avoided or corrected in order to the furtherance of this work of God. He confesses that things have never yet been set agoing in their right channel; that if they had been, *the work* would have so prevailed as to carry all before it, and to have triumphed over New England as its conquest. He apologizes for assuming so high and important a rôle, on the score of his youth (he was then in his fortieth year); he speaks of himself, in the conventional phraseology, as an "inferior worm;" he is anxious not to appear as taking too much upon him, as if he were dictating or determining the duty of his fathers or superiors or the civil rulers. But it is a day when great liberty is allowed to the press, when every author may freely speak his mind concerning the management of civil affairs, as in the war then raging with Spain. When he considers the sad jangling and confusion that has attended the revival, it seems plain that somebody should speak his mind, and that not in a way to inflame and increase the uproar, but to bring the bitter contention to an end. If he is right, he hopes his work will be received as a manifestation of the mind and will of God. If any will hold forth further light to him he will thankfully receive it. He feels his need of greater wisdom, and makes it his rule to lay hold of light, though it come from a child or an enemy.

Edwards' book, with the title, Thoughts on the Revival, was published in 1742. It not only bears the traces of being written in haste, but it lacks unity of impression, owing to the conflicting motives which impelled him to his task. To defend the movement as divine, while pointing out its flagrant abuses, was no easy task. But the defence of *the work* comes first in the order of treatment, for on this point Edwards had an overwhelming conviction that demanded a full and earnest utterance.

One of the arguments on which he most relies to prove the movement from God is the great transformation it has worked among the churches. "Who that saw the state of things in New England a few years ago," he exclaims, "would have thought that in so little a time there would be such a change!" Notwithstanding all the imprudences and sinful irregularities, it was manifest and notorious that throughout the land there had been an increase of a spirit of seriousness. The fruits of this seriousness were seen in a disposition to treat religion as a matter of great importance, to perform the external duties of religion in a more solemn and decent manner. There had been an awakening of the conscience of the people, which had led to deeper views of human sinfulness. There was a strange alteration almost all over New England amongst young people. A powerful invisible influence must have been at work which had induced them to forsake their devious ways, when hitherto they had clung to them despite the warnings of the ministers, or the vigilance of the civil magistrates. They had now abandoned their frolicking, their night-walking, their impure language and lewd songs. And among all, whether old or young, there was to be seen a change in their habits of drinking, tavern-haunting, profane speaking, and extravagance of apparel. Notoriously vicious persons have been reformed. The wealthy, the fashionable, the gay, great beaus and fine ladies, have relinquished their vanities. Through the greater part of New England the Bible has come into much greater esteem than it had formerly been, as also other books of piety. The Lord's day has come to be more religiously observed. Much had been done in making up differences, in offering restitution, and in the confession of faults one to another, — probably more within these two years than had been done in thirty years before. And in view of all this, was it not strange that, in a Christian, orthodox country, and in such a land of light, there should be many at a loss whether *the work* is of God, or of the devil? For this is certain, that it is a great and wonderful event, a strange revolution, an unexpected, surprising overturning of things, such as has never been seen in New England, and scarce ever has been heard of in any land. If it is a work of God, it is a most glorious work, or, if a work of the devil, then a most awful calamity. There is but one alternative. God and the devil may work together at the same time and in the same land; but they cannot work together in producing the same event.

For these reasons he calls upon the magistrates, as well as the clergy, to acknowledge God in this work, and to put their hand to its promotion, if they would not expose themselves to the curse of God. He recommends also that the press should be utilized to this end. They that handle the pen of the writer should come up to the help of the Lord. He warns those who are publishing pamphlets, in which they endeavor to discourage or hinder the work, that God may go forth as fire to consume all that stands in His way, and so burn up those pamphlets; and there may be danger that the fire which is kindled in them may scorch the authors. He intimates that jealousy or envy may be among the motives which influence the ministers to show themselves out of humor, or sullenly refuse to acknowledge the work. Let them not decline to give the honor that belongs to others because they are young or inferior to themselves, or may appear unworthy that so much honor should be put upon them. But among the clergy who may be thus tempted he includes himself, for he had experienced the trial of seeing a young man in his pulpit at Northampton whose moving power on the congregation proved greater than his own. There is a hint in all this that the old régime was coming to an end, when the minister might grow old in his parish with the increasing reverence of his people, even though the fire of a fervent oratory had declined. But Edwards was inclined to acquiesce in the change. "It is our wisest and best way to bow to the great God in this work, and to be entirely resigned to Him with respect to the manner in which He carries it on."

Among the reasons which explain the error of those who have had ill thoughts in regard to the revival, Edwards assigns the neglect of the Bible, — the sole rule by which such things should be judged. They follow, instead, their à priori notions, or they make philosophy instead of Scripture their rule, and so reach the conclusion that religion is running out into transports and high flights of the affections. These persons separate the affections from the will, as if they did not belong to the noblest part of the soul, so that the relation of the affections to Christianity is regarded as something adventitious or accidental.

Those gentlemen who hold such a view labor, he thinks, under a great mistake both in their philosophy and divinity. The religious affections appertain to the essence of Christianity; the very life and soul of all true religion consists in them. The affections, he argues, should not be separated from the will as though they were two distinct faculties. Acts of the will are simply acts of the affections. The soul wills one thing rather than another, no otherwise than as it loves one thing more than another. The greater, therefore, and the higher the exercises of love toward God and of self-abhorrence for sin, so much higher is Christ's religion, and the virtue which He raises in the soul.

But another cause which helps to explain the disaffection toward the revival is to be found in the failure to discriminate between the evil and the good which are associated in the movement. Because of this want of discrimination, things are condemned as abuses which Edwards refuses to condemn. Among these was the style of preaching then coming into fashion, — what Edwards calls a very affectionate manner of speaking, with great appearance of earnestness both in voice and gesture. It was objected that this method of preaching stirred the affections without reaching the understanding. Edwards admits the importance of clear and distinct explanation of the doctrines of religion, — a method in which lay his own strength, in great part, as a preacher. But it is evident that in meeting this objection he is distracted by contrary impulses. It would have been a more congenial task to have upheld the importance of the scientific, speculative aspects of Christian truth. But on the other hand he recognizes in the objection the desire to eliminate the emotions from the sphere of practical piety, and in the emotions he considers the chief part of religion to consist. Hence he maintains the correctness and necessity of this mode of preaching which appeals to the affections. He endeavors, by a subtle distinction, to show that the affections cannot really be excited except by light in the understanding. We are to infer, therefore, that this *affectionate* mode of preaching must somehow reach the mind before it stirs the passions. The mind may be enlightened without a learned handling of the doctrinal points of religion. Edwards now goes so far as to maintain that speculative knowledge of divinity is not what is chiefly needed at this time, but rather warmth of devotion. The age, he thinks, abounds in this kind of knowledge. " Was there ever an age," he exclaims, " wherein strength and penetration of reason, extent of learning, exactness of distinction, correctness of style, clearness of expression, did so abound? And yet was there ever an age in which there was so little sense of the evil of sin, so little love to God, or holiness of life? What the people need is, not to have their heads stored, so much as to have their hearts touched." Here, also, Scripture comes to his assistance. It seems to be foretold that in the latter days there will be a loud and earnest preaching of the gospel. *O Jerusalem, that bringest good tidings, lift up thy voice with strength, cry aloud, spare not*, is the divine injunction. This is to be the way with the church at the supreme moment when the *Christ mystical* is about to be brought forth.

The next abuse mentioned, which Edwards will not admit as such, is preaching terror to the people when they are already under great terrors, instead of preaching comfort. He admits of course that something else besides terror is to be preached. But before a sinner's conversion through repentance and faith, there is no danger, he thinks, of overdoing the terrors of the law. To bring in the gospel too soon would be to undo the previous distress. The phase of distress and terrors is the moment of the minister's opportunity. He must strike while the iron is hot; then only will the work be thoroughly done. He himself is not afraid to tell sinners, who are most sensible of their misery, that their case is a thousand times worse than they imagine; for this is the truth. If all this should lead in some cases to religious melancholy, it is not the fault of the ministers. The same objection might be urged against the Bible as against awakening preaching. There are hundreds and probably thousands of instances of persons who have murdered themselves under religious melancholy, which would not have been the case if they had remained in heathen darkness.

That which more especially gave offence to

many was the frightening of poor, innocent children with talk of hell fire and eternal damnation. This, also, Edwards maintains, is not an abuse. Those who complain of the ministers who follow this method raise a loud cry, as if such conduct were intolerable. But this complaint only betrays weakness and inconsideration. Here follows the passage which has been remembered against Edwards to our own day: —

"As innocent as young children seem to be to us, yet, if they are out of Christ, they are not so in God's sight, but are young vipers, and infinitely more hateful than vipers, and are in a most miserable condition as well as grown persons; and they are naturally very senseless and stupid, *being born as the wild ass's colt*, and need much to awaken them."

Upon this point Edwards makes no qualification whatever. In theory and in practice he extended the revival to the case of children. He himself presided over children's meetings. He thought that God really descended from heaven to be amongst them. He declares that he has seen the happy effects of dealing plainly with them in the concerns of their souls, nor has he ever known any ill consequences to result from such a method. Indeed, God in *this work* has shown a remarkable regard to little children. Let men take care that they do not despise the religion of children, as did the scribes and high priests who complained of the children when they cried *Hosanna* in the temple, to whom also Jesus had replied: "Have ye never read, Out of the mouth of babes and sucklings thou hast perfected praise?"

Much also was said against frequent religious meetings, and spending too great an amount of time in religion. This objection Edwards meets with ease and in his usual manner. He affirms, as a matter of course, that people ought not to neglect the business of their daily calling. But having admitted the principle, he seeks in some degree to counteract its force. He urges that it may not be so improper after all, if, while people are seeking eternal riches and immortal glory, they should in some measure suffer in their temporal concerns. On extraordinary occasions a whole nation spends time and money in the ceremonies of a public rejoicing. Why, then, should we be so exact with God as to think it a crime if we injure our temporal interests in His service? But, whichever way he looks, he has the best of the argument. He is sure that of late, more time has been gained than lost; more time has been saved from frolicking and tavern-haunting, unprofitable visits, vain talk and needless diversions, than has been spent in extraordinary religion; "and probably five times as much has been saved in persons' estates, at the taverns and in their apparel, as has been spent by religious meetings."

There was one other accompaniment of the revival which its opponents regarded as an abuse and delusion, which Edwards still refuses to condemn. Once more we must revert to the "bodily effects" which waited upon the movement, as Edwards believed, by a divine appointment. It has been already remarked that he clung to these manifestations, impelled as it were by some inward necessity. In his Thoughts on the Revival he resumes the subject, placing it in the foreground of his treatment, determined, as it would seem, to have it out with his opponents. It is a subject which is confessedly difficult and mysterious, nor is his attitude wholly free from contradiction. But he guards himself as far as possible from misapprehension. These bodily affections and high transports, he affirms, have nothing to do with true religion, which consists only in a right state of mind and correct moral conduct. They are to be regarded as incidental, not to be sought after or encouraged, not to be valued as a sign of the divine favor. "The degree of the influence of the Spirit of God on *particular persons* is by no means to be judged of by the degree of external appearances." But, taking the movement as a whole, these effects are also probable tokens of God's presence. Where they exist, they are arguments for the success of the preaching. A great crying out in a congregation, in consequence of the powerful presentation of the truth, seems to him a thing to rejoice in, much more than if there were only an appearance of solemn attention and a show of affection by weeping. "To rejoice that the work is carried on calmly, without much ado, is in effect to rejoice that it is carried on with less power, or that there is not so much of the influence of God's Spirit."

He regards it also as a specious objection against *the work*, that there have been cases where the body is injured, or the health impaired. Did not Jacob wrestle with God for a blessing, and gain the blessing, though he was sent away halting upon his thigh, and went lame ever after? Is it strange that if God pleases a little to withdraw the veil, to let in light upon the soul, giving a view of the things of another world in their transcendent and infinite greatness, that human nature, which is as the grass, a shaking leaf, a weak withering flower, should totter under such a discovery? When Daniel saw the majesty of Christ, there was no strength left in him; when John the apostle saw Him, he fell at His feet as one dead. The prophet Habbakuk, when he saw the awfulness of the divine manifestation, exclaims, "When I heard, my belly trembled, my lips quivered at the voice, rottenness entered into my bones." The Psalmist also was affected as persons of late have been: "I opened my mouth and panted, for I longed for thy commandments." God may be pleased at times to make the cup of blessing to run over. "It has been with the disciples of Christ, for a long time, a time of great emptiness upon spiritual accounts; they have gone hungry, and have been toiling in vain during a dark season, a time of night with the church of God; as it was with the disciples of old, when they had toiled all night for something to eat and had taken nothing. But now, the morning being come, Jesus appeared to his disciples, and takes a compassionate notice of their wants, and says to them, *Children, have ye any meat?* and gives them such abundance of food that they are not able to draw their net; yea, their net breaks, their vessel is overloaded and begins to sink." In this process God may not only weaken the body, but may take the life also. In this way it has been supposed that the life of Moses was taken. Indeed, God may so impair the frame of the body, and particularly of the brain, that persons shall be deprived of the use of the reason. And if God does give such discoveries of Himself as to lead to this result, the blessing is greater than the calamity, even though the life should be taken away; yea, even though the soul should not be immediately taken away, but should be for years in a deep sleep, or be deprived of the use of its faculties before it should pass into glory. Considering what a number of persons have been overpowered of late, it is remarkable that their lives should have been preserved, and that the instances of those who have been deprived of their reason should have been so few.[1]

In accounting for Edwards' attitude on this subject, it has been already suggested that a system like his, of such transcendent idealism, needed some tangible or physical counterpoise, in order that it might not be detached altogether from the

---

[1] *Thoughts*, etc., vol. iii. pp. 282–285.

external world, and so be in danger of terminating in unreality. It is one of the characteristics of his system that he makes no attempt to trace an organic relationship between man and nature. The external world existed only mentally and in the mind of God. The purpose of nature in relation to man, its necessity to his spiritual existence, the conflict of man with nature, the victory which is reached through perpetual struggle, and is manifested in the ever-increasing transmutation of the natural into the spiritual, — these are thoughts which find no expression in his works. He had reacted against the low materialistic tendency of the age which glorified the miracle as the highest evidence for the validity of a spiritual revelation. He had adopted a definition of the supernatural which did not include the miracle, finding the evidence for the truth of spiritual things in the inward consciousness, the insight or intuition of the soul. But he saw no significance for the miracle as in itself a spiritual process, — as in the triumph of Christ's perfected humanity over the law of necessity in nature. His earnest defence of the bodily manifestations may be taken as an intimation that he felt the need of some element which his system did not afford. He might have found the desired relief, — the response of nature to the invocation of the Spirit, — had he been willing to lay supreme emphasis on moral practice as the test of the Spirit's presence and power. But from this mode of escape he had shut himself off by placing conscience, together with the greater part of the moral sphere of human life, under the control of God's common grace, which carries with it no saving efficacy. And yet at times he was on the eve of accepting this mode of deliverance: he hovers about the ethical result as the tangible evidence of the life of God in the soul. And, indeed, though he never retracted his testimony in behalf of bodily manifestations, it was to this conclusion that he seems to have been gravitating as he closed the long discussion.

There is, however, another explanation of Edwards' relation to this subject, which is too interesting and important to be passed over without a brief allusion. We cannot be wrong in assigning to Mrs. Edwards a place in the Great Awakening hardly inferior to that occupied by her husband. The young girl whom at the age of thirteen he had eulogized as a favorite of Heaven, whose rare beauty had satisfied his fastidious taste, was still exercising as a mature woman the same attractive influence over his mind and heart. There is abundant evidence of the spell which she exerted over those around her by the beauty of her person, and the singular and refined loveliness of her manner, as also of the character which inspired it. Her reputation had gone abroad in the colony, she was even said to surpass her husband in her endowment of Christian graces. Like him, she was a mystic devotee, with a natural capacity for the highest fervors of devotion. It was her experience

— which seemed to Edwards as genuine as it was remarkable — which would have compelled him to believe, even against his will, that the divine visitation might overpower the human body. At his request she wrote a statement of these vicissitudes of her inner life,[1] to which Edwards often alludes, and which he finally incorporated in his own words, though not mentioning her by name, in his Thoughts on the Revival in New England. He presents it to his readers as if it were decisive of the question at issue.

Apart from its religious significance, Mrs. Edwards' statement is valuable as throwing light upon her husband's personal history, as well as her own. Indeed, it must be confessed that the pure womanliness of her statement, the traces of feminine pride in her husband, her jealousy for his reputation, and her desire to retain undiminished his respect and love, are more interesting to the ordinary reader than the expressions of mystic rapture with which it abounds. It was towards the close of the year 1738, and at the age of twenty-nine, that "she was led under an uncommon discovery of God's excellency and in a high exercise of love to God, and of rest and joy in Him, to make a new and most solemn dedication of herself to His service and glory, — an entire renunciation of the world, and a resignation of all to God." The occasion which led her to long for a deeper resignation and a more entire renunciation of the world

[1] Dwight, *Life of Edwards*, pp. 171–190.

was a casual suggestion of Mr. Edwards that she had failed in some measure in point of prudence in a conversation with Mr. Williams, of Hadley. As she looked into her mind, she found that it seemed to bereave her of quietness and calm not to have the good opinion of her husband. She saw that two things interfered with an act of complete renunciation, — the desire to keep her own good name and fair reputation among men, and especially the esteem and just treatment of the people of the town, and more especially the esteem and love and kind treatment of her husband. And again, on another occasion, she had felt that the eye of God was upon her to observe how she was affected by the respect shown to Mr. Edwards, who had then been sent for to preach at Leicester. She was sensible that the incident had ministered to her pride in her husband, rather than to a pure interest in the extension of God's work. When she heard that Mr. Buel, a young man recently ordained, was coming to Northampton to take Mr. Edwards' place during his absence, she had a struggle with herself before she was willing to pray that God would bless his labors. She gained, as she thought, the resignation and the submission for which she longed, although Mr. Buell's preaching was attended by greater success than had attended her husband's preaching before he went to Leicester. Even if God were never again to bless the labors of Mr. Edwards, or were to make use of Mr. Buell to the enlivening of every saint and the conversion of every sinner in the town, she thought her resignation would enable her to rejoice in the result. She was not only willing that her pride in Mr. Edwards should be humbled, but the moment came when she felt that she would be able to bear, if God so willed it, these two greatest evils, — the ill-treatment of the town and the ill-will of her husband. "I was carried above even these things," so she writes, "and could feel that, if I were exposed to them both, they would seem comparatively nothing."

We may doubt if she had succeeded so completely as she thought to have done; for ever and anon in her confession she repeats how entirely willing she had become that "God should employ some other instrument than Mr. Edwards in advancing the work of grace in Northampton." It may have been also that her sensitive instincts divined afar off the impending calamity for her family; she may have been foreboding and preparing for an event which would call forth the requirements of stoical fortitude, when, her husband's power as a preacher having declined, and his hold upon his congregation lost, they should be driven forth as it were into that wilderness which, in her imagination, she had descried, amid the scorn and contumely of the people. But however this may be, none the less did she have her reward for her consecration to what she believed to be the divine will. For a period of nearly three years she remained in a state of such spiritual exhilaration as lifted her above the world, and brought her into intimate communion with Heaven. Although in a condition of firm health, she was constantly overcome by the power of her emotions and the vividness of her appprehensions of divine things, so much so as to faint, or to be deprived of her strength. At other times she rose up leaping with joy and exultation. The depth of her sense of assurance of her own salvation surpassed anything her husband had experienced. Her soul seemed to be on the eve of sundering its tie with the body.

"I had a constant, clear, and lively sense of the heavenly sweetness of Christ's excellent and transcendent love, of His nearness to me and of my dearness to Him; with an inexpressibly sweet calmness of soul in an entire rest in Him. I seemed to myself to perceive a glow of divine love come down from the heart of Christ in heaven into my heart in a constant stream, like a stream or pencil of sweet light. What I felt each minute of this time was worth more than all the outward comfort and pleasure which I had enjoyed in my whole life put together. . . . To my own imagination my soul seemed to be gone out of me to God and Christ in heaven. God and Christ were so present and so near me, that I seemed removed from myself. . . . I had an overwhelming sense of the glory of God as the great Eternal All. I knew that I certainly should go to Him, and should as it were drop into the Divine Being and be swallowed up in God."

Edwards' comment upon his wife's experience may be read at length in his Thoughts on the

Revival. He was so afraid that he should be misled by it, that he scrutinizes it with the cool manner of a disinterested observer. As he studied it, it seemed to answer every test which he applied. Mrs. Edwards was led into no extremes of behavior; she retained her good judgment and sound common sense. She followed no *impulses;* she was the subject of no *impressions.* Her high experience seemed to strengthen and purify her Christian character. She was free from censoriousness, with no disposition to judge of others: she was filled with charity and humility. She did not neglect the necessary business of a secular calling in order to spend time in the exercises of devotion, but rather realized, in worldly business performed with alacrity, the service of God, and as it were a substitute for prayer. What she had felt could be, therefore, nothing else than the response to the exalted expressions of Scripture: *The peace of God which passeth all understanding; the joy and peace in believing, which is unspeakable and full of glory.* "Now if such things," he exclaims, "are enthusiasm and the fruits of a distempered brain, let my brain be evermore possessed of that happy distemper! If this be distraction, I pray God that the world of mankind may be all seized with this benign, meek, beneficent, beatifical, glorious distraction."

A critical student, concerned only with what is unique in psychological manifestations, might be inclined to inquire, whether, in all this, Mrs. Edwards may not have been adapting herself unconsciously to her husband's views, striving in a spirit of devotion and loyalty to embody her husband's ideal of what a saint on earth should be. To some extent this may be true. But no such suspicion crossed his mind. He staked the whole question at issue on his wife's experience. It is quite possible that hers was the stronger influence.

To the task of exposing the abuses of the revival Edwards seems to come with reluctance. He lingers on the gloriousness of the work, the reasons why all should unite in promoting it. But when he has once committed himself to the business of criticism, he shows the same disposition to thoroughness of treatment which characterizes all his writings. His tone is kindly, for he is addressing the friends of the movement rather than its foes. But he lays his axe at the root of the tree.

The first evil which he attacked went under the name of *impulses* or *impressions*.[1] He declares that one of the wrong principles which had given rise to grave errors was the notion "that it is God's manner in these days to guide His saints by inspiration or immediate revelation, to make known

---

[1] Edwards' *Thoughts on the Revival* was republished in England by Wesley with the title, *Thoughts Concerning the Present Revival of Religion in New England*, by Jonathan Edwards. Abridged by John Wesley, A. M. London, 1745. It is characteristic of the nature of the abridgment that, while the discussion of "bodily effects" is retained, all that relates to "impulses and impressions" is omitted.

to them what shall come to pass hereafter, or what it is His will they should do." That people should have been misled into such a notion was a thing to have been expected. To admit the immediate action of the divine Spirit in the soul seemed to warrant the vulgar conclusion that the future would now be revealed, and their course of duty under all circumstances made plain. What else, they might have argued, did they need more than this, — an infallible directory within? In what other way could the divine Spirit, which was distinct and different from the human, manifest itself as an inward reality, unless by doing that which the human spirit could not do? Edwards himself had at first sounded a wrong note when, in his Narrative of Surprising Conversions, he attributed importance to the circumstance that, in the process of an awakening soul, passages of Scripture suddenly came to the mind as if suggested by the Holy Spirit. But he now deprecates this idea as part of the same delusion as the *impulses* and *impressions*.

But while Edwards has emancipated himself from all complicity with the various manifestations of this evil principle, we search his pages in vain for a satisfactory enunciation of the method by which the root of the evil is to be reached. He is sure that the principle is wrong, that it has a tendency to supplant Scripture, to bring in confusion, to nourish pride, to draw off the mind from the one thing needful. Why cannot men be content with the divine oracles? Why should they desire to make Scripture speak more than it does? There is nothing necessarily spiritual in this idea of special direction. Even if God were to reveal anything by a voice from heaven, there is in it nothing of the nature of true grace; it is but a common influence of the Spirit; it is but dross and dung in comparison with the gracious leading that a real saint possesses. As much as this God gave to Balaam, revealing to him what he should say or do. But there is a more excellent way than inspiration in which the Spirit of God leads the sons of God, — their transformation by the renewal of their mind, proving to them what is the good and acceptable and perfect will of God.

All this is as true as it is admirably said. Whatever the deficiencies of Edwards' theory may have been, a true instinct warned him away from all *impulses and impressions*, as having a tendency toward the degradation of the spiritual, or to a sensuous confounding of the spiritual with the material. To suppose that these physical or external impressions were in any way caused by God, was " a low, miserable notion of spiritual sense." If he had only felt at liberty to develop this principle, his attitude would have been clear and consistent. The grace divine could then have been conceived as the implantation in the soul of an attraction toward the good, mingling insensibly with the springs of human action, yet so as to be wholly divine, while seeming to be wholly human. The love of the good would then become the basis of faith in the spiritual, the very essence of God within the soul. Edwards was inclined to such a view of the divine action, but fears of Arminianism prevented its full acceptance. He has before him the Arminian statement that "the manner of the Spirit of God is to coöperate in a silent, secret, and undiscernible way with the use of means and our own endeavors, so that there is no distinguishing by sense between the influences of the Spirit of God and the natural operations of the faculties of our own minds."[1] But if he admitted this principle, how could he maintain, what lay so close to his heart, that the great revival was an exceptional moment in history when God was working more powerfully than was His usual manner, in a way unique and spasmodic, producing even physical manifestations as in the great upheaval of the apostolic age? And still further, if he admitted such a view, it would have required a reconstruction of his ideas of humanity, a practical abandonment of the distinction between elect and non-elect, a modification of his views of original sin and the freedom of the will. In fact every feature of his theology was involved in the issue to which he had now been brought. That issue was no other than the momentous inquiry as to the relation between the divine and the human,—whether they were by nature incompatible with and foreign to each other, or whether they tended to flow together by an in-

[1] *Religious Affections*, vol. iii. p. 29.

ward affinity, forming an union in which they cannot be divided or separated, even if they may be distinguished from each other.

The following passage shows Edwards as attempting a sort of compromise with a truth which strangely attracts him, while he cannot accept it: —

"However all exercises of grace be from the Spirit of God, yet the Spirit of God dwells and acts in the hearts of the saints in some *measure* after the manner of a vital, natural principle, a principle of new nature in them; whose exercises are excited by means in some measure as other natural principles are. Though grace be not in the saints as *a mere natural principle*, but as a sovereign agent, and so its exercises are not *tied to means* by an immutable law of nature, as in mere natural principles; yet God has so constituted that grace should dwell so in the hearts of the saints that its exercises *should have some connection with means*, after the manner of a principle of nature." [1]

Because Edwards failed to reach a satisfactory solution of this fundamental problem, his attitude was an uncertain and inconsistent one. He could not effectually overcome the evils of the revival, nor meet the arguments of those who contended for *impulses and impressions* as evidences of the Spirit's presence and power. He must be held partly responsible for these very evils. Nay, more, he was forced into a worse situation, if that were possible, than those who were following their own impressions, under the delusion that they were

[1] *Thoughts on the Revival*, iii. p. 378.

divine. Dr. Chauncy and his sympathizers, who opposed the revival, showed their keenness in fastening upon this delusion as its vulnerable point. They may have been in error in attributing too much to human action, or in reducing the divine Spirit to a mere humble, unrecognized servitor upon the human spirit. Edwards denounces them for refusing to confess *the work* as divine: he is fearful lest they should commit the unpardonable sin by denying the presence and activity of the Holy Ghost in the religious contagion which was spreading throughout the land. But what shall we say in reference to the ground which he was driven to take in order to defend his own position? Assuming, as he did, that the action of the Spirit in the revival was extraordinary, manifested in bodily effects, and always distinguishable from the human activity, he was obliged to admit that the tendency of this divine action was to excite inclinations which if gratified would lead to confusion. Human judgment and discretion must therefore come to the rescue, in order to prevent the unlimited influence of the divine. He illustrates this necessity of checking and curbing the divine influence, by showing how absurd it would be, if those who were moved by the love of souls were to spend all their time, night and day, in warning and exhorting men, giving themselves no opportunity to drink or sleep. Such a course of action would do ten times more injury than good. And yet, upon Edwards' principles, not to do this presents the extraordinary spectacle of the divine influence controlled and kept within bounds by human prudence. But we must believe that Edwards was not wholly satisfied with his own attitude. A mind like his, whose own obstinate self-questionings were more embarrassing than the objections of his opponents, still remains a more profitable as well as interesting study than the writings of an antagonist like Chauncy, who had no misgivings when deciding on the course of action to be pursued. We turn away from the consideration of this abuse, the impulses and impressions, to another evil which grew out of them, whose result was to subvert the ecclesiastical order in New England.

Allusion has been made to the itinerant preachers and lay exhorters who went travelling over the country, intruding into parishes, censuring the clergy as unconverted, calling upon God either to convert or to remove them, advising their people to form separatist churches in the interest of their own salvation. Such were the Whitefields, the Tennants, the Davenports, and the young men who were inspired by their example. There had grown up in New England, in the hundred years that had elapsed since its settlement, a consolidated ecclesiastical system which was as tyrannical[1] in its way as anything from which the Puritans had sought escape in England. "The whole country was divided into parishes, in each of which a

[1] Cf. Tracy, *The Great Awakening*, p. 414. "The revival gave a mortal wound to parish despotism."

church was organized and a pastor settled according to law, with whose rights none was allowed to interfere. The minister of the parish was held responsible for the religious instruction of its inhabitants. The idea grew up very naturally that those who held him thus responsible should not put themselves under other teachers without his leave, and that other teachers ought not to derange his plans of usefulness by breaking in upon his parish contrary to his judgment. The pastor had at least a moral right to control the giving and receiving of religious instructions within the geographical bounds of his parish." [1] For this ecclesiastical system Edwards had a genuine respect and affection. Such was his own position in the town of Northampton. This feeling partook in some measure of an inherited tradition. Herein he differed from Whitefield, Davenport, and others, who were restrained by no sympathy with New England history, and no desire to uphold the interests of the standing order. But Edwards could not go as far as Chauncy in his opposition to the itinerants. He evidently recognizes them as having a place and a work to do, though he cautions them as liable above all other clergy to spiritual pride. "When a minister is greatly succeeded from time to time, and so draws the eyes of the multitude upon him, and he sees himself flocked after and resorted to as an oracle, and people are ready to adore him and to offer sacri-

[1] Tracy, p. 416.

fice to him, as it was with Paul and Barnabas at Lystra, it is almost impossible for a man to avoid taking upon him the airs of a master or some extraordinary person." If Edwards had had any such experience himself, he had resisted the temptations to which it led. But the description might be said to apply word for word to Whitefield.

If Edwards was willing to recognize the itinerant clergy, although it was an invasion of the established order, yet at this point he sharply draws the line and will go no further. He condemns severely the lay exhorters who assume the clerical rôle. In the same connection he asserts the necessity for an educated ministry. It would be a calamity at all times, and especially at that time, if men without a liberal education, who according to the rule of the prophet *had not been taught to keep cattle from their youth*, were to be admitted to the work of the ministry on the ground of having had remarkable experiences. These would be the very men to mislead the people with impulses, vain imaginations, and such like extremes. But the time had come when such as these were called for by a large part of the people. The *lowly preaching* encouraged by the Baptists was making inroads on the favored flocks of the educated clergy. It was acceptably received by many as coming closer to their needs, than the sermons which according to right reason should have been the most effective. In this respect the age was changing: an ecclesiastical democracy was asserting its rights and needs, and in its presence the Puritan oligarchy broke down.

The ground on which Edwards condemns the lay exhorters who intrude into the ministerial field is most interesting to study, for at this point Congregationalism and Presbyterianism should be distinguished from the later movement which was led by Wesley. Wesley had his qualms of conscience upon this point, springing from his high-church principles; but he overcame them, and lay exhorting became one of the features of Wesleyan Methodism. Edwards was also a high-churchman from the Puritan point of view, carrying the principle of church authority to almost extreme results. The high-churchman, whatever his ecclesiastical affiliation, is inclined to limit the divine influence by the bounds of organization, or to make the spread of the truth keep pace with the extension of the institution. The ecclesiastical idea is one to which Edwards never gave much attention; but he was resting upon it when he objected to admitting men to the ministry who did not possess a liberal education, simply on the ground of their having an unusual experience, or as being persons of a good understanding. On this point he exclaims naïvely that, if it should become a custom to admit such persons to the ministry, how many lay persons would soon become candidates for the office! He doubts not but he has become acquainted with scores of persons that would have desired it. And then how shall we know where to stop? In other words, the agencies for the diffusion of Christianity might surpass the scope of the institution to provide for them.

The chief ground on which Edwards deprecates the lay exhorters is the necessity of ecclesiastical order. He speaks of order as among the most necessary of external means for promoting the spiritual good of the church. He denounces the erroneous principle that external order, in matters of religion and the use of the means of grace, is a thing of no importance. He has no sympathy with those who condemn these things as ceremonies and dead forms, inasmuch as God looks only on the heart. He may have had Hooker's eloquent words in mind when he writes that order is most requisite even in heaven itself and among angelic intelligences. God has also implanted it, as by a wonderful instinct, throughout the ranks of the animal creation. A church without order is like a city without walls, lacking the means for self-defence. He is willing, however, to admit that some measure of lay exhorting is proper, and may be a duty, if it does not overstep its bounds and infringe on the authority of the clergy. There is a sharp distinction, as he conceives, between preaching and what he prefers to call *Christian conversation*. Let laymen confine themselves only to the latter. The main characteristic of preaching is authority. This authority only ministers should exercise. Ministers are clothed with the authority of Christ; they alone have the power to preach the gospel and to speak in His name. They are commanded to speak, rebuke, and exhort with all authority. But private Christians, *who are no more than mere brethren*, if they exhort, should do so by way of entreaty, and in the most humble manner. And even "if a layman does not assume an authoritative manner, yet if he forsakes his proper calling, and spends his time in going about from house to house to counsel and exhort, he goes beyond his line and violates Christian rules." For teaching is the *business* of the clergy. All are not apostles or prophets, all are not teachers. According, then, to the apostolic command, *He that teacheth let him wait on teaching.* "It will be a very dangerous thing for laymen, in these respects, to invade the office of a minister! None ought to carry the ark of God but the Levites only. And because one presumed to touch the ark that was not of the sons of Aaron, therefore the Lord made a breach upon them, and covered their day of rejoicing with a cloud in His anger." No strenuous upholder of the notion of an apostolic succession could desire more explicit language than this.

Such was Edwards' devotion to the principle of church authority that he seems almost willing to limit the spread of the *movement*, if there is danger of its weakening or overthrowing the power of the clergy. Mingled with these strict principles of ecclesiastical authority, we may discern traces of the aristocratic pride which marked the manner of the ancient Puritan clergy. It was right, as Edwards thought, that "they should have the outward appearance and show of authority, in style and behavior, which was proper and fit to be seen in them." Hence he was inwardly shocked at the way in which the "meanest of the people" took upon them to criticise the most eminent ministers, sitting in judgment upon their deficiencies, or pronouncing them converted or unconverted. So far as his own relations with the ministers were concerned, he had solemnly exhorted and adjured them to recognize *the work* as divine, and labor zealously for its promotion. If this impossible advice could have been received, there would have been an end of the difficulty. But even if the ministers did not accept the work as divine, or if they were really unconverted, yet Edwards does not propose that the *mere brethren* shall be the ones to take them to task. The power of judging and openly censuring others should be in the hands of particular persons or consistories appointed for the purpose. Upon the question whether it was a duty for people to desert the ministry of those who unqualifiedly and openly condemned the revival, — upon this point Edwards maintains a prudent reticence. For himself he remarks: "I should not think that any person had power to oblige me constantly to attend the ministry of one who did from time to time plainly pray and preach against this work, or speak reproachfully of it frequently in his public performances, after all Christian methods had been used for a remedy and to no purpose."[1] His reserve upon this subject, the burning question of the day, may be construed as indicating a subordinate sympathy, not easily reconciled with his view of the importance of ecclesiastical order.

However definite and rigid may have been Edwards' idea of conversion, he was unwilling for himself to pronounce upon the condition of his fellow-ministers. He was even willing to admit that they might be in a state of grace, and yet oppose *the work* through prejudice or other reasons. His moderation was in strong contrast with the over-zealous converts who denounced the unconverted ministers as if they were guilty of desecrating the church, like the ancient money-changers in the Jewish temple. These zealots, as they may be called, claimed for their justification the words of Christ, that He came to send not peace, but a sword. One of the scourges which they employed in order to drive the unconverted ministers from the temple was the most violent imprecatory language. Those who indulged in this profane vocabulary defended its use on the ground that they only said what was true, — that they must be bold for Christ's sake, and not mince matters in His cause. Edwards complains that the language of common sailors is introduced among Christian peo-

---

[1] Compare on this point a letter of Edwards in which he gives advice as to how to deal with repentant separatists. Dwight, p. 204.

ple under the cloak of high sanctity. "The words 'devil' and 'hell' are almost continually in their mouths." While he admits that every kind and degree of sin is justly characterized as devilish, cursed, hellish, his refined nature, as well as his aristocratic instincts, revolted within him when such epithets were hurled by those whom he calls the meanest of the people against the most eminent ministers or magistrates. It was as improper as it would be for a child to say concerning his parents, "that they commit every day hundreds of hellish, damned acts, or that they are cursed dogs, hell-hounds, devils." He draws a distinction between characterizing sin in the abstract in these truthful terms and giving them a concrete application to individuals. But the zealots made no such distinction. Nor is it greatly to be wondered at that, when such a vocabulary was thought proper for the pulpit, it should find its way to general use among the people.

Edwards was hardly in a position which could be called consistent, when he advised the zealots to drop their denunciation of the unconverted ministers. The zealots maintained that to allow them to remain in their parishes was a "bloody, hell-peopling charity." Edwards thought it would be no such dreadful danger if they were left undisturbed. It almost seems as if a change were passing over his mind, — as if he were condemning his own practice. He now advises the ministers to be careful "how they discompose and ruffle the minds of those that they esteem carnal men, or how great an uproar they raise in the carnal world, and so lay blocks in the way of the propagation of religion." But certainly no one could have ruffled the carnal mind more than Edwards had done, as in his sermon at Enfield. It may be that the caution now exhibited is no evidence of a retractation. It was a peculiarity of Edwards that he becomes at times so intent upon the point before him, as to leave all the other pieces upon the board unguarded. One would like to think that the intense fervor of his youth, as well as his inexperience at an exceptional moment, constitute an apology for those features of his earlier preaching which have injured his memory.

IV.

TREATISE ON THE RELIGIOUS AFFECTIONS.

WHEN Edwards published his book on the Religious Affections, in 1746, the Great Awakening as a religious movement had come to an end. To use his own language, the devil had prevailed against what seemed so happy and so promising in its beginning. But the dust and the smoke of the controversy were still in the air; an endless variety of opinions prevailed as to the nature of true religion. The Religious Affections was written as a series of sermons in the years 1742 and 1743, following immediately the meditations which had found utterance in his Thoughts on the Revival. We may be mistaken, but it seems as if Edwards' attitude toward the revival was never again quite the same after he had allowed his mind to dwell on its abuses. It must have pained him beyond measure to witness his ideal dragged as it were in the dust. Under these circumstances he did what so many other lofty souls have done in similar situations. Rather than behold his ideal profaned, he sought to withdraw it beyond the reach of vulgar religionists, — to make it a thing so difficult to attain that very few could be certain that they had achieved the prize. As he looked upon the variety of false experiences, the hypocrisies, the degeneration, which waited upon the revival, he was chiefly impressed with the words of Christ: *Strait is the gate and narrow is the way that leads to life, and few there be that find it;* or those other memorable words, *Many are called, but few are chosen.*

It is this conviction in Edwards' mind which like a sad undertone pervades the Religious Affections, even when not expressed, that has given the book, in the eyes of many, only a painful interest. But the treatise is a masterpiece in its way, — a beautiful and authoritative exposition of Christian experience. It is a work which will not suffer by comparison with the work of great teachers in theology, whether ancient or modern. It fulfils the condition of a good book as Milton has defined it, — "the precious life-blood of a master spirit." It is in reality Edwards' Confessions, as much as if it were directly addressed to Deity. It corresponds also to the Consolation of Philosophy in the midst of failure and disappointment. Some, as they have read, have not been able to forget the dark background in Edwards' mind, — the distinction between the elect and the non-elect, the destiny which awaits the many who are called but are not chosen. To such as these, the Religious Affections is a book which they must avoid as they hope to preserve their faith in God. The subjectivity which characterizes it, the incessant and profound introversion, the variety of delusions which entangle a soul on its way to God, — these only add horror to the situation which Edwards may have been able to contemplate with serenity, but to which the modern mind is unequal. It is possible, however, to forget the negative side of Edwards' theology as we study this pure, sublimated ideal of Christian experience. Let the book be taken by itself, as if by some anonymous writer, and its excellence will appear. It is occupied with one great motive, — to distinguish a true from a false experience, to draw the picture of a human soul which under grace has become worthy of union with God.

The Religious Affections is Edwards' answer to the question which confronted him in his youth as to the nature of true religion. He then determined, as is recorded in his Resolutions, "that he would look most nicely and diligently into the opinions of our old divines concerning conversion." Such was his unconscious confession that in the depth of his mind there lay uncertainty as to how the great reality should be defined. Although his book on the Affections has a positive and constructive purpose, yet there lingers about it something of the controversial spirit, — the old hostility against the Arminians which had been increased by the revival. He devotes considerable space to demonstrating against them that the principal part of religion consists in the affections or emotions.[1] But if his dislike to Arminianism remains unchanged, he has also seen something on the Calvinistic side which he dislikes still more, — the evangelical hypocrisy to which the revival had given birth was a greater evil than Arminian legalism.

The second part of his book is devoted to showing that the signs of conversion, upon which so great stress had been laid by many in the Revival, had no necessary connection with true religion. It was to be taken as no sign one way or the other that the religious affections were greatly stirred, or that they produced great effects upon the body. He has not abandoned his former attitude on this

[1] It is sometimes difficult to determine Edwards' meaning when he speaks of the affections, for under this term he includes also the will. He does not follow the modern method of classification according to which the faculties are divided into intellect, emotions, and will. He made a twofold division, the first of which includes the intellectual powers, and the second is variously named as the affections, the heart, or the will. It is evident that, in the first part of this treatise on the Religious Affections, it is the emotions, as we should call them, for whose recognition in religion he is contending.

point, that the action of God on the spirit may overpower the body, but he now condemns those who are looking for *bodily effects* as a sign of the spirit's action. Persons may be fervent and fluent in talking about religion and yet not possess the reality. Texts of Scripture, suddenly and unaccountably brought to the mind, are no evidence of the Spirit's work. Religious affections of many kinds may exist which are not genuine, but only counterfeits of the true. There may have been a certain order in the phases of experience by which comforts and joys may follow after awakenings and convictions, and yet there may be nothing real in it all. People may spend much time in religion, and be greatly moved in the external duties of worship, without having experienced a true conversion. The strong sense of assurance of salvation possesses in itself no value. Nor can anything be concluded from the circumstance that those professing themselves the subject of gracious experiences gain the love and win the confidence of true saints. The revival had demonstrated how vast was the field for delusion and mistake in judging of the condition of others. In a word, it was with the things of religion " as it is with blossoms in the spring. There are vast numbers of them upon the trees which all look fair and promising, but many of them never come to anything. And many of these, that in a little time wither up and drop off and rot under the trees, yet for a while look as beautiful and gay as others."

What, then, is the reality? How shall the spiritual as distinct from the natural be defined? Or, in Edwards' words, what are the distinguishing signs of truly gracious and holy affections?

The divine reality is asserted to be something entirely distinct and different from anything that is human. The human and the divine have nothing whatever in common. No improvement of natural or human tendencies ever passes by slow stages into the divine. The divine is different in kind from the human. It is in true religion as if a new sense were imparted utterly diverse from any of the other senses. The difference between those who have the spiritual gift and those who have it not is to be compared to the difference between two men, one of whom is born without the natural sense of taste, to whom the quality of sweetness is unknown. Edwards does not, in so many words, define in what the human consists, as distinct from the divine. We might infer that he regards the human as if it were the absence and the negation of the spiritual. There is nothing in his system to prevent the human from being identified with the principle of evil. He does not deny that there is much which is beautiful and even admirable in human nature, — it may bring forth moral fruits of a high order; it may have graces and charms, and even possess affections which may simulate the divine influences. But these may be the result of what he calls the *common* influence of the Divine Spirit, — that influence which once breathed on the face of the natural world in the chaos of the creation. The common influences of the Spirit are widely diffused. Edwards, as we have seen, was in philosophical language a monist, and in one sense all things are attributable to God. But these effects which are wrought by the common influence of the Spirit may be also wrought by satanic agency. Up to a certain point, the magicians of Egypt did with their enchantments what Moses did by a divine power. There is no redemptive power in the common influences of the Spirit. They are but the operation of an omnipotent force overcoming the human spirit from without, for certain ulterior purposes in the divine economy.

In those who are truly spiritual the Spirit of God does not merely act from without, as an influence apart and not their own, but it enters into them as an abiding, indwelling, integral factor of the soul. The Spirit of God even lives in them as in its peculiar home, the bosom of God. The Spirit becomes a seed or spring of life, making the soul a partaker of the beauty of God and the joy of Christ. That which is born of the Spirit *is* Spirit. But this language reminds him that he verges upon pantheism. The saints, then, do not become actually partakers of the divine essence in the abominable and blasphemous language of heretics who speak of being "Godded with God."[1]

---

[1] Who were the heretics who used this expression which Edwards quotes, "Godded with God and Christed with Christ"?

But the protest, which is a necessary one, having been made, Edwards continues to use language which conveys the same idea. And indeed that is his meaning, whether he owns it or not, — the saints through an indwelling Spirit, which is the highest, fullest essence of Deity, become as it were one with God. This is the Spirit that bears witness with our spirit that we are the children of God. The bond of union is beheld intuitively. The saint feels and sees plainly the union between his soul and God. The Spirit of God bearing witness with our spirit must not, however, be taken to mean the action of two independent, collateral witnesses. The human spirit is passive in the affair, receiving only and declaring the witness of the divine.

From this abstract and unethical statement of the difference between the spiritual and the natural, the thought moves on to the affirmation that the response of the human affections is to the excellent and amiable nature of divine things as they are in themselves, and not as they have any relation to self or self-interest. Popular Calvinism exhibited a tendency toward religious selfishness, whose manifestation increased in proportion to the degree of religious activity. In opposition to this tendency, Edwards maintained that affection to-

And where did Edwards come across it? It is used in a work by Lowde, *New Essays*, a writer engaged in controversy with Norris, the author of the *Theory of the Ideal World*, and a disciple of Malebranche. Edwards' use of it may point to some familiarity with the controversy. Cf. Lyons, *Idéalisme*, etc., p. 200.

ward God which arises from self-love is a mere product of the natural man, having in it nothing of the supernatural or divine. The heart must first discern that God is lovely in Himself, and then follows the realization of what the love of such a being toward man must be. Some might be ready to allege against this position the assertion of St. John, *We love Him because He first loved us*, as if God's love to His people were the first foundation of their love to Him. Edwards' interpretation of the passage is hardly a satisfactory one. But however these words of Scripture may be taken, they contain no argument against the truth that human love arises primarily from the excellence of divine things as they are in themselves, and not from any relation they have to human interests.[1]

But in what consists the excellency and loveliness of the divine nature? What are the tests by which these qualities are to be known? Questions of this kind we need not fear to ask, even when reading a treatise which is concerned with practical piety; for to Edwards these speculative issues are of supreme and absorbing interest. We may follow him in

---

[1] Upon this point Edwards' thought varied. In his *Notes on the Mind* he held that love to God was based upon the recognition of the divine existence apart from its moral excellence. He again maintained this view in his *Treatise on Virtue*. But in his *Treatise on Grace* he returns to what he had asserted in the *Religious Affections*, that the foundation of delight in God is His own perfection. Beneath these variations may be traced divergent conceptions of the nature of Deity.

sincere agreement as he distinguishes between the moral attributes of God and His natural perfections. These last include His infinite greatness, power, and knowledge, as well as His terrible majesty. But the spiritual beauty of the divine nature does not consist primarily in these. Even natural men may have the perception of God's physical perfections: the devils also may believe and tremble. The moral excellence of Deity is in His holiness. And this word, charged with a sense of remote Hebrew origin, a word more frequently used than defined, exactly how much and what does it mean? According to Edwards, as used of God it includes His righteousness, truth, faithfulness, and goodness, His purity and His beauty as a moral agent. Holiness when applied to men comprehends their true excellency as moral beings; it includes all the true virtues of a good man, his love to God, his gracious love to men, his justice, his charity, his meekness and gentleness. It is of these things that it is said: *Thy word is very pure, therefore thy servant loveth it; the law of the Lord is perfect, converting the soul; the statutes of the Lord are right, rejoicing the heart; the commandment of the Lord is pure, enlightening the eyes.*

But here one is tempted to ask whether these moral qualities, which are included in the general designation of holiness, do not have some natural foundation also in the constitution of the human soul. Edwards has been so emphatic in declaring that there is something new which is imparted by the Spirit in conversion, something entirely distinct from all that is human, that, when we come to the category of moral excellences as they exist in God, we look for something more and other than he furnishes. Righteousness, truth, faithfulness, goodness, these are qualities which have their root in human nature, of which the germs may be discerned in those who would not be recognized as converted. Edwards apparently feels the difficulty. But in conducting his controversy with the Arminians it was impossible for him to admit that any traces of what he calls the gracious affections should be found in the unawakened. There must be something in those whom God's Spirit has touched which is wholly new, totally unlike what existed in them before. To deny this would be equivalent to denying the distinction between the converted and the unconverted; it would be disowning the truth that the Spirit dwells in the saints in some unique manner, a manner direct and immediate, integral, and vital; and the final result would be to deny another fundamental conviction, — that the divine and the human are utterly diverse and incompatible with each other.

"We cannot rationally doubt but that things that are divine, that appertain to the Supreme Being, are vastly different from things that are human; that there is a Godlike, high, and glorious excellency in them, that does so distinguish them from the things which are of men that the difference is ineffable, and therefore such *as, if seen*, will have a most convincing, satisfying influence upon any one that they are what they are, viz., divine."

All this is undoubtedly true, but again one is tempted to ask in what direction lies the difference. Shall we be content to say that the difference is ineffable? But that would be almost tantamount to affirming that it is incomprehensible also. Or shall we say that the difference between God and man may be compared in kind to the difference between the speech of some great literary genius and the talk of a little child? Edwards uses this comparison, but it is not meant to express his entire thought. He falls back upon the statement, that God is able to make this ineffable difference manifest to those whom He chooses to enlighten by His spirit. He now reaffirms, what he had asserted so eloquently in his sermon on The Reality of Spiritual Light, that in truly spiritual men there is a direct intuitive insight into divine things which not only convinces of their reality, but discloses them in all the reach of their ineffable superiority to human things. Not only are the prejudices of the heart dissolved, but the hindrances to the pure speculative reason are removed, so that divine truth stands forth revealed in all its beauty and splendor. It is not by miracles or external evidences that this supreme result is attained, useful as, under certain circumstances, these may be. But even to ignorant men and children, incapable of weighing evidence or appreciating historical research, the same revelation may be made, the same profound spiritual intuition may disclose the reality of spiritual light. And here for the present Edwards pauses in his treatment of a point possessing vital importance. We are haunted with a painful sense of unreality in the result of his efforts to escape all human limitations. Unless there be something in God which is very like what is most distinctive in humanity, unless the human has its deepest root in the divine, the soul must be baffled in its search after God, sinking back in despair, as if its highest flight had disclosed only an empty void in the place of Deity. That Edwards may have had some suspicion of failure there is reason for believing. In the later years of his life he returned again to the great search which enthralled his nature.

Looking at the immediate influence of such a treatise as this on the New England churches, it must be admitted that it was not altogether a healthy one. Edwards had now begun to feel a deep dislike to the prevailing laxity in admitting to the membership of the church, which had been sanctioned by the Half-way Covenant. But the opposite evil, which he overlooked, seems almost as great as that against which he was contending. There now grew up, and mainly in consequence of Edwards' teaching, a hesitation about " joining the church," on the ground of unfitness, or the lack of certainty of one's conversion. The introversive tendency begat religious weakness and vacillation. The phrase, " not good enough to join the church," points to a wrong conception of the church which still lingers in New England, and has proved an obstacle to the church's growth. It has been said that any one who could read Edwards on the Affections, and still believe in his own conversion, might well have the highest assurance of its reality. But how few they were who gained this assurance may be inferred from the circumstance that Dr. Hopkins and Dr. Emmons, disciples of Edwards and religious leaders in New England, remained to the last uncertain of their conversion.

It has been impossible in this brief review of the Religious Affections to give any adequate conception of the religious ideal as Edwards portrays it. The defects which have been pointed out do not diminish from its beauty and value as an exalted presentation of Christian character. The evil which it may have wrought was surely owing, to some extent, to the nature of the ground into which it fell as seed. The conclusion of the whole matter, as Edwards labors at great length to show, is that Christian character and practice are the only tests of the presence of the divine Spirit. Whatever may have been his mistakes in the excitement of the years of the Great Awakening, he emerged from its unhallowed confusion with the conviction that in the life alone can be made manifest the sincerity of Christian faith. The Religious Affections should be read as we read the Imitation of Christ, making allowance for its defect in severing the spiritual from the world of human interests and realities. If we can supply what seems to be wanting in Edwards' speculative attitude, his book may yet be recovered from the neglect of generations. Works on topics kindred to this are not uncommon, but for the most part they are unredeemed from a certain tameness and commonplace because they lack the combination of intellectual power with the spiritual imagination, such as Edwards brought to the treatment of his theme. One can understand how an enthusiastic disciple as well as descendant of Edwards should feel impelled to write, "that, were the books on earth destined to a destruction so nearly universal that only one besides the Bible could be saved, the church of Christ, if aiming to preserve the volume of the greatest value to man, that which would best unfold to a bereaved posterity the real nature of true religion, would unquestionably select for preservation the treatise on the Affections." [1]

V.

"UNION IN PRAYER." — DAVID BRAINERD.

IN the year 1746 a memorial was sent from Scotland inviting the people and the churches in America to combine in one great united effort to gain the blessing of God; and to bring about, if it

---

[1] Dwight, *Life of Edwards*, p. 223.

were His will, such a revival of religion as would usher in the millennial reign of Christ. During two years previous to this date, there had been united prayer for this purpose in many of the churches in Scotland and also in America. It was now proposed to give to this informal movement a more organic and universal character, and to this end the memorial signed by twelve Scotch clergymen had been circulated in this country. The proposal commended itself to Edwards. He was now in somewhat intimate relations with the Church of Scotland, carrying on a correspondence with several of its leading ministers. His books, which had been republished there, had gained him great renown among the stricter school of Calvinists. It was natural, therefore, that a proposition coming from Scotland should arouse his interest, if for no other reason than that he saw reflected in it the extension of his own peculiar influence. The method by which the great end was to be sought was the setting apart a certain time, on Saturday evening and Sunday morning of each week, to be spent in prayer, and also the first Tuesday in each quarter of the year. Individuals were invited to pray separately at these stated seasons, as well as in concert, where it was practicable. In order to further the movement, Edwards preached on the subject to his congregation, and out of his sermons there grew another treatise, published in 1747, entitled Union in Prayer. It is a book of less interest and value than those we have been reviewing; but it has importance as presenting his views on the subject of prayer, as also a glimpse of his attempt at a philosophical interpretation of history.

Edwards had been disappointed in the results of the Great Awakening in America. It had subsided almost as quickly as it had arisen, leaving in its train a crop of evils from which the churches were still suffering. The degree of his disappointment may be measured by the high expectations in which he had indulged as to the probable extension of the movement until it should bring the world, even in his own lifetime, into the love and obedience of Christ. At one time he was so sanguine of this vast achievement, that he indulged at some length in a fanciful speculation in regard to America as the place indicated by prophecy where the Christ spiritual was to be reborn. To the old world had been assigned the honor of bringing forth the historical Christ; to the new world it would belong to present the Christ mystical, generated after a higher birth, as America's offering in return for what it had received.[1] This vision faded away, not to appear again. But he still believed as firmly as ever that there was a day in waiting for the church, and it might be near, when the glory of God should be made manifest as it had not been since the beginning of Christianity, — a time when, in the language of prophecy, the glory of the Lord should cover the earth as the

[1] *Thoughts on the Revival*, pp. 313, ff.

waters cover the sea. His faith in the coming of that day sustained him in the midst of disappointment. These movements that had come and gone, ending in seeming failure, might, after all, be forerunners of a greater movement; just as the wind, the earthquake, and the fire on Horeb were forerunners which heralded the coming of the Lord. He does not attempt to explain the ways of God in thus delaying the manifestation of His power and presence. But the mystery of the contrast between the present and the future impresses his imagination. The time that is to be, will be the chief time for the bestowment of the divine blessing. *Before this the Spirit of God is given but very sparingly and but few are saved.* But that future time is represented in Scripture as eminently the elect season, *the accepted time, and the day of salvation.* The comparatively little saving good which there now is in the world, as the fruit of Christ's redemption, is granted, as it were, by way of anticipation, — glimpses of the light before the dawning of the day, or as the first-fruits are gathered in before the harvest.

But could the coming of such a day as Edwards looked for be accelerated by prayer? If its time had been determined in the secret counsels of God, could prayer, however united or protracted, change the divine will and hasten the accomplishment of the divine purpose? Edwards did not think so. He had already put himself on record to the effect that the object of prayer is not to change God's will, but suitably to affect our own hearts, and so prepare us to receive the blessings we ask.[1] Indeed, this view of prayer, as mainly if not exclusively *subjective* in its effect, was the only view compatible with Edwards' idea of Deity. Nor does he anywhere contradict formally this emphatic statement of his belief. His book on Union in Prayer shows him presenting the motives which should induce people to pray for a great specific purpose. He meets objections which are presented as if they came from others, but it is more probable that he was here as elsewhere solving the difficulties which his own mind suggested. It is proper to pray for the general outpouring of the divine Spirit on the world, because there are many signs that such an event is near, — so very near that before the appointed seven years of prayer are ended, the day determined by divine decree may be ushered in. If there should be a universal movement toward prayer, it would be an evidence that God had also decreed the prayer as the condition of fulfilling His decree. "Whenever the time comes that God gives an extraordinary spirit of prayer, then the fulfilling this event is nigh. God, in His wonderful grace, is pleased to represent Himself, as it were, at the command of His people, with regard to mercies of this nature." But though Edwards comes as near as he can to the popular notion regarding prayer, he

---

[1] *Religious Affections*, vol. iii. p. 15; cf., also, vol. ii. p. 514, "On the Decrees."

is not willing to conceal his conviction. Again we have the subjective doctrine of prayer clearly affirmed without qualification : " Though it would not be reasonable to suppose that merely such a circumstance of prayer, as many people's praying at the same time, will directly have any influence or prevalence with God to cause Him to be the more ready to hear prayer, yet such a circumstance may reasonably be supposed to have influence on the minds of men." And this, it is argued, is a reason and justification for the union in prayer which has been proposed.[1]

Among the reasons assigned for believing that the day is near when the Spirit shall be poured out from on high are God's recent dealings with New England in its political relations, which are taken as an evidence of His interest in the land and its people, as if He were preserving them for some great consummation. The deliverances which have been wrought during the French war, "God succeeding us against Cape Breton and confounding the armada from France last year," these wonderful works of God are only to be paralleled by His works of old in the days of Moses, Joshua, or Hezekiah. And it is worthy to be noted, he remarks, that "God sent that great storm on the

[1] A sermon of Edwards, vol. iv. p. 561, entitled *The Most High a Prayer-hearing God*, though intended as a popular inducement to the practice of prayer, contains nothing at variance with the views presented above. Edwards was cautious, it would seem, lest he should encourage the notion that prayer may change the will of God. Cf., also, vol. iv. p. 105.

fleet of our enemies the last year, that finally dispersed and utterly confounded them, and caused them wholly to give over their designs against us, the very night after our day of public fasting and prayer for our protection and their confusion."

These deliverances are the more memorable because in other respects, and so far as the condition of the church is concerned, the present is a time of great apostasy and confusion. From a pamphlet recently printed in London, he has learned that luxury and wickedness of almost every kind is well-nigh come to the utmost extremity in England. The Church of Scotland has lost much of her glory, greatly departing from her ancient purity and excellent order. Lamentable also is the moral and religious state of these American colonies, and of New England in particular. The kind of religion which was first professed and practised has grown out of credit. Fierce and violent contentions abound. The gospel ministry is growing into contempt. Church discipline is weakened, and ordinances are disregarded. Wild and extravagant notions, gross delusions of the devil, and strange practices, prevail under the pretexts of great spirituality, or of zeal against formalism. The following passage is interesting as giving Edwards' view of his own time. To the minds of many, it would apply *mutatis mutandis* to our own age. After alluding to the discoveries in the arts and sciences, and to the learned and elaborate treatises written in defence of Christianity, in which it seemed to him that the eighteenth century surpassed anything seen in the world before, he remarks: —

"It is an age, as is supposed, of great light, freedom of thought, and discovery of truth in matters of religion, and detection of the weakness and bigotry of our ancestors, and of the folly and absurdity of the notions of those that were accounted eminent divines in former generations; which notions it is imagined, did destroy the very foundations of virtue and religion and enervate all precepts of morality, and in effect annul all difference between virtue and vice; and yet vice and wickedness did never so prevail like an overflowing deluge. It is an age wherein those mean and stingy principles, as they are called, of our forefathers, which as is supposed deformed religion and led to unworthy thoughts of God, are very much discarded and grown out of credit, and supposed more free, noble, and generous thoughts of the nature of religion and of the Christian scheme are entertained; but yet never was an age wherein religion in general was so much despised and trampled on, and Jesus Christ and God Almighty so blasphemed and treated with open, daring contempt."[1]

But the argument that is based upon the conviction that the world is evil, and therefore that the time is waxing late, might easily be pushed too far. And here Edwards separated himself from many contemporary theologians. It was an opinion prevailing at the time when the proposal was made for united prayer, that the coming of Christ's kingdom must be preceded by extreme calamity to the church of God, and even the tem-

[1] *Union in Prayer*, p. 459.

porary prevalence of Antichristian enemies against her. Such a feeling must of course make union in prayer impossible. To hasten the coming of the day of Christ would be to involve those who prayed, their children, and all that they held dear, in a terrible time, a time of extreme suffering and of dreadful persecution. Edwards devoted, therefore, a large part of his work on Union in Prayer to the refutation of this obnoxious belief. His argument is drawn from the prophetical books of the Bible, from obscure hints in the Book of Daniel and the Book of Revelation, which he interprets in the light of history as their fulfilment. Into his argument it is not necessary to enter. The fashion of it has passed away. But the conclusion which he reached was a service rendered to his own and succeeding ages. Much as he felt at liberty to denounce his own time for its ungodliness, it was impossible for him to admit so irrational a foreboding, which found no countenance in history, and which must neutralize every effort for the extension of Christian work. The argument from Scripture was but incidental to his own good judgment, which uttered its verdict in advance.

One other objection against the Scotch Memorial deserves notice as illustrating Edwards' attitude toward a stereotyped Puritanism inherited from the conflicts of the sixteenth century. There were those who might condemn the observation of stated seasons for united prayer, on the ground that it was only reintroducing the principle of the Christian Year as it had been retained in the Church of England. To do this would be doing what men had no right to do; what eminent Christians and divines had protested against: it was adding to God's institutions, it laid a bond upon men's consciences, and it naturally tended to superstition. Edwards admits the force of this argument. He tacitly condemns the Christian Year as an unwarrantable burden of human appointment, which, in proportion as it is regarded as sacred, is productive of superstition. But having made this admission he looks at the other side of the question, and finds that much which is already practised in the customary Puritan worship has no authority from Scripture. The only safeguard lies in not regarding these things as sacredly fixed as if by divine law. Hence there is no objection to stated seasons for prayer, if this caution be observed, any more than to an annual fast day. And it is added that the Scotch memorializers have been particular to make it apparent that it was not their intention to commit the Puritan churches to any superstitious entanglements in sacred times or seasons. The Puritans were still sensitive, two hundred years after their origin, to anything which approximated the worship of the English Church.

Edwards seems to share in the same prejudice. The objection is apparently one of his own raising. And yet one cannot avoid the feeling that he had not so great a repugnance, after all, to this or similar innovations. Anything which made the worship of God seem real and glorious he was prepared to welcome. If it had not been for the conservatism of a Puritan people holding tenaciously to their traditions, it is not impossible that he would have ventured some innovations of his own. It was, for example, one of the Puritan ways to reduce the frequency of celebrating the Lord's Supper. In the Church of Scotland semi-annual communions had taken the place of the old order of the mass which every Sunday had reminded the worshipper of the benefits of the death of Christ, in however distorted or perverse a manner. On this point Edwards' admissions are significant. He laments that the revival had not resulted in an increase of the ministrations of the Lord's Supper; that God's people should not more frequently commemorate the dying love of their Redeemer than they have been accustomed to do. It was evident from Scripture that the primitive Christians kept the memorial on every Lord's day; and so he believes it will be again with the church of Christ in the days that are approaching. This desire for more frequent celebrations of the Lord's Supper differentiates him from the Quaker, the spirit of whose theology he had appropriated. His philosophical and spiritualistic idealism seemed to demand some external manifestation, as if it needed to be made more tangible and real by the outward visible sign. There are traces in his writings which show that he was not insensible to the pomp and ceremony of worship : only given the inward spirit, and the outward form could not be too beautiful or glorious. But he would not have reversed the method, — an elaborate or sensuous ritual as a means of spiritual life.

We have now reached a point in the biography of Edwards where it becomes necessary to sum up briefly those remoter consequences of the revival, which were imperfectly understood at the time, but which were big with seeming disaster to the fortunes of Edwards and his family. But at this point we must also pause for a moment in order to introduce the story of David Brainerd, — an important episode in the last years of Edwards' pastorate at Northampton.

David Brainerd's short life filled a large place in the consciousness of the stricter Calvinistic sort during the last century; nor has the memory of his devoted career entirely faded out in our own day. We may think that the significance attaching to his name is an exaggerated one, but the life of Edwards would be incomplete without at least an allusion to him.

Edwards first met him in 1743 at New Haven, where he had gone to attend the Commencement exercises of Yale College. Some two years before, Brainerd, while then a member of the college, had expressed himself disrespectfully, not to say contemptuously, of the religious character of certain members of the faculty. He had said of them, in fact, that they possessed no more religion than the chair on which he was leaning. This language having been reported to the faculty Brainerd had been expelled. He had now returned to New Haven when his class was graduating, in the hope, by humble confession of his fault, that he might receive his degree. Great efforts were made to induce the faculty to accede to his petition. The Rev. Aaron Burr, of New Jersey, came on to New Haven for the purpose of using his influence in his behalf. Edwards also was one among others who attempted to make reconciliation between the offended teachers and their indiscreet pupil. But the degree was refused, nor was it ever accorded to him. It was this incident which first drew out the sympathy of Edwards for one with whom he afterwards became intimately associated. Into the merits of the case we do not propose to enter. Brainerd seems to have behaved well at the time he was seeking his degree. He made, says Edwards, " a truly humble and Christian acknowledgment of his fault." When his degree was refused " he manifested no disappointment or resentment." It must be remembered that he was at this time a young man with a reputation for high religious attainments, and he came to New Haven from a remote settlement known as Kaunameek, what Edwards calls a howling wilderness, where he was meeting with unexampled success as a missionary to the Indians. Under ordinary circumstances it would have seemed only natural if the authorities had overlooked his offence, and had granted to such an exemplary youth, who represented the fervors of the revival, the degree which he desired in order to enhance his usefulness. But these were not ordinary circumstances. The college had taken its stand against the evils and abuses which the Great Awakening had generated. Brainerd was a typical instance of that spirit of censoriousness which, following the New Lights, as they were called, was breaking up the harmony and unity of the New England churches. The offence was therefore a serious one, which could not easily be forgiven without conveying the appearance of indifference towards the evils of separatism.

On the other side there was also much to be said, and more that was deeply felt. Brainerd became, as it were, a living martyr for the cause with which the college at New Haven had little or no sympathy. His case became notorious throughout the colonies, lending a fictitious interest to his name; and the interest was deepened and made abiding by his early death when only thirty years of age. He was an ardent, enthusiastic soul, moving with great impetuosity in whatever he undertook, one whose zeal for religion was even consuming his life. Four years after the degradation which he had received at New Haven (1747), he came again into New England, an invalid in the last stages of consumption. He was now invited by Edwards to take up his abode in his own house. His story from this time is an extremely painful one. The progress of his disease is recorded by

Edwards, who was watching his case with a morbid interest. There must have been something in Brainerd of high excellence that he should have won the confidence and affection of Edwards. But there is so much that is repellant in the situation that we gladly pass over what appears to belong to a morbid psychology rather than to a genuine religious experience. Edwards professed himself as thankful for the privilege of having conversed so freely with Brainerd in his last days. It was as if he were permitted to gain a new and striking evidence of the reality of the religious affections. He was accumulating, through Brainerd's religious experience on his death-bed, fresh confirmation of the truth of his own theories as against Arminians and deists. As in the case of Mrs. Edwards, he was making an intellectual study of Brainerd's rapturous condition, not suspecting at all that he might be watching in some measure the effects of his own influence. For Brainerd's confessions so entirely accord with all that Edwards had taught as high and desirable in a true conversion, that one cannot avoid the conclusion that he reflected unconsciously the effects of his association with his friend and master.

But the painful interest of Brainerd's case does not stop here. There must have been something of an attractive spell in the man who could win the affections of a daughter of Jonathan Edwards. This daughter, his second child, whose name was Jerusha, and who had then attained the age of seventeen, was allowed to become the constant attendant upon the invalid. She travelled with him on a visit which he made to Boston, and returned with him to Northampton. Edwards speaks of her as the flower of the family, and as a person of much the same spirit with Brainerd. But this betrothal was a strange one, with an unnatural, unearthly character. For nineteen weeks she devoted herself to attending Brainerd in his illness. She delighted in the task, because she looked on him as an eminent servant of Christ. And yet even her young heart must have been chilled on its human side, when, shortly before his death, Brainerd, in taking his leave of her, spoke of his love for her, but also added that it was his brother John for whom he had the greatest affection of any person on earth. She filled only a subordinate place in his heart, and yet was to offer up her young life as a sacrifice to his service. Only a few months after his death she was called away, leaving an aching void in her father's heart.

Edwards preached the funeral sermon of Brainerd, and afterwards edited his diary, adding to it observations and reflections of his own. It was this life of Brainerd by Edwards which is said to have been the means of the conversion of the famous missionary, Henry Martyn. Credit for the missionary spirit, which was so rare a gift in the eighteenth century, should be freely accorded to David Brainerd. But the story of his connection with Edwards resembles the case of Sterling and Carlyle.

In each instance there is the history of a human soul, which, if we can only see it so, is always interesting, wherever we may look at it. But, as in the case of Sterling, there was no special reason for furnishing a biography. Private motives impelled Carlyle to the task. Edwards was moved by a desire to furnish irresistible evidence against the Arminians or deists, who denied the validity of religious experiences.

VI.

DISMISSAL FROM NORTHAMPTON. — "QUALIFICATIONS FOR FULL COMMUNION."

EDWARDS may have found support and refreshment in his association with Brainerd as with a kindred spirit. And of such consolation he stood in need, for he was now approaching the catastrophe of his life. The results of the Great Awakening were to prove bitter fruit to the pastor at Northampton and his household. The time was at hand when, as Mrs. Edwards had contemplated among the possible contingencies of life, they were to be driven forth from the town, when, after years of devoted service, the unrivalled preacher, the theologian who had not his like or his equal, was to be banished by the almost unanimous voice of the congregation. He had expected, as was then generally the case with New England ministers, to end his days with the church over which he had been set in his youth. But not only were the sacred ties which bound him to his people broken, — there was a manifestation toward him of anger, of malice, and of contumely, the story of which, even at this distance of time, it is painful to read. Such an event had no precedent in the history of the New England churches. It may help to appreciate the situation if a general summary be given of the effects, near or remote, of the Great Awakening, before treating of the peculiar cause which explains the misfortunes of Edwards.

First among these may be ranked the prominent place assigned to the emotions, which becomes an almost new element in popular Christianity. The appeal to the emotions had been attended, it is true, by gross evils, caricatures, distortions, and perversions of true religion, which had made sensible men stand aloof in the conviction that the movement was doing more injury than good. But the good was in the long run to predominate over the evil. To rouse the emotions in the interest of religion was equivalent to asserting the inwardness of religion, instead of leaving it a cold routine of external duties. The emphasis placed upon the affections in religion marks a new step in the development of the people. Sacerdotal and sacramental theories of a divine grace, conveyed through external channels, vanished under the influence of the principle that the divine action on the soul is direct and immediate, capable also of imparting such a shock to the whole nature as to divert it from its old current into a higher ethical as well as spiritual existence. The appeal to the emotions, in behalf of which Edwards plead so earnestly, not only made possible a religious enthusiasm, but was the indirect cause of other popular enthusiasms by which great reforms were to be accomplished. To rouse the emotional nature was to emancipate the powers of the soul which had so long lain dormant that their very existence was unsuspected. Without such a preliminary quickening movement as the Great Awakening, it is doubtful if the sentiment of humanity, which has been such a powerful factor in modern civilization, could have made its successful record. The hardness and cruelty of the last century, the want of sympathy with human suffering, the injustices which had long reigned undisturbed, were gradually overcome when men ceased to remain strangers to their inmost selves. It will always remain the peculiar glory of the religious body known as Friends, or Quakers, that their theological principle made them the first to awake to the evils of human slavery. The Puritans now fall into line with those whom they have despised or persecuted; and it is a circumstance to be noted, that a friend and pupil of Edwards, the famous Dr. Hopkins, became the leader in the social reform which effected the abolition of slavery in New England.

Another result of the revival in New England

was to make the inward process of conversion the foremost consideration in the religious consciousness. Not but what it had been recognized before, in name as well as in substantial result. But yet the revival so magnified the importance of conversion that it may be regarded as a new and distinct creation of the last century, whose acceptance by the Calvinistic churches has had the effect of subordinating their differences to such an extent as to give them a unity and resemblance which overshadows their divergences. And further, the idea of conversion, dividing as it did the world into two great classes, was a distinction so tangible, so potent, as to eclipse the distinction between the elect and the non-elect, which from this time was destined, however slowly, to disappear. The necessity of conversion was asserted by the great founder of Methodism, with a vigor and success which Calvinism could not rival, so long as it was embarrassed by the prior distinction between elect and non-elect, which Wesley totally rejected. Although Edwards had aimed to revive the old distinction, and not without success, yet the attempt to retain election, as a coördinate ruling idea in the religious life, threw New England theology into a confusion out of which it was long in emerging. The idea of conversion involved the freedom of the will, and was silently undermining all false distinctions by which human freedom was denied or made inoperative. The question has been asked why revivals should have been unknown in the American churches after the Great Awakening in 1740, and should not have reappeared until two generations had passed away. The answers to this inquiry have been various, such as the evils which the Awakening produced, or the political complications which ended in the American Revolution. Both answers contain a germ of truth. But there is another answer still. It took the lifetime of two generations of Puritan preachers and theologians to get rid of the distinction between the elect and non-elect. It was not until Hopkins and Emmons had had their day that the new school of Puritanism arose, cordially admitting the freedom of the will in terms which Edwards would have regarded as impossible or absurd.

The excitement and even consternation into which the revival plunged New England is not wholly explained from the religious stand-point alone. As we study the time, it becomes apparent that a change was going on which was affecting also the political order, whose result was to undo the bonds of sympathetic relationship which for ages had united the church and the state. The readjustment of the relation between the church and the world was now attended by the same accompaniments as had waited upon the Montanistic movement or the Donatist controversy in the ancient church. These signs of agitation and distress in the ecclesiastical sphere are but the correspondents to war in the political sphere, — the necessary evils which accompany a great transition. The interest in studying such a transition does not lie in measuring the extent and bitterness of the agitation, which have passed away, but in reaching an adequate idea of the principle at stake, — the form which the reconstruction was assuming.

There are times when the church and the world are seen drawing more closely together, when it looks as if the church were deteriorating in its effort to embrace within itself, as far as possible, the outlying life of humanity. Whether the church actually deteriorates or not, may be an open question. It may lower itself, but if so, for the purpose of raising itself again, bringing with it, in its resurrection to a higher standard, the world which it would not have reached if it had not known how to abase itself in order to its exaltation. Puritanism in New England had shared in the oscillations of this vast process. Hardly had the Puritans reached the new world when church and state flowed together in close and harmonious relationship. But if the church and the world at times approximate for mutual benefit, it may also be regarded as an equally legitimate process when they draw apart, when the church is seen jealously separating and holding itself aloof from the world, as if fearful of its contamination. The feeling grows within the church that its ideal is in danger of degradation unless it may go apart by itself, to nourish the strength of holy things in silence and seclusion.

Edwards had been the leader in a movement, of which this was the outcome; to separate the church from the world, to raise such barriers between them that their life should flow on separate and apart. He had grown up in the church, as if it were the only necessary sphere for the religious man. From childhood on, his attention was concentred on the church, as if the state hardly existed, so little attention did he give to its affairs. Throughout his life he was in search of a principle whose acceptance by the church would give to it a vigorous and independent life of its own. There is one notable allusion to the relation which the state should hold to the church, and but one, so far as we know, in Edwards' works. It is found in his Thoughts on the Revival, and is couched after the manner of the Theocracy. He there alludes to the indifference displayed by the civil authority to the glorious work that was going on in the churches. At least, he thought, the government might have proclaimed a day of public thanksgiving for so unspeakable a mercy, or a day of fasting and penitence for past deadness and unprofitableness under the means of grace; or it might have entered upon consultation as to what should be done to advance so great a reformation. If a new governor comes into the province, those who are in authority arise and go forth to meet him with addresses and congratulations. Not to do so would be construed as a denial of his authority, or a refusal to receive and honor him. And when the Lord of the universe comes down from heaven in so wonderful a manner, shall the civil rulers stand at a distance and be silent and inactive! He would humbly recommend them to consider whether their behavior will not be interpreted by God as a denial of Christ, or whether God is not adjuring them: *Be wise now, O ye rulers; be instructed, ye judges of New England*.[1] But the rulers kept silence notwithstanding Edwards' complaint. Nor was the protest which he had made indicative of any deep-seated purpose. He did not feel impelled to write a treatise in order to expound or enforce his meaning. The allusion seems to have been intended rather for rhetorical ends, as if to complete his thought; or it may have been the conventional echo of an earlier age. Church and state were drifting apart, and Edwards not only made no effort to prevent or retard the process, but furnished the formula for their withdrawal and separation. In accordance with his sharp and ruthless distinction between common and special grace, the state is deprived of a truly divine or supernatural character, while the church becomes the exclusive home of the spiritual. The same distinction had run through Christian history from the time of Augustine, until Wycliffe broke its spell by the annunciation of a higher teaching, — that the state is equally divine with the church, holding its sacred authority, not mediately, as popes in the Middle

---

[1] *Thoughts on the Revival*, vol. iii. p. 326.

Ages had asserted, but immediately from Christ Himself. Edwards, like Wycliffe, stands at the beginning of a new cycle in the history of the church. But though the outcome of his teaching was to reverse the thought of Wycliffe, and to separate church and state as if their union were the alliance of things incompatible with each other, he showed no disposition to draw the inference which popes had drawn, which Calvin and the early Puritans had also drawn, that because the ecclesiastical was more important than the civil, therefore the state should be subordinated to the church. The state had now become too strong, and it may be because of its clearer recognition of its divine call, to sacrifice its mission at the bidding of the church. The only alternative was to awaken in the church an independent life, so that it should not feel its need of dependence on the state; to create an interest so powerful and absorbing within the ecclesiastical fold as to render the clergy content with their restricted sphere. Such was the significance of the doctrine of conversion when viewed in its relation with the dissolution of the Puritan theocracy. The church now became not only reconciled to its new lot, but soon learned to denounce the old relation as a baneful mingling of the things of Cæsar with the things of God.

It was still another result of the new distinction between the converted and the unconverted that it made impossible any longer the retention of the Half-way Covenant, and especially in the form which it had assumed at Northampton. As originally set forth in the Synod of 1657, and again in 1662, the Half-way Covenant had been a concession on the part of the church, mainly in order to its more facile working in relation with the state. When the number of those was increasing who asked for membership in the church in order to a voice in the affairs of the state, but who had not the qualification for church membership in either ability or willingness to make the required profession of religious experience, the church relaxed its requirement, and allowed admission to the civil privileges of membership on the ground of baptism alone. But to those joining the church on this Half-way Covenant, as it was now called, the Lord's Supper was still refused until they should enter into full covenant by presenting before the church satisfactory evidence of the Spirit's work within them. But this was not the form of the Half-way Covenant which awoke the distrust and opposition of Edwards. At Northampton a further step had been taken by Mr. Stoddard, Edwards' grandfather and predecessor, who had introduced on his own authority a radical modification of the Half-way Covenant, in accordance with which baptized persons were admitted to the Lord's Supper without making a credible profession of Christian experience, or even if they knew that they were destitute of any work of divine grace within them.

Although Mr. Stoddard's attitude had met with

much opposition,[1] the custom which he introduced at Northampton had very generally prevailed among the surrounding churches, as well as elsewhere throughout New England. Edwards, when he first went to Northampton, felt instinctive misgivings as to the method in vogue, but he suppressed at the time any impulse to inquire further into the matter for the satisfaction of his mind. After the Revival of 1735, and again after that of 1740, he admitted large numbers to the communion without requiring from them any distinct profession of Christian experience. But in his sermons on The Religious Affections, he intimated plainly his dislike to a further continuance of the custom. This was in the year 1744. From that time until 1748, no one was presented for admission to the sacred rite of the Lord's Supper.

[1] Among those who resisted the innovation at Northampton was the celebrated Dr. Increase Mather, the last great champion of the theocracy. But though he answered Mr. Stoddard's defence of his position, he felt no great interest in the subject and regarded it as of minor importance. Cf. Stoddard's *Guide to Christ* (1735), which contains a prefatory epistle by Increase Mather in which he remarks: "It is known that, in some points not fundamental, I differ from this beloved author." Mr. Stoddard's position was not a clearly defined one, and was easily liable to misapprehension. In his *Appeal to the Learned*, in which he makes his defence, he remarks: "My business was to answer a case of conscience, and direct those that might have scruples about participation of the Lord's Supper because they had not a work of saving conversion, not at all to direct the churches to admit any that were not to rational charity true believers." — p. 27. Cf., also, the *New-Englander*, vol. xliii. p. 615, for an account of Mr. Stoddard's own religious history, which has only recently come to light.

Then, in the case of a person who solicited the privilege, Edwards stated what he should require as the terms of full admission to the church. The person in question declined to accept them, and the issue was now broached which resulted in his dismissal.

It is possible that the difficulties in which Edwards was now involved might have assumed a different shape had not affairs been complicated by a peculiar case of discipline in the parish in which Edwards had failed to carry with him the coöperation of the people. As the story runs, a discovery had been made that certain books of an obscene character [1] were in circulation among the young people of the parish of both sexes, the result of which was licentious conversation and immoral practices. The first act of the pastor was a sermon in which the facts were made known to the congregation, — an impressive sermon, which led the officers to unite with him in calling for an examination of the offenders. But when Edwards came to read from the pulpit the names of the guilty persons, and of those also who were summoned to give their witness in the case, it appeared that almost every family in the church of any consideration was involved. Those who had hitherto favored an investigation now resisted it. The consequence was that the proposed discipline was

[1] The suggestion has been made that the books were some of the popular novels of the time, such as *Pamela*, etc. Cf. Leslie Stephen, *Hours in a Library*, vol. ii. p. 63.

dropped, while a certain disaffection towards Edwards began to be felt which put an end to the extraordinary influence he had hitherto exercised. From this time Edwards laments the ineffectiveness of his preaching. Whether it was that his speculative cast of mind had carried him too far away from the range of the popular interest, his sermons no longer aroused the unconverted. A general decline of religious interest began to prevail which he was powerless to overcome.

Edwards was inclined to attribute the difficulty to the custom of admitting to the inner shrine of the Christian worship those who had made no profession of a Christian purpose. He now proposed to discuss the subject in a series of sermons, and asked permission of the church to that effect. The permission was not only refused, but a storm of human rage and furor now broke forth against him, and nothing would allay the angry passions of the people but his final and immediate dismissal from his post. In vain he asked permission to be heard, aware as he was that his views were bitterly misrepresented. He finally gained consent to write a book on the Qualifications of Full Communion, which might be read when his voice would not be listened to from the pulpit. But while the work was in preparation the people became impatient that it did not appear, in order that they might hasten his dismissal, which had become a foregone conclusion. When the book appeared but few of them read it. He then deter-

AN ECCLESIASTICAL COUNCIL. 261

mined by the advice of the surrounding churches to lecture on the subject. But his lectures were thinly attended by his own congregation, though many came from a distance who made up the greater part of his audience. When the question arose of calling an ecclesiastical council for the purpose of hearing the case, there was long and unseemly wrangling, because the church at Northampton was afraid that, if Edwards went out of the county to invite ministers and churches to sit upon the council, as he was entitled to do, the case might result in his retention of the pastorate; and they were determined that he should go. When the council met, it was decided by a majority of one that the pastoral relation should be dissolved. But the vote of the church ratifying the decision of the council was two hundred in favor of it, and only twenty who were opposed. The date of Edwards' dismissal was June 22, 1750. Although he continued to live in the town for some months after his connection with the church was severed, great reluctance was felt at allowing him to preach, even when the services of no other minister could be obtained. And at last a town meeting was called which accomplished its object in the formal vote that he should not again be permitted to enter the pulpit of the church in Northampton. So Jonathan Edwards was turned adrift at the end of twenty-three years of service, and at the age of forty-seven, with a large family of children, and with no means of support, and doubtful if he should ever obtain another parish. The spirit of the man under these circumstances shone forth so beautifully that one's sympathies and love go forth toward him as if the scene were still visibly enacting before our eyes. He had sat down and counted the cost before he proceeded to action. He knew that to overturn the established usage meant disaster to himself and his family. After all, the man was greater than the metaphysician or the theologian. In his mature years he is exhibiting the final product in high Christian character, of which he had set before himself the ideal in the Resolutions of his youth. It must have been a strange scene at Northampton when he preached his farewell sermon. The discourse is still tremulous with the intense feeling of the hour. The whole man stands forth in it, with his moral indignation at a great wrong; with the solemnity of accusation in which he had no equal; with the tender pathos in which he takes his leave of the dear children whom God had given him, warning them all of the final meeting at the judgment day, when the case should be reheard before the tribunal of Heaven.

No attempt can be made here to review at any length the questions at issue regarding the reorganization of the Puritan churches. The confusion in this time of transition was so great that no one could do justice to the motives of his opponent. All parties alike complain of misrepresentation. It was Edwards' misfortune that he labored under the suspicion of being a separatist. He was charged with seeking to establish a church on principles opposed to those of the standing order; of demanding the evidence of an inward change on the part of postulants for admission, the stages of which should be sharply defined; of sitting in judgment on the religious condition of others. In the excited condition of the people, it was almost impossible that he should assuage these hostile suspicions. But in this case as in others the indomitable will of Edwards rose above all obstacles. He was determined to make his position clear. In his Qualifications for Full Communion, written while the controversy was at its height, he resisted that tendency in the Puritan churches, represented by Mr. Stoddard, which endowed the church as an organic institution with a life-giving efficacy. Mr. Stoddard's doctrine of the Lord's Supper might easily be interpreted as giving to the feast of the Holy Communion a magical effect apart from the spiritual fitness of the recipient. Hence he had spoken of the Lord's Supper as a converting ordinance; he invited persons to the Holy Table even though they knew themselves to be destitute of Christian sincerity. This sacramental tendency was banished from the Puritan churches by Edwards' influence. His book on the subject became a standard authority, holding Congregationalism to its original principle, that only by a living faith did Christ become the living bread in the sacrament of His body and His blood. A reply to this work on the Qualifications for Full Communion was made by Williams, a neighboring minister and a kinsman of Edwards, which drew forth from him a few years later another large treatise which practically closed the controversy. In this work he pursues his antagonist into the hidden recesses of those groundless suspicions which were rife among the people. He endeavors to clear himself of the charge of setting up a separatist church, or of calling for evidence of conversion, or of insisting that conversion should assume a uniform character. All that he had insisted upon as a requisite for admission to the Lord's Supper was a simple, moderate formula of self-consecration, hardly going beyond the confirmation vow of the Church of England.[1]

But on the other hand Edwards does not seem to have been aware of the revolution which the popular idea of conversion was working in the churches. As a consequence of that sharp distinction, the baptism of infants was losing its sig-

---

[1] Edwards has given two of these formulas in his *Reply to Williams*, vol. i. p. 202. The first of them reads: "I hope I do truly find a heart to give myself wholly to God, according to the tenor of that covenant of grace which was sealed in my baptism, and to walk in a way of that obedience to all the commandments of God which the covenant of grace requires, as long as I live." The alternative formula reads: "I hope I truly find in my heart a willingness to comply with all the commandments of God, which require me to give myself up wholly to Him and to serve Him with my body and my spirit; and do accordingly now promise to walk in a way of obedience to all the commandments of God as long as I live."

nificance. Until they had been converted, they stood in no relation to God; they were as far from Him as if they had never come within the scope of Christian influence. Edwards made no effort to meet the difficulty, nor did he feel called upon to examine the subject of infant baptism. He admits [1] that all the baptized are in some sort members of the church. But there he leaves a subject which had no interest for him. He had no doubts about it, as he remarks, but it was "a topic liable to great disputes, and called for a large dissertation to make it clear." The opponents of Edwards on this subject had a clear and valid position. In maintaining that baptism admitted to all the privileges of church membership,[2] they were resisting the evil effects of the doctrine of conversion, which easily degenerated into a baneful subjectivity, where the organic character of the church threatened to disappear, where the shifting feelings about one's inner state became the test of one's acceptance with God. In adhering to the

---

[1] *Qualifications*, etc., vol. i. p. 89.

[2] Among those who actively helped in the expulsion of Edwards from Northampton was another kinsman, Ashley, of Deerfield. Edwards' bitterest foes seem to have been those of his own household after the flesh. Cf. *The Historical Magazine*, June, 1867, for a sermon preached by Ashley containing a defence of the principle that baptism admits to full church membership, and represents an organic relationship to Christ. Ashley suffered for his devotion to this principle, as well as for his opposition to Edwards. He saw his own congregation divide on the issue, the larger part going to Greenfield to found a church on Edwards' ideas. It was on this occasion that he preached the sermon.

Half-way Covenant, they were also struggling against what was called the Anabaptist heresy, which discarded infant baptism altogether, postponing the performance of the rite until it could gain a real significance by coinciding with the experience of conversion. It had been, indeed, one object of the Half-Way Covenant to overcome the Anabaptist principle by attaching increased importance to baptism. With the rejection of the Half-Way Covenant, and under the influence of the popular notions about conversion, that was now coming to pass which the early Puritan fathers had dreaded. An opportunity was afforded to the Baptist sect of which it was not slow to take advantage. With this communion most of the separatist organizations in New England threw in their lot, and were lost to the Congregational order.

There are clearly, then, two sides to this controversy. It is not altogether true, as is sometimes remarked, that Edwards was simply restoring the early order of the Puritan churches in New England. He could not restore that order without restoring also the Theocracy, with which its connection was a vital one. Those who were resisting Edwards were also legitimate descendants of the Puritan fathers in the spirit, as also largely in the letter. We are tracing here the rise of the schism in the New England churches which came to an open rupture in the beginning of the present century. The opponents of Edwards who insisted on the importance of baptism as admitting to full membership in the church, who rejected the distinction between the converted and the unconverted, were also representatives of the old Puritan purpose which was seeking some normal connection between the church and the world, keeping the church in a larger and healthier attitude by its relation to the state, insisting on the objective side of Christian truth, and in this spirit vanquishing the antinomian spectre as it appeared in Mrs. Hutchinson, or the subjective moods of the Quakers, or the disintegrating tendency of the Anabaptists, who threatened the supremacy of the standing order.

The world is weary of discussions about the nature of baptism. The only apology for presenting the subject here is the fact of its historical importance, and its close relation to the ecclesiastical divisions which now began to mark the face of New England. Speculations about what might have been, although they are intangible, imponderable considerations, are nevertheless inevitable to any one who cannot help seeing both sides of a controversy. If the two positions in this embittered party strife could have been combined; if baptism could have been imparted freely to all and accepted as a rite admitting to full membership in the church; while the ratification of the unconscious vow of infancy was required as a natural step in maturer years, as well as a condition for receiving the Lord's Supper, — the divisions into hostile sects might have been to some degree averted. But the churches of the Congregational order, both before and after Edwards' time, narrowed the number of recipients of the rite, in the case of infant baptism, to the children of believing parents. There was thus opened a door for the introduction of another church, an older ecclesiastical order, which rejected no child from its fold, whatever its parentage, asserting of all baptized children that they were divinely and authoritatively declared by baptism to be the "children of God, the members of Christ, and heirs of the kingdom of heaven." For such a church, with such a profession, there was surely a demand. Edwards must have looked upon its declaration of the meaning of baptism with a feeling of deep repugnance. And yet it might become the basis of a theology quite as spiritual as his own, and without his limitations.

The controversy on the nature of the church was carried on by Edwards without knowledge of previous discussions which had covered much the same ground in ancient history. His Reply to Williams, as well as his Qualifications for Full Communion, remind one constantly of Augustine's controversy with the Donatists in the fifth century. The parables of the good and bad fish taken in the net, or the tares and the wheat growing in the same field, recurring in both controversies, are the hinge on which the discussions turned. Edwards had something of the Donatist spirit, which was seeking the purity of the church, but he might not have been averse to Augustine's compromise of an *ecclesiola*, — the little church within the larger church. Augustine was also adjusting afresh the relations between the ecclesiastical and the civil power. Here the divergency is wide and real. In the ancient church everything tended toward the union with the state in some organic relationship, — the church, however, possessing the advantage; while the state trembled in its impotence as it saw the imperial sceptre gradually ceasing to be the symbol of power. But in the eighteenth century the situation was reversed. It was becoming the watchword of modern Christianity, as it had been among the Donatists, that the church should have no relation to the civil power. The times were with Edwards in his efforts to mould the church in accordance with the distinction between the converted and the unconverted, — a distinction which should serve to keep the church within its own too narrow sphere. Edwards seemed to be carrying back the Congregational order to its early purity, when a profession of Christian experience was demanded from every postulant for admission to the church. But the difference is greater than the resemblance between his work and that of the Puritan fathers. To the original churches there had opened the attractive opportunity of ruling the state and the social order in the name of God. When this opportunity and privilege were withdrawn, there was danger of an unhealthy pietism invading the religious circle, which would not only destroy its attractiveness for the outer world, but might rob the church itself of a robust manliness, if it did not empty religion of its positive significance. There are not wanting signs of a certain hollowness and unreality in the speculative thought of Edwards, which may owe their origin in some part to this defect.

Having made these qualifications, it only remains to add that Edwards may be justly called the father of modern Congregationalism. If he seemed to have been defeated by his expulsion from Northampton, his expulsion made the issue clear and he triumphed in his fall. Most of the Puritan churches accepted his principles, banished the Half-way Covenant, and took on the form which they still retain. As one by one they went over to his side, they found it hard to understand how there ever could have existed a different practice. It became the custom to refer to the times of the Theocracy as "those unhappy days when things secular and religious were strangely mixed up in New England."[1] And yet the Congregational churches have never been able to escape altogether from the effects of that "unhappy" connection, if so it must be regarded. It has given them a certain distinction, the consciousness of which they prize. They have continued to retain a sense of relationship to the state, and to feel themselves responsible for its welfare. Nor have

---

[1] Dwight, *Life of Edwards*, p. 303.

the cases been rare in which its clergy have given themselves to political and legislative duties, as if a natural and congenial work.

But if Edwards was the father of modern Congregationalism, he came very near disowning his offspring. In those dark days after his expulsion from his parish, when he did not know which way to turn for a common livelihood, he was approached by one of his Scotch correspondents, who offered to procure for him a church in Scotland. To this correspondent he wrote: "You are pleased very kindly to ask me whether I could sign the Westminster Confession of Faith, and submit to the Presbyterian form of church government. . . . As to my subscribing to the *substance* of the Westminster Confession, there would be no difficulty; and as to the Presbyterian government, I have long been perfectly out of conceit of our unsettled, *independent*, confused way of church government in this land; *and the Presbyterian way has ever appeared to me most agreeable to the word of God and the reason and nature of things.*"[1] It is no gratuitous assumption if we view this language as expressing only the alienation of the passing moment. The case of Edwards is similar to that notorious instance in the ancient church where Gregory Nazianzen, the Patriarch of Constantinople, was driven from his see by the violence of his enemies. The language in which, from the soreness of his heart, he condemned all general councils and

---

[1] Dwight, *Life of President Edwards*, p. 412.

synods of bishops as productive only of evil, may be compared with Edwards' strictures upon the ecclesiastical polity of New England. In both instances allowance must be made for human infirmity. Congregationalism as a church polity may have its defects and disadvantages; but it has also merits for those who know to discern and appropriate them. Among this number Edwards should certainly be ranked. He was born a Congregationalist, if we may use the expression. The appeal to the reason in defence of truth, rather than the prescription of authority, is his leading characteristic. He was, all his life through, an innovator, following the lead of his speculative faculties, rather than anxious for the conservation of theological formulas. His rejection of the church polity, whose workings he stimulated and adorned, is not consistent with the freedom and independence of his own career.

THIRD PERIOD.

THE PHILOSOPHICAL THEOLOGIAN. 1750-1758.

I.

REMOVAL TO STOCKBRIDGE AS MISSIONARY TO THE INDIANS.

IN the straitened circumstances in which Edwards was placed after his dismissal from Northampton, he was remembered by his friends in Scotland, who sent generous contributions for his relief.[1] It is also touching to read how his wife and daughters endeavored to increase the family income by various feminine pursuits. Toward the close of the year 1750 he received an invitation to become the pastor of the church in Stockbridge, the frontier town of the colony, forty miles west of Northampton. He had already declined to further a movement in Northampton whose object

---

[1] Among these Scotch friends and correspondents of Edwards the most distinguished was Dr. John Erskine. He forwarded to him supplies of books, urged him to his great controversial writings, and superintended their publication in Scotland. He has been immortalized by Sir Walter Scott in his *Guy Mannering*, where he is presented in his old age leaning over the pulpit of Greyfriars. He was the leader of the Evangelical Calvinists in the church of Scotland. It is interesting also to note that he was the great-uncle of the late Mr. Thomas Erskine, of Linlathen.

had been to establish there another church of which he should become the pastor. He had hardly accepted the invitation to Stockbridge when he received a call from a church in Virginia, which also promised him a generous support. These and similar indications must have been grateful in his despondency, as showing that a career of active usefulness was still open, despite the reflection on his name by his treatment at Northampton. The removal to Stockbridge, however it may have first appeared, was in reality an expansion to him, offering opportunities which had hitherto been denied for the full display of his highest powers.

He still continued to feel, after his removal there, the effects of the great disruption which had followed his attempts at reform. It was there that he wrote his rejoinder to Williams, who had ventured a reply to his work on the Qualifications for Full Communion. When Edwards undertook a task of this kind, he showed his adversary no quarter. In this case he brought his subtle exhaustive method to an examination and refutation of every fallacy, every misrepresentation, however slight, in order that the reader who was willing to examine the subject might become fully aware how the case had stood between him and his opponents. But irrational and perverse elements were so mixed up with that disastrous time at Northampton, that one must not expect, and from Edwards least of all, an intelligible account of the situation. There came to him while at Stockbridge some sort of an apology from his former parishioners, which seemed to him entirely inadequate. His reply,[1] which is addressed to Major Joseph Hawley, shows how deeply the sense of his personal dignity had been affronted, and also the lofty and authoritative tone of the ancient Puritan minister. From the same Joseph Hawley there came personal letters which even to Edwards' exacting mind must have disclosed an adequate repentance. Hawley, who had been active and influential in fomenting the disaffection among the people, had now condemned his own conduct, and with it that of the people with whom he had acted, as sinful and criminal in every respect: as he reflected upon it, he had been confounded and filled with terror. He appeals to the 51st Psalm as the confession of his soul in view of his crime. He calls upon the church at Northampton to consider whether it had not been guilty of great sin before God in parting as they did with such a minister as Mr. Edwards. Their words against him he denounces as odious and ungodly and vile, full of unchristian bitterness and of gross slanders. Mr. Hawley had received from Edwards the assurance of his forgiveness and prayers. But, not content with this private confession, he published a letter, after Edwards' death,[2] in which he gave to the world the confession which he had rendered in

[1] Cf. *Bibliotheca Sacra*, vol. i. p. 579.
[2] Dwight's *Memoir*, pp. 421, ff.

private; and as no remonstrance appeared from the congregation, it may be taken as indicating more than a personal apology. There is now a church at Northampton which is called after the name of the once dishonored pastor; and the highest distinction which the town can claim, after one hundred years and more have passed away, is to be identified with the labors and reputation of Jonathan Edwards.

The family of Edwards when he went to Stockbridge included ten children, one daughter having died, to whom allusion has been made. Two of the older daughters were married about the time when their father's difficulties were at their height, — Mary at the age of sixteen, and Sarah at the age of twenty-two, — events which must have called off his mind from his troubles, and renewed his interest in the changes and chances of this mortal life. Of the daughters who went with him to Stockbridge, Esther was one, to whose beauty inherited from both parents, as well as her intellectual brightness, tradition bears ample testimony. She had attracted the attention of the Rev. Aaron Burr, a noted personage in those aristocratic days, and to Stockbridge the devoted lover followed her, gaining her consent to matrimony in a short courtship. Mr. Burr was a man of brilliant qualities, who had recently been called to the presidency of Nassau Hall, — what was afterwards to become known as Princeton College. His career was cut prematurely short at the age of forty-two, but not before he had achieved a reputation for piety and culture which long survived him. He left two children, one of them a boy named after his father, in whom a curious interest has always centred, partly on his own account, and partly also for the thoughts and misgivings which are suggested by the fact that such a man should have been the grandson of Jonathan Edwards. Aaron Burr was the murderer of Alexander Hamilton in a duel; he became vice-president of the United States; and his career reached its height for notoriety in a conspiracy against the government, which led to his arrest and trial for treason. He was a man with an unusual, almost a weird power of fascination, — to some extent the same charm which may be traced in his ancestors, where it had found scope and satisfaction in the things of religion and the church. Diverted from these channels, the fascination reappeared under the aspect of a worldliness as intense as had been the other worldliness of its previous associations.

Among the younger children of Edwards was a son named Jonathan, six years of age at the time of the removal to Stockbridge, who illustrates in a directer way the principle of heredity. He lived to become a metaphysical theologian, following to a great extent in his father's line of thought, but without his father's genius or poetic fire, or that mystic glow which lends interest and beauty to the works of the elder Edwards. There was also another son, an infant still in his mother's arms when the migration took place, who bore the united names of his parents, Pierrepont Edwards.

The town of Stockbridge, when Edwards went there in 1751, was almost exclusively an Indian settlement. Only a small amount of land had been allotted to the few white settlers, who were for the most part drawn to the place by plans for the improvement of the Indians. Though Edwards had received and accepted a call to the church in Stockbridge, his chief responsibility was for these Indians, to whom he was appointed missionary by the Board of Commissioners for Indian Affairs residing in Boston, with the concurrence of a society in London which also contributed to his support. These were the days when there existed in England a romantic interest in the American Indian, — an interest which had drawn Wesley to Georgia, which had inspired Pope to write his well-known lines; an interest which Rousseau and his school had also felt, as giving support to their reverence for nature as something higher than either culture or grace. But in America so far, little or nothing had been achieved in the way of converting the Indians either to civilization or religion. Two ardent missionaries, or apostles as they have been called, Eliot and Brainerd, had consecrated their lives to this end, but without any permanent result beyond their own manifestation as types of the great Protestant missionaries of the future.

To this work Edwards was now called at a time of life when it was too late to adapt himself to a task for which he had no special fitness. His duty required him, in addition to preaching twice on Sunday to his white congregation, to preach one sermon to the Indians through an interpreter. How he performed this function may be seen in the plan of one of his sermons, prepared expressly for the purpose.[1] It shows an effort at adaptation of statement, but one can hardly think it was successful. The minute divisions and sub-divisions still remind us of the author of the Freedom of the Will. Edwards, however, may have gained the confidence and love of his Indian auditors by his untiring and disinterested labors in their behalf. In this, too, he was assisted by his family, of whom he speaks in one of his letters as being greatly liked by the Indians, and more particularly his wife. The moment when he arrived at Stockbridge was one of great confusion in Indian affairs. There was no lack of money to carry on the work among them, but on the part of some of the white settlers there was a disposition to secure the money for themselves, and leave the Indian to his own devices. The story of Edwards' relations with the Indians reads like an extract from a modern newspaper, detailing the conflict between the enemies and friends of this unfortunate people; private avarice diverting funds from their appointed course, while an honest, incorruptible man refuses to make himself a party to the trans-

[1] Cf. Grossart, *Selections from the Unpublished Writings of Edwards*, p. 191.

action. Edwards was an evil genius to those who were using the Indians for their private emolument. Among these was a member of a certain prominent family in the colony, who had done what he could to prevent Edwards' call to Stockbridge. The account of Edwards' connection with this family suggests some bitter feud, which is left unexplained. When Edwards first proposed to preach against Arminianism in 1734, it was from another member of the same family that he met with strenuous opposition to his project. Still other representatives of this family, residing in or near Northampton, had abetted the disaffection which led to his dismissal. In Stockbridge he was again confronted with the same hostility. Edwards' fortunes recall those of Athanasius, who seemed to arouse against himself a certain malignant hostility, and apparently for no other reason than his unflinching integrity.

Edwards would not be called a practical man. But no man of affairs could have been better fitted than he was to detect the avariciousness which crippled the Indian mission, and to follow it through all its disguises. He had not studied in vain the tortuous ways of the Arminians in the field of theology. The man who had devoted a volume to exposing the misrepresentations of Williams, or followed up in elaborate letters the inaccurate statement of Rector Clap, had learned how to deal with any adversary, whether in the sphere of ecclesiastical controversy or of practical life. When it came to showing up the true state of Indian affairs, there was no one who could stand in comparison with him. In this case it was no ecclesiastical council to whom his appeal was carried, but sensible men devoted to a Christian purpose, who only asked for the truth. He was sustained by those to whom his long correspondence was directed. For two years or more he carried on the hard fight, till he was rewarded by seeing the man who was the chief source of the trouble abandon Stockbridge, and leave the field a free one for the friends of truth and righteousness. But in the mean time the Indians had suffered from this struggle over their welfare. Pulled about as they were between contending factions, realizing but little good from the efforts in their behalf, — from this and from other causes, they ceased to regard Stockbridge as their reserve. The peace which had come to Edwards was little more than a deeper solitude.

II.

THE FREEDOM OF THE WILL.

EDWARDS was now at leisure to take up some larger work than any which he had hitherto attempted. At this time, also, he seems to have reverted to the speculations which had interested him when he was a boy in college writing his Notes upon the Mind. But the gulf of more than a quarter of a century lay between him and that early dream, so suddenly and strangely relinquished, of interpreting the universe in accordance with the absolute reason. Meantime his thoughts had been running so long in the grooves of a religious controversy which was still unfinished, that he could not escape the fascinations which it offered, — the temptation to make some final and permanent effort for the maintenance of the Calvinistic theology. So far as he reverted to his early speculations, it seems to have been mainly for the purpose of laying a deeper basis for the argument against Arminianism.

Hitherto he had assaulted the foe chiefly on religious grounds. But it had long been apparent to him that the hinge of the whole controversy was the speculative issue regarding the freedom of the will. Out of the Arminian doctrine that the will was free, in the sense of possessing a self-determining power, grew, as he thought, the arrogant disposition to despise the Calvinistic notions of God's sovereignty and moral government, the contempt for "the doctrines of grace," the dislike to experimental religion, the cultivation of a morality which read out the divine existence from the sphere of human interests. Everything vital was at stake in the doctrine of the human will. So strongly was he convinced of this that in his most impressive manner he declared himself ready to admit, that if the Arminians could demonstrate the self-determining power of the will, they had an impregnable fortress against every Christian doctrine which he held most dear. To the task, then, of demolishing this stronghold he devoted himself with the momentum of thought, and energy, and indignation which had been gathering for many years. So intense was the spirit with which he labored that in four months he finished the composition of the work on which, more than on any other of his writings, his world-wide reputation has rested, — a work which produced so deep an impression that it still continues to be spoken of as "the one large contribution which America has made to the deeper philosophic thought of the world."

The treatise on the Will was published in 1754, and may be regarded as one of the literary sensations of the last century. It was more than that, — it was, to a large part of the religious world, a veritable shock, staggering alike to the reason and the moral sense. The age was accustomed to similar views from infidels and free-thinkers such as Hobbes, and Collins, and Hume were reputed to be. There were others, too, calling themselves Christians, such as Hartley, and Tucker, and Priestley, who denied the freedom of the will, but without awakening the indignation which was caused by Edwards' assertion of the same principle. For here was one who rose up in the name of religion and morality, whose high character was acknowledged by all, whose genius was indisputable, whose reasoning seemed invincible, and who seemed to be clasping hands with materialists and atheists in behalf of the doctrine that the will was not free to choose between good and evil. Edwards' teaching, also, was associated in the public mind with his other beliefs, — the divine sovereignty, decrees of election and reprobation, an everlasting hell which was yawning for the reception of a majority of the human race. It now added an element of inexpressible horror to the situation if it was also true that the will was not free to choose between good and evil.

Edwards' work on the Will was but the culmination of the reaction which he had signalled when he preached his Boston sermon on Dependence in 1731. His work was received by his fellow-religionists with exultant testimonies to its power and value. There was among the Calvinists a general conviction that he had annihilated Arminianism. From being ashamed of their cause, they now felt themselves forever absolved from the disgraceful necessity of bowing in the house of Rimmon, which had led so many of their number, a Doddridge or a Watts, to admit the self-determining power of the will. In the enthusiastic words of Jonathan Edwards the Younger: "Now, therefore, the Calvinists find themselves placed upon firm and high ground. They fear not the attacks of their opponents. They face them on the ground of reason as well as of Scripture. Rather have they carried the war into Italy and to the very gates of Rome."[1] Long after its first appearance the same testimony continued to be borne. "There is no European divine," said Dr. Chalmers, "to whom I make such frequent appeals; no book of human composition which I more strenuously recommend than his Treatise on the Will, read by me forty-seven years ago, with a conviction that has never since faltered, and which has helped me more than any other uninspired book to find my way through all that might otherwise have proved baffling, and transcendental, and mysterious in the peculiarities of Calvinism."[2] In a passage frequently quoted, Sir James Mackintosh speaks of Edwards' power of subtle argument as "perhaps unmatched, certainly unsurpassed, among men."[3] Dugald Stewart regarded him as not inferior to disputants bred in the best universities of Europe. It is said that in conversation he once remarked that the argument of the Freedom of the Will had not been and could not be answered. The late Isaac Taylor, who edited an English edition of the work, esteemed it "a classic in metaphysics," though regretting the mixture of the metaphysical with the Scriptural argument. He also thought that Edwards had achieved his immediate object of demolishing the Arminian notion of contingency, and that his influence had been much greater than those who had yielded to it had

[1] Edwards the Younger, *Works*, vol. i. p. 484.
[2] Chalmers, *Works*, vol. i. p. 318.
[3] *Progress of Ethical Philosophy*, p. 108, Am. ed.

always confessed. Among other things which Edwards had taught the world was "to be less flippant."[1] A writer in the Christian Spectator for 1823 expressed the prevalent opinion when he remarked that it was curious to observe how few attempts had been made formally to answer any of those larger works in which Edwards put forth his strength. "Nibbling enough about the points of his arguments there has certainly been, but for the most part it has been extremely chary; and we suspect that the few who have taken hold in earnest have in the end found pretty good reason to repent of their temerity." The general impression that Edwards' argument was invincible drove those who resisted his conclusion to making an appeal to the consciousness in opposition to the intellect, as the only available alternative; or, in the words of Dr. Johnson to Boswell, "We know that we are free and there's an end on 't." Even so late as 1864, a distinguished American writer, Mr. Hazard, introduced his Review of Edwards on the Will by remarking that the soundness of his premises and the cogency of his logic were so generally admitted that " almost by common consent his positions are deemed impregnable, and the hope of subverting them by direct attack abandoned."

In view of these tributes of admiration, and many others which could be adduced, it is unnecessary to remark that a high place must be as-

---

[1] Introductory Essay to his edition of *Freedom of the Will*, p. xxv.

signed in literature to Edwards on the Will. Like Butler's Analogy, it belongs among the few great books in English theology. It may claim the great and peculiar honor of having first opened up to the world a new subject of interest, — the neglected and almost unknown sphere of the human will in its vast extent and mystery. It attempted to fill an empty niche in the corridors of human thought. From an historical point of view, no one can question its significance. Whether its importance is now more than historical, it is fairly open to doubt. The book is a difficult one to read, and this difficulty has been generally supposed to lie in the nature of the subject rather than in the author's method of exposition. But the close scrutiny to which it has been subjected has revealed a confusion in Edwards' mind as one source of the difficulty which the student encounters.[1] The work starts out with a definition of the will as "that by which the mind chooses anything," — a definition which might be allowed to stand, though far from being an adequate one. But even to this definition Edwards does not adhere. Hardly is he launched in his argument when he is found resting upon another ground, — that the will is that by which the mind

---

[1] Among other American critics of Edwards' argument besides the late Mr. Hazard, are Bledsoe, *Examination of Edwards on the Will;* Whedon, *The Freedom of the Will as a Basis of Moral Responsibility;* Tappan, *Review of Edwards' Inquiry,* etc. In Mr. Martineau's recent work, *A Study of Religion,* there is an admirable criticism of Edwards' attitude. Cf. vol. ii. chap. 2.

desires or inclines to anything; and this ambiguity of the word "choice" runs throughout the treatise. In his Notes on the Mind he had identified inclination with will: to this principle he had clung throughout his career as a practical theologian; it now turns up again in this speculative treatise, and becomes the basis of his opinion regarding the nature of freedom and of human responsibility. If a man possesses an inclination, however derived, and has the natural power to gratify it, he is free. If his inclination be evil, he is a proper subject of condemnation, or of approval if his inclination be right. But the ability to reverse the inclination, or to choose between the good and the evil, is no prerogative of the will.

The most striking feature of Edwards' position is its close agreement with the attitude of the physical or materialistic school of philosophy in his own and in a later age. There is no difference between his doctrine and that of the ancient Stoics, or of the famous philosopher Hobbes, who shocked the religious world of his day by his unspiritual method of dealing with religious things.[1]

---

[1] Edwards declared that he had not read Hobbes. Hume he seems to have read after his own work was published. One would like to know whether he had read Collins' *Philosophic Inquiry Concerning Human Liberty*, in which views identical with his own are advocated. It has been remarked that Collins' little work would have made an admirable introduction to Edwards' treatise. Edwards makes no allusion to him, though his book must have been widely known. Cf. Professor Fisher's valuable remarks in *Discussions*, etc., pp. 234, 235.

There is no perceptible difference between Edwards and David Hume on the vital question of the nature of causation. A cause is defined to be, not only that which has a positive tendency to produce a thing, but it includes also all antecedents with which consequent events are connected, whether they have any positive influence in producing them or not. He assumes that uniform causes are followed by uniform results. In this respect he is also at one with the late John Stuart Mill, affirming the common principle that the life of humanity, like that of outward nature, is involved in the meshes of necessity. The invariableness of the order of nature, man as the creature of outward circumstance, the iron chain of necessity which controls human character and conduct, — these things, as Mr. Mill has taught them, are paralleled by Edwards' view of a world in which every event in nature or in human experience is decreed by an Infinite Will, and in the nature of the case cannot be otherwise than it is.

Edwards' argument against the freedom of the human will, in the sense of a power to choose between good and evil, gains its force from the assumption of the thing to be proved. There is no movement in his thought beyond this assumption that every event must have some external cause. But the question at issue is, whether the will be not itself a creative cause, endowed with the power of initiating acts, of choosing between motives, nay, even of creating a motive to itself.

The illusion under which Edwards labors is in looking at man as part of nature, instead of as a personal being, who, rising above nature, has in himself the power of new beginnings. It is unnecessary to follow him in the phases of his argument as with matchless subtilty he reiterates the principle that every event must have a cause. It only requires to start with another definition of the will, as, like the divine will, "a creative first cause," — wherein also lies the image of God in the creature, — and Edwards' objections not only fail to overcome this counter principle, but even tend to its confirmation.

But it is, after all, the religious argument, and not the metaphysical, upon which Edwards' chief reliance depends in refuting the doctrine of the self-determining power of the will. If the will were free to choose between good and evil, then there would be uncertainty as to the result of its choice, and God's foreknowledge of the volitions of moral agents would be impossible. If the Divine Mind could not foreknow with infallible certainty the acts of the creature, how could events be decreed with the infallible certainty of their accomplishment? The divine action must in consequence be subject to constant revision, the divine immutability give way to infinitely numerous changes of intention. But this seemed to Edwards as contradictory to Scripture as it was to reason and to the moral sense. The Bible, as he read it, abounded in the prediction of events attributed to God. To admit the possibility of the uncertainty of human actions seemed also to involve a tacit atheism. Such an admission limited the divine omniscience, and endangered the omnipotence of God. The divine Being would then be conceived as standing at the mercy of man, waiting for the human will to determine its course. For such a deity, too feeble to govern the world which He had made, a Calvinist like Edwards could have no respect. The God of the Arminians was to him no God at all.

The issue which is here raised is a serious one, confronting every earnest thinker. While we are concerned in this discussion, not so much with the replies that have been or may be made to Edwards' position, yet it may be said in passing that we are not necessarily shut up to the alternatives of sacrificing human freedom, or limiting the divine omniscience. It is not difficult to conceive that the Infinite Mind may be competent to take into account every use that man may make of his freedom, and to govern the world accordingly. Even if it were required to conceive the divine omniscience as self-limited in order to the free development of the creature, this does not make impossible the divine moral government. It then would become a feature of the world-process as God has ordered it, that the free will of man shall be the means through which the divine purpose is to be accomplished. To govern the world, and yet allow full scope to human freedom, is a task more difficult, and therefore worthier of God. It is a grave objection to Edwards' conception of the universe that, when God has once decreed the course of human affairs down to its smallest detail, there remains no further opportunity for the creative divine activity. The same result would be obtained if for God were substituted the action of force or of unchanging law.[1]

It had formed an essential part of Edwards' plan in the treatment of his subject, to show that the Arminian idea of the freedom of will — as implying a self-determining power, or power to choose between good and evil — was not only untrue in itself, but was not necessary to moral agency. He had done this, apparently to his entire satisfaction, in the third part of his book, where he elaborates his thought at some length. But the scholarly recluse may become so accustomed to his own line of reflection as to be out of touch with the popular mind, which draws inferences from premises of its own, the ground of which lies too deep to be disturbed by speculative discussion. The popular inference from Edwards' argument was, that he had denied the freedom of the will, and in so doing had shaken the truth of moral accountability. In Scotland, where his work had

---

[1] Edwards' biblical argument is a defective one. But it involves questions of Biblical criticism, — the relation between the revelation and its record, — and cannot here be criticised. According to Edwards, Scripture reads like one continuous chapter of fulfilled prophecy. His interpretation of history is in harmony with his view of life, as ordered by divine decrees.

been long expected and was eagerly received, this inference was also drawn by the celebrated Lord Kames, who was entangled in speculations of his own on the same subject, and who hailed Edwards as a kindred spirit coming to his relief. Lord Kames had deduced the natural conclusion that, " if motives are not under our power or direction, we can at bottom have no liberty." He also reasoned that the human consciousness, which attests a sense of liberty, must be therefore a delusion, implanted in the soul in order to give men a sense of responsibility for their acts. An anonymous pamphlet was also issued in Scotland in which it was maintained that, if Edwards' teaching were true, it was better that it should not be known, as it would endanger the feeling of human accountability. Edwards seems to have been surprised and indignant when he learned through his friend and correspondent, Dr. Erskine, how his views were interpreted by those with whom he had no sympathy. In order to put his meaning beyond the power of misinterpretation, he wrote an open letter, which has ever since been appended to his treatise on the Will, in which he defined his attitude against those who understood him to hold that the will was not free.

How, then, did he discriminate his position from philosophical necessitarians, as they are called, who agreed with him in holding that the will has no power to choose between good and evil? It is a curious and remarkable case of how a subtle and powerful mind may fall into captivity to the bondage of words. Edwards now declared that he held to the freedom of the will, because freedom consisted, not in one's power of choosing between alternatives, but in his power to pursue his inclination without restraint. Because a man's actions were necessitated, or certain to take place just as they did, it did not follow that he acted under compulsion. Indeed, he was quite willing to give up all such words as "necessity" or "inability" when applied to the will. What he contended for was only the certainty that men's actions would take the shape they did, and that without any feeling, on their part, of compulsion or restraint. So long as there was no sense of compulsion, a man was free, no matter how he came by his inclination, or how infallibly certain that his action should be what it was.

It is rather to the credit of the necessitarians, with whose principles Edwards agreed while he disliked their alliance, that they refused to escape the consequences of their theory by what seems a hollow evasion or mere jugglery with words. Calvin also had held consistently to the same conviction that the will did not possess the power to choose between good and evil. He had even denounced with something of scorn in his tone the manner of those who, while accepting this view, still maintained that a man was free "because he acts voluntarily and not by compulsion." "This is perfectly true," he adds, "but why should so small a matter have been dignified with so proud a title? An admirable freedom! — that man is not forced to be the servant of sin, while he is, however, a voluntary slave; his will being bound by the fetters of sin. I abominate mere verbal disputes, by which the church is harassed to no purpose; but I think we ought religiously to eschew terms which imply some absurdity, especially in subjects where error is of pernicious consequence. How few there are who, when they hear free will attributed to man, do not immediately imagine that he is the master of his mind and will, and can incline himself either to good or evil!"[1] But this small matter, as Calvin rightly deemed it, Edwards chose to dignify, in the emergency of his conflict, with the proud title of freedom. There is even a tone of passion in its advocacy. He contends that he differs from necessitarians like Lord Kames by holding to freedom in the highest sense. "No Arminian, Pelagian, or Epicurean," he exclaimed, "can rise higher in his conception of freedom than the notion of it which I have explained.... And I scruple not to say, it is beyond all their wits to invent a higher notion or form a higher imagination of liberty; let them talk of sovereignty of the will, self-determining power, self-motion, self-direction, arbitrary decision, liberty *ad utrumvis*, power of choosing differently in given cases, etc., as long as they will." But Calvin was right when he foresaw the consequences of dignifying so small

[1] *Institutes of Christian Religion*, book ii. ch. ii. p. 7.

a matter with so proud a title. From a fear of being understood to deny the freedom of the will, coupled as it was in the popular mind with the sense of responsibility, the preachers who followed Edwards magnified his meagre conception of freedom, and felt justified in using the Arminian nomenclature. In this way Edwards' idea of freedom became a bridge of transition to a modern Calvinism in which liberty is conceded in the fuller sense as a power to choose between good and evil.

But we reach the momentous outcome of Edwards' argument when he applies this same idea of freedom to the sovereign will of God. To the conclusion that this was the only freedom predicable of God, he was driven by the necessities of his thought. He was laboring to show that man is free, although possessing no power to choose between good and evil, — free even though his action be necessary or certain; and if free, then responsible for his action, and deserving of praise or blame. To establish this point he drew an illustration from the person of Christ, with whom there was a necessity to the right and an impossibility to sin, and yet He was morally responsible, and his conduct a proper subject of moral approval. From this very inadequate conception of the personality of Christ, he passed on to the consideration of the being of God. God also is free only to do what is right, — free only in the sense that He has the power to carry out the divine inclination. The divine freedom is therefore but another name for a divine and eternal necessity. Behind the divine will there lies an immutable divine wisdom, to which the will of God must in the nature of the case conform. But here one is forced to ask what becomes of the doctrine of the divine sovereignty, which played so large a part in Edwards' earlier writings, which, as he had presented it, implied in the divine will a power to the contrary. How often had he asserted, that God was under no obligation to save man after the fall; that when, in the exercise of His sovereign will, He had determined to do so, it was still a matter of His arbitrary will whom He would save and whom He would reject! "He chooseth whom He will, and whom He will, He hardeneth." The two doctrines are plainly incompatible. Sovereignty, as he had preached it, contradicts necessity. The divine sovereignty was the last relic of freedom, when it had been denied elsewhere. But it now appears as having no justification at the bar of reason. Even in Edwards' consciousness from the first, it had been a mysterious conviction, the genesis of which he could not explain. It is plain that a change is now taking place in his mind as to the nature of God, which is fundamental and revolutionary in its character. The Augustinian idea of God as arbitrary, unconditioned will, is growing weak in the presence of another conception, — the definition of God as the one substance of whose thought the world of created things is the necessary manifestation. But throughout the universe there is no place for the freedom of the will.

At this point, which is the culmination of Edwards' argument, there opened before him diverging lines of thought, and which of them he should take depended on whether his interest was stronger in following out the line of speculation about the nature of God and its relation to man, or in tracing the origin and history of that evil inclination in humanity which is known as Original Sin. The discussion of the latter topic was required in order to supplement the treatise on the Will. For it is a noticeable feature of this treatise that no effort is made to account for that inclination to evil in every man, which man does not originate within himself, which he is not free to reverse or overcome. Elsewhere Edwards had boldly declared that the will is determined by God. But we do not meet this statement in any such emphatic form in his work on The Will. He preferred to abide by the negative demonstration that the acts of the will are rendered certain by some other cause than the mere power of willing. What that remoter cause may be is not specially considered. He does not go beyond the statement that the will is determined by that motive which, as it stands in the mind, is the strongest, or that the will always is as the greatest apparent good is. In the vast and obscure region of human motives there is disclosed an ample sphere where God may work unfelt or unperceived, where He may so influence or direct the agencies which control the will that a man shall do the divine bidding while still acting in accordance with his own inclination. To the natural objection that such a view makes God the author of sin, he offers a brief reply, at the same time remarking that he has not space to consider at length the question of the first entrance of sin into the world. The subject of original sin was then clearly before his mind. But the idea of God had a deeper charm than the nature of man, and its exposition more imperatively demanded his attention. Before writing his work on Original Sin, he stopped to consider the nature of True Virtue and the Last End of God in the Creation.

With one brief remark we must dismiss the treatise on the Freedom of the Will. It no longer holds the same preëminence which was once accorded to it. The spell with which it was invested by an almost sacred tradition has been broken. Marred as it is by its controversial purpose, it cannot be regarded as a disinterested effort to reach the truth. It is disfigured also by methods of biblical interpretation which have been discarded by a later scholarship. It has been superseded by the advances made in psychology, — a study which in Edwards' time was still in its infancy, — to whose progress we owe the idea of the education of the will, of which he takes no account whatever. Although the labors of modern students in this field of inquiry regarding the will have by no means resulted in agreement, yet the tendency of later investigation has not been in the direction which Edwards was following, but for the most part tends toward the assertion of that freedom which it was his aim to disprove. But none the less does his work still possess a worth which is its own, — that peculiar quality of his spirit, which gives to all his writings their interest and value. He impresses the imagination, as does no other writer, with the truth that, in some way unexplained, human freedom, however real or undiminished, must yet move and have its being within the sphere of a divine determinism. While it is true, as Rothe has taught, that moral freedom lies in a mastery over one's motives, in the ability to form and modify them or to react against their influence, yet this process goes on in a world where God is supreme, where the divine will mingles with human action; or, to adopt the words of Coleridge, "Will any reflecting man admit that his own will is the only and sufficient determinant of all he is and all he does? Is nothing to be attributed to the harmony of the system to which he belongs, and to the preëstablished fitness of the objects and agents, known and unknown, that surround him as acting on the will, though doubtless with it likewise? — a process which the co-instantaneous yet reciprocal action of the air and the vital energy of the lungs in breathing may help to render intelligible." [1]

From Edwards' point of view, this inward union

[1] *Aids to Reflection, Works*, Am. ed., vol. i. p. 150.

or reconciliation of the divine with the human was an impossibility, since the human is conceived as having in itself no spiritual affiliation. But if we may be allowed to interpret him, to distinguish what he may have meant to affirm from what he actually teaches, it was his aim to enforce that real freedom which is in harmony with necessity, — that service of God which is the only perfect freedom. The Arminians, against whom he was contending, also misrepresented themselves, so as almost to make it appear as if it were a desirable thing for the will to remain in a state of equilibrium, instead of regarding the liberty of choice as a means of rising to a higher freedom where the power to the contrary disappears, where a state is reached in which the will is fixed in its devotion to righteousness beyond the possibility of change. As Edwards contemplated this higher freedom, he rejoiced in the necessity which it involved. In this respect he is in agreement with Augustine and Anselm, with Luther and Calvin, with devout souls in every age whose eyes are set on God, with the spirit of all genuine worship, whose essence it is to disown self in order to the enthronement of the divine.

III.

DEFENCE OF THE DOCTRINE OF ORIGINAL SIN.

After the publication of the Freedom of the Will in 1754, Edwards wrote two dissertations, on the Nature of True Virtue, and on God's Last End in the Creation, as well as other treatises or essays which will be described in an ensuing chapter. It was after the preparation of these works that he proceeded to write his book on Original Sin, which was finished in 1757, and was going through the press at the time of his death. For some reason unexplained, he preferred to delay the publication of these earlier dissertations. A question therefore arises as to the order in which these works should be treated. If we were to follow the movement of Edwards' mind, in which there lay a certain significance, it would be proper to take up these remaining works in the order in which they were written. But as the treatise on Original Sin was published with the sanction of his personal approval, which is lacking in the case of the other treatises, it cannot be amiss to give it the precedence. In the case of the other dissertations, there is reason for thinking, that if he had lived he would have recast them in some different shape. Whichever course we take, there will be seen the profound suggestiveness of the intellectual and spiritual process in which he was engaged.

The connection is a close one between the treatise on Original Sin and the doctrine of freedom set forth in the treatise on the Will. Edwards now proceeds to show how man comes into possession of that evil inclination which he is free to follow, but not free to reverse or overcome. It is needless to remark that this conception of freedom implies a low and degrading view of human nature. The younger Edwards, who defended his father's teaching in a logical treatise which won for him great distinction, plainly asserts what this doctrine of the will clearly implies: "Beasts, therefore, according to their measure of intelligence, are as free as men. Intelligence, therefore, and not liberty, is the only thing wanting to constitute them moral agents."[1] But Edwards himself has left us in no doubt as to his meaning. The spiritual element, he teaches, forms no necessary part of the human constitution. It is something added to man over and above his nature as man, — the *donum supernaturale* of mediæval theology. Virtue, though it may be necessary to the perfection and well-being of man, does not belong to man as man. One may have everything needful to his being a man where virtue is excluded.[2] For one brief moment Adam, indeed, possessed this spiritual element, what Edwards calls the divine nature, in conjunction with his human nature. But

[1] Edwards the Younger, *Improvements in Theology*, etc., *Works*, vol. i. p. 483.
[2] *Original Sin*, ch. ii. p. 477.

when Adam sinned and became a rebel against God, it was only just that the divine nature should be withdrawn from him, and in consequence from all his posterity. The merely human was then left standing by itself, superior only in its intelligence to the brute creation, or in its greater capacity for evil.

The interesting question now arises, How came Adam to rebel against God, possessed as he was of the spiritual complement to his nature which, it would seem, should have been a strong barrier against a rising inclination to sin? To this question theologians from the time of Augustine almost uniformly had replied that Adam formed an exception to his descendants in possessing the self-determining power of the will, and thus originated his sin by his own act. Such also was the answer of the Westminster Assembly of Divines whose Confession was accepted by English Calvinists. At this point Edwards made his first great innovation. He denied that Adam had any other freedom than was possessed by his posterity. He, too, was free only in the sense that he could act according to his inclination. For if Adam had possessed a self-determining power of the will, it would have implied uncertainty as to how he would act, and thus made impossible the divine foreknowledge. There was but one alternative in Edwards' mind,— that God had decreed to permit Adam's sin; and in his own words, " sin, if it be permitted, will most certainly and infallibly follow." [1] Although he

---

[1] *Freedom of the Will*, § 9, p. 157.

does not like the expression, yet he is willing to admit, if need be, that God is the author of sin. The only qualification which he is anxious to urge is, that the action of God in causing the fall shall appear as indirect and not immediate. He again takes refuge in the land of motives, where the divine will may be active, but where its action is not seen. "It was fitting," he remarks, "that the transaction should so take place that it might not appear to be from God as the apparent fountain." [1] Yet, as he also remarks, "God may actually in His Providence so dispose and permit things that the event may be certainly and infallibly connected with such disposal and permission."

In all this, Edwards emphatically disclaims the inference that God implants or infuses any evil thing in Adam's nature. Let the disclaimer be put to the credit of his heart which prevented him from admitting in words what his thought implied. The first man, as he has portrayed him, becomes, as to his personality, a shadowy, impossible thing, a type of existence solitary and unclassified, as if neither animal, or man, or angel, — an opportunity as it were for the operation of the divine will, or the manifestation of the divine wisdom. But how does the case stand with his descendants? We are now told that when Adam sinned by rebellion, it was only just and fitting that God should withdraw from his posterity those superior principles of the divine nature which had been implanted in

[1] *Freedom of the Will*, p. 161.

Adam, and wherein consisted the image of God. "The Holy Spirit, that divine inhabitant, now forsook the house." It was with man as with a room where the light ceases when the candle is withdrawn. Nothing was left but human nature, a state of woful corruption and ruin. But as the coexistence of a divine nature with human nature in the case of Adam had served no purpose, unless it were as an advertisement of God's idea of what man should be, the withdrawal of this divine nature was like taking away its ideal from humanity. Edwards argues that it was just and proper in God to sever the divine image from man in his fallen estate, and to remove the possibility of the divine communion. But one does not see why it was not quite as fitting that this divine ideal should still be allowed to remain, even though it should serve no other purpose than as a divine protest against the predominance of the animal nature.

Edwards' argument for original sin is, to a great extent, a familiar one, and needs no rehearsing. His book was intended partly as a reply to a work very popular in the last century, by Dr. John Taylor, which proposed to subject this time-honored doctrine to a "free and candid examination." Edwards regarded Taylor as a specious writer, and seems to have found satisfaction in tearing his "candid examination" to shreds. Both were agreed in admitting the prevalence and heinousness of sin. But Dr. Taylor doubted its universality as including infants from the hour of their birth; he refused to admit that the general diffusion of sin was owing to the corruption of human nature, nor did he think it explained anything to refer the origin of evil to Adam. It was enough to suppose the force of evil example, the weakness of our nature, together with the freedom of the will, in explanation of the sin which originated with every man. Edwards' reply consists in unrolling upon a larger canvas the picture of humanity under the universal predominance of sin, drawing his materials from experience and observation, the history of the race, the teaching of Scripture. He urges the inference that human nature must have been corrupted at its original source as the only adequate explanation. But how could human nature as a whole have become inwardly depraved unless through the sin of its progenitor who carried humanity in himself, and in whom, as at its primal fount, the springs of life had been contaminated? Until this point had been established, Edwards' argument halted and fell short of its aim. But in seeking to establish this point, he was confronted by the moral sentiment and reason of the age. Was it just that all men should be adjudged guilty of Adam's sin, and doomed to suffer its endless consequences? In the earlier ages of the church, when what is called realism was the prevailing philosophical bias, it had been easy to defend such a doctrine on the ground that all men had sinned in Adam. But the spirit of nominalism, prevailing widely in the eighteenth century, made such a statement seem as contrary to the reason as it was repulsive to the moral sense. Nor was the statement more acceptable in its modified form, — that God had decreed a certain relationship with Adam, in consequence of which his sin was imputed to his descendants, even though it were not their own. Such opinions were indignantly challenged as irrational or immoral. Every man stood by himself before God, responsible only for his own guilt, and not punishable for the sin of another.

Edwards met the opponents of the doctrine with no compromise of its ancient rigor. Nor was he content merely with an appeal to Scripture. But in calling reason to his aid, he produced an argument so novel and extraordinary in the history of the doctrine that it seems to have struck his readers, for the most part, dumb with astonishment. He asserted not only that all men sinned in Adam, but that every man is identical with Adam, and has therefore actually committed Adam's sin. His argument turned on the metaphysical question of the nature of identity. The mysterious principle, by which a man remains the same being through the mutations of experience, he declares to be no other than "the sovereign constitution and will of God." We have here again the principle of Berkeley carried beyond the sphere of sense perceptions to which Berkeley confined it, and regarded as controlling the whole range of human consciousness or intellectual activity.[1] God is not only the

[1] There is a passage in the treatise on *Original Sin*, pt. iv., ch.

universal mind which constitutes the substance of the external world, but He is also the essence which lies behind the phenomena of consciousness or mind. There is no essential difference between the process by which we know the oak to be identical with the acorn, and the self-consciousness by which a man knows himself to be one and the same being from childhood to maturity. The hidden reality or substance in both cases is the immediate and continuous action of the stable will of God. Or, to follow Edwards' reasoning: "There would be no necessity that the remembrance of what is past should continue to exist but by an arbitrary constitution of the Creator. It does not suffice to say," so he continues, "that the nature of the soul will account for the existence of the consciousness of identity, for it is God who gives the soul this nature: identity of consciousness depends on a law of nature, and therefore on the sovereign will and agency of God. The oneness of all created substances is a dependent identity. It is God's immediate power which upholds every created substance in being. Preservation is but a continuous creation. Present existence is no result of past existence. But in each successive moment is witnessed the immediate divine agency. All depen-

2, p. 479, which contains an allusion, probably, to the Berkeleyan philosophy, though without mentioning it by name. "The course of nature is demonstrated, by late improvements in philosophy, to be indeed what our author himself says it is, viz., nothing but the established order of the agency and operation of the author of nature."

dent existence whatsoever is in a constant flux, ever passing and returning; renewed every moment, as the colors of bodies are every moment renewed by the light that shines upon them. And all is constantly proceeding from God, as light from the sun."[1] The same law, then, by which a man knows himself as one and the same being, despite the differences of time and appearance, also binds every man to Adam, and creates a common consciousness of identity with him in his sin and fall. The sin of Adam, including his guilt, is therefore properly imputed to every man, because by the law of identity it is his own.

While this argument from the nature of identity did not commend itself to Edwards' contemporaries or followers, his free handling of the subject long continued to be imitated. The doctrine of original sin became the battle-field in New England of a great controversy. In some cases the doctrine was greatly modified, in others almost explained away, while there were those who rejected it altogether. Edwards, of course, is not to be held responsible for every deduction from his premises. But the tendency of an attitude so literal and extreme was to neutralize the earlier meaning of the doctrine, if not to give rise to a new and diverse interpretation. It required but a step from the principle that each individual has an identity of consciousness with Adam, to reach the conclusion that each individual is Adam and repeats his experience.

[1] Vol. ii. p. 490.

Of every man it might be said, that like Adam he comes into the world attended with the divine nature, and like him sins and falls. In this sense the sin of every man becomes original sin. The old feudal conception grows weak which regarded Adam as having a proprietorship in the race of his descendants. Instead of being the head of humanity, he becomes rather its generic type on that side of its existence which is of the earth earthy.

If there is any literary interest in the treatise on Original Sin, it lies in the revelation of Edwards' character. He was penetrated with the mystic's conviction of some far-reaching, deep-seated alienation which separates man from God. Out of his ideal of the divine perfection springs his consciousness of sin. But his conception of sin is after all lacking in what may be called an ethical motive. He defines sin as a negation, — the absence of reality. But in this negation he seems to include the infinite gulf which divides the creature from the Creator. All imperfection, finiteness as contrasted with the infinite, the interest in earthly things or all which is not God, — these, as well as the lack of entire disinterested devotion, or the darker vices which disfigure human life, enter into Edwards' conception of sin. Naturally, therefore, was he indignant at what seemed the shallow theory of Dr. Taylor, that "corruption and moral evil are not universally prevalent, that good predominates, that virtue is in the ascendant." To Edwards' mind, humanity in itself was identified with evil.

He treats with disdain the objection which may be raised, that his view of human nature is derogatory to its sacredness or dignity. He does not condescend to its consideration. To another question which arises, whether, under these circumstances, the propagation of the race be not a sin, he replies that such is the will of God.

Of this treatise on Original Sin, Mr. Lecky has remarked that it is "one of the most revolting books that have ever proceeded from the pen of man." Where, if it may be put briefly, lies the fallacy of a work which can evoke such a criticism? There is a passage in the opening pages in which Edwards states the method he proposes to follow: "That is to be looked upon as the true tendency of the natural or innate disposition of man's heart which appears to be its tendency when we consider things as they are in themselves or in their own nature, without the interposition of divine grace." But had he any right, in considering things as they are, to leave out of view the divine action within the soul? Is not God's grace as real as human sinfulness, — the divine interposition as inevitable as Adam's fall? To separate things which accompany each other is not to see things as they are. It is to commit the familiar fallacy of supposing that because things may be separated in abstract thought, they are also separated as a matter of fact. The grace of God is as organic in its relation to man as is the evil in his nature. Grace also reigns wherever justice reigns. To draw a picture of humanity apart from God, is an injustice alike to God and man. Such an attempt transgresses the limits of a lawful rhetoric, even when seeking to impress the imagination with a sense of the evil of sin.

IV.

TREATISE ON THE NATURE OF TRUE VIRTUE.

The Augustinian or Calvinistic theology was not a favorable soil for the growth of ethical systems. The study of ethics, indeed, had been made almost impossible by the doctrine of original sin from the time of Augustine onwards. It was not till the latter part of the seventeenth century, when the traditional interpretation of this ancient dogma was losing its hold on the popular mind, that attention began to be given to ethical theories. The deistical and Arminian writers, more particularly of the eighteenth century, who were seeking to vindicate for character and conduct a higher place in religion, as if it were the most essential element, found it necessary to seek for some principle which should explain and justify the utterances of the moral nature, and bind them together in the unity of a system. Edwards was watching them in this constructive process, so far as it came under his vision, eager to detect from his own point of view the deficiency of the result. No subject could have been more congenial to the natural bent of his mind. It had interested him, as we have seen, from the moment when he became conscious of his intellectual power, occupying the foremost place in his early Notes on the Mind. Had he been free from the trammels of controversy, or the self-imposed necessity of making his conclusions square with the narrow principles of his theology; could he have trusted humanity as redeemed in Christ, it would seem as if he must have won his chief distinction in the field of ethical inquiry. But while his treatise on Virtue has never held the place of honor among his writings, it is worthy of careful study. His conception of virtue, viewed apart from the negations which accompany it, has much that is sublime and inspiring. In making the motive of true virtue consist in devotion to an Infinite Being, he marks the first beginnings of a transition in the Calvinistic churches to a theology in which love is the central principle of the creation, and the law of all created existence.

A peculiar interest attaches to the treatise on Virtue, as being the reproduction of Edwards' earliest thought with no essential modification. Virtue is again identified with the beautiful. It has its primary root in love to God for Himself alone. All true excellence or beauty, all proportion and harmony, is traced back to an ultimate foundation in the necessities of pure existence or being. There can be no virtue where the gradation is not preserved between the existence which is infinite, and that which is created and finite. It is not the moral character of God that first awakens a moral response in the creation. It is rather the infinite preponderance of existence which Deity possesses, compared with which the amount of created existence is as nothing, that awakens the feeling of reverential awe which is the beginning of true virtue. For being as he calls it, or substance as it might be called, Edwards like Spinoza felt a profound and awful reverence. That which is called great, even in the moral universe, is great because it has more of existence than that which is small. The comparison is that of a large piece of gold to a tiny fragment of the same material. The value depends upon the quantity. In the relative amount of being possessed by the archangel and the worm lies the difference which distinguishes and separates them. In the last resort, it is being which is the most sacred and awful of realities. And being possesses sanctity and value because it is the furthest remove from nonentity, which is the greatest evil.[1]

This doctrine of Edwards seems to imply a physical or at least an unethical basis as the ground of the moral or spiritual. It is not difficult to see

---

[1] "*Being*, in what we should call an awful nakedness, not unconnected surely (how can it be?) with life and action; not separated, as it is in Spinoza, from a personal will, but almost as separate from all relations, almost as far removed from humanity as it is in his metaphysics; — is the ground of the divinity of Edwards, is the ground also (subject to the exception we have just mentioned) of his ethics."— Maurice, *Hist. Modern Phil.*, p. 473. Cf., also, Chapter I., First Period, pp. 6–10, *ante*.

how he came to identify the two. The physical or the material did not in his view possess any real existence except in the will of God. In God's will lies the only substance. A monism more absolute it is impossible to conceive. As bodies have no real existence, and spirits are but the communication of the Infinite Spirit, it was necessary for him to insist upon the infinite quantity of the Divine existence, as contrasted with the human, if he would escape the consequence of his theory which tended to identify all existence with God. So deeply is he impressed with this necessity of his thought, that he reads it into the minds of others even when it would be disowned. He applied it to the doctrine advocated by Hutchinson and the Arminian school, that virtue consisted in love or benevolence to all men, or in regarding the good of all, or of the greatest number, in preference to the interest of self. He assumes that the reason why these writers give the preference to the greatest number must be on account of the larger quantity of being which all men, taken together, possess when compared with the amount of being in the individual. On this ground he calls upon them to carry out the principle in its application to God. They seem to him inconsistent when they make morality consist in love to men, and do not rather make it consist primarily and even exclusively in the love toward God. That Edwards had struck a note of profound significance must be confessed. But it can hardly be called an ethical principle. It is a principle which underlies religion, if religion be defined as, in its origin, the sense of awe in the presence of the mystery of the universe. But how unethical it is may be illustrated by a passage which Edwards was fond of quoting, — "The devils also believe and tremble." But he seems to have clung to his position the more strenuously for this reason, — that it enabled a totally depraved humanity to discern clearly the ground of its condemnation. Even if the wicked could not appreciate God's moral excellence or rejoice in His beauty, yet they could recognize His infinite greatness, resistance to the attraction of which constitutes evil. In the consummation of things at the last judgment, the verdict against sinners would be sufficiently justified by this principle alone.

The ethical principle of Edwards is defective in grounding morality in the immeasurable, incomprehensible essence of God. The landmarks disappear by which the good in itself may be recognized. His insistence on this principle reveals at the heart of his theology a defect which he had not been able to overcome. Infinite power or force, a physical attribute of Deity, becomes the ultimate reality. Had he carried out his principle, it must have made impossible the Incarnation. For Christ is the revelation of God as a spiritual or moral being. The goodness of God can be revealed in humanity when God in the depth and mystery of His infinite existence is unknown. Though Christ emptied Himself of the infinite glory and majesty of the divine existence, yet, in making Himself of no reputation, he still revealed in the flesh the essential image or quality of God. What else was the significance of the Incarnation but the entrance of God into humanity, the confinement of Deity as it were within human limits, in order that He might be measured by human capacity, and known and loved as the divine? The mysticism of Edwards here appears as overreaching itself, till the soul is in danger of being lost in the abyss of the incommensurable.

But this is not all of Edwards' doctrine concerning virtue. The truly virtuous soul, who begins with loving God for His infinite existence, advances to the love of God for His moral excellence. To such a soul God appears as preëminently lovable, because of the infinite love wherewith He loves Himself supremely. To be in unison with this love is to rest in the ultimate harmony of things. It is to be one with God, for it is to be governed by the same principle, rejoicing in God as God rejoices in Himself. The love for individual or particular beings, in order to be genuine, must spring out of the love toward God as its motive and sanction. But a difficulty arises here in the interpretation of Edwards' meaning. It was thought by the distinguished Robert Hall that his teaching must result in making individual affections useless, or even pernicious, supposing that they were any longer possible; for, in order to observe the right proportion between the love of God and that of the individual, the latter love must be infinitely less than the former, — a distinction of which the human mind was incapable.[1] Mr. Hall, also believed that Godwin, the poet Shelley's father-in-law, was indebted to Edwards for his leading arguments against the private affections.[2] Edwards' silence on this point is a reason for doubting if he would have sanctioned such an inference from his position. There is but one passage in the treatise on Virtue in which he appears to hold that love or benevolence must be proportioned to the degree of existence. What he does urge is the tendency of love toward God to produce exercises of love toward particular beings as occasion may arise, — that he who has true love towards God will be more disposed than others to be moved with benevolence towards individuals. But the ordinary mind draws its own inferences. One can hardly read this treatise without feeling that he is putting God in contrast with man, as if to weigh them in the scales of thought. And the result is, that either the individual affections become impossible, or God is robbed of his infinitude.[3]

[1] Hall, *Works*, p. 284, Bohn ed.
[2] Godwin, *Political Justice*, vol. i. p. 301, Amer. ed.
[3] There is a contradiction in this treatise on *Virtue*, of which Edwards may not have been aware. If he had said plainly, what his thought implies, that the creature has no existence outside of God, his attitude would have been clear and consistent. But he seems also to grant an infinitesimal portion of an independent existence to humanity. He halts between these two opinions, neither of which is quite acceptable to him.

That Edwards had not made his meaning clear, or that its perversion was an almost necessary consequence of so high an ideal, was shown in the next generation, when his disciple, Dr. Samuel Hopkins, was wrestling with the difficulties created by the treatise on Virtue. Dr. Hopkins drew the inference that to love God for Himself alone required that every man should be willing to be damned, if thereby God's happiness and glory could be promoted. Dr. Hopkins was also puzzled by another difficulty. He assumed that it was fitting for man to love only those who were loved by God. But it was impossible in this world to know with certainty who were God's elect, to whom He vouchsafed His love. Under these circumstances, if one's love went forth to his fellows it must be a sort of hypothetical or tentative affection. The incongruities, the absurdities even, to which Edwards' teaching gave rise, were not altogether inherent in his theory, but sprang from its association with the Calvinistic doctrine of election or predestination. If this doctrine be dismissed from view, his conception of virtue bears a close resemblance to the ethics of Spinoza. One might be justified in thinking that Edwards would have approved these propositions from the *Ethica:* "God loves Himself with an infinite intellectual love" (v. 35); "The intellectual love of the mind towards God is that very love whereby God loves Himself" (v. 36); "The good which every man who follows after virtue desires for himself he will also desire for other men, and so much the more in proportion as he has a greater knowledge of God" (iv. 37); "He who loves God cannot endeavor that God should love him in return" (v. 19). Transcendent ethical impulses like these were struggling in the bosom of the old New England Calvinism, in sharp conflict with the selfishness which it naturally engendered. We may smile at the ungainly shape which the principle of disinterested virtue assumed in Hopkins' theology. But the same principle assumes a fair, attractive guise in its large and human presentation by the great German poet. Goethe writes, after reading Spinoza: "A large and free view of the sensible and moral world seemed to open itself before me. But what specially chained me to him was the boundless disinterestedness which shone forth from every proposition. That wondrous word, 'who rightly loves God must not demand that God should love him in return,' with all the premises on which it rests, and all the conclusions that flow from it, entirely filled my thought.[1] To be disinterested in all, and most disinterested in love and friendship, was my highest joy, my maxim, my practice; and so that later petulant saying of

---

[1] "Mr. Brainerd's religion," says Edwards, "was not selfish and mercenary: his love to God was primarily and principally for the supreme excellency of His own nature, and not built on a preconceived notion that God loved him, had received him into favor, and had done great things for him, or promised great things to him: so his joy was joy in God, and not in himself." — *Reflections on the Memoirs of Mr. Brainerd*, vol. i. p. 659.

mine, 'If I love thee, what is that to thee?' was spoken from my very heart."[1]

The resemblance is close between Edwards and Spinoza; but so also is the divergence great. One of Spinoza's propositions reads, "No one can hate God" (v. 17). It was Goethe's method in persuasive speech always to address men as if they were already what it was desirable they should become. Spinoza had also written: "He who clearly and distinctly understands himself and his emotions loves God, and so much the more in proportion as he more understands himself and his emotions" (v. 15). And again: "The more we understand particular things, the more do we understand God" (v. 24). If the tendency of Spinoza's ethics was toward moral laxity, in consequence of his obliterating the distinction between God and man, Edwards stood at the other extreme, and made virtue so difficult as to be almost impossible. The greater part of the treatise on Virtue is devoted to the negative effort of showing that there is no virtue in acts which are prompted by self-love, or the action of the natural conscience. The principle is affirmed and reiterated that "whatever benevolence or generosity toward mankind, or other virtues or moral qualifications which go by that name, any are possessed of, that are not attended with a love of God which is altogether above them and to which they are subordinate and on which they are dependent, there is nothing of the

[1] Hedge, *Ways of the Spirit*, p. 265.

nature of true virtue or religion in them." The private affections, unless they spring from the conscious love of God, have no moral value. There are instincts in humanity which in some respects resemble virtue, but they are only instincts, springing only from self-love. Such is the love of parents for their children, or the pity which is natural to mankind when they see others in distress. Even if the soul of a man should go forth in love and devotion toward the whole race, without regard to God's existence, such love or benevolence would not be of the nature of true virtue. It is as if Edwards stood in an attitude of defiance toward the process of the divine revelation as given in human history or experience. His principle seems a grand and inspiring one, that true virtue must begin and end with loving God supremely. But is not this rather the ultimatum, the final goal to which virtue tends, rather than its incipient motive? The divine training of humanity begins with and leads through the human in order to end in the divine. Out of the love of children for parents, the divinest of all analogies, there arises the love toward God. "He that loveth not his brother whom he hath seen, how shall he love God whom he hath not seen?"

The moralists of the last century spoke of a moral sense endowed with a direct insight into the nature of virtue, — of a natural conscience capable of approving right and condemning evil. Edwards refused to admit that the action of conscience implied any virtuous principle, inasmuch as it could not rise to the love of Being in general, which is God. Even though the conscience approved things that are excellent, or condemned their opposites, this did not imply any spiritual sense or virtuous taste. The natural conscience, when well informed, will approve of true virtue, and condemn the want of it, without seeing the beauty of true virtue. Edwards was impressed with the fact which came under his vision, that there prevailed a striking analogy between the benevolent deeds of the natural man which have no true virtue in them, and the deeds of the virtuous man which are made valid and beautiful by consecration to the divine love. It was certainly incumbent on him to inquire into the analogy in order to detect its full significance. But he waives the question, as if it had no special bearing on his theme. Why there should be such an analogy, he remarks, it is not needful to inquire. It is sufficient to observe that God is pleased to maintain such an analogy in all His works. Wherever we look, it may be seen that God has established inferior things in an analogy to superior things. Brutes are, in many instances, in analogy to the nature of mankind, and plants to animals. The external world is in analogy in numberless instances to things in the spiritual world. And so also it is with natural men, or the great majority of human kind, in their conduct and character, when compared with the few who are truly virtuous. All that can be said is, that

God has been pleased to make this kind of consent and agreement as a beautiful and grateful vision to all intelligent beings, — an image, as it were, of the true spiritual, original beauty which is in God. While the action of the natural conscience does not rise into the sphere of virtue, it still serves a useful purpose in the divine economy. Gratitude, sympathy, pity, charity, the spirit of public benevolence, the love of country, the domestic affections, or conjugal or filial love, — these do not have in them the nature of true virtue, and yet they are necessary to the order and happiness of social institutions. These qualities have in them also a certain negative goodness, implying in greater or less degree the absence of moral evil. For these reasons many mistake them for truly virtuous actions. But upon this point Edwards is uncompromising in the rigidity of his attitude. There is no virtue in them unless they are subordinated to the conscious love of Being in general, which is God.

It is difficult to treat Edwards' teaching on this subject with that impartial justice which it demands. One is in danger of spurning what is true and sublime in his thought, because of its close conjunction with what our moral nature condemns as false. A reaction has long been in process against his ruling conviction, which has not yet reached its limit. So far has the modern mind gone in the opposite direction, that to some the idea of God seems like a waste of energy in the presence of appeals to the moral nature. The philosophy of the unconscious, if we may so call it, underlies to a great extent our modern theology and ethical systems. Upon it rests the larger hope for the myriads who have come and gone, doing their work apart from any conscious service of God. As if by tacit assent, the intellect or the conscious will is subordinated to the instincts. To live by the emotions, to grow by unconscious effort, has become the modern ideal. In all this there may be a justifiable protest against the narrowness of the conclusion that God is not where He is not consciously known or served. There are words of Christ Himself, spoken to those who have served Him in unconsciousness, as when He was in hunger or in thirst, in sickness or nakedness, or in prison, which seem to justify what Edwards labored to disprove. "Forasmuch as ye have done it unto one of the least of these my brethren, ye have done it unto me." There is truth in Edwards' position if conscious knowledge be the goal toward which we are moving, which even here we struggle to attain. His error lay in cherishing true virtue as the precious pearl, to the neglect of that other illustration to which Christ compares the life of God in the soul, — the leaven slowly penetrating but destined to revolutionize the world. He neglected the small beginnings, the tedious process, in order to fasten his gaze upon the remote result when the course of ages should have done its work. He looked to the distant end when the kingdom should be delivered up to the Father, and God should be all in all. So absorbed was he in the prospect that he counted humanity as nothing, so far as it still existed unconscious of its destiny, or as an obstacle in the way of the fulfilment of the beatific vision.

V.

GOD'S LAST END IN THE CREATION.

ONE more treatise remains to be considered, and Edwards' long controversy with the Arminians is over. The title which he gave to his work, The Last End of God in the Creation, is an interesting one. It suggests the profound and fascinating speculations of Gnostic theosophies. It recalls the mystic thinkers of the Middle Ages, an Erigena or an Eckart; the wonderful poetry or the vast reaches of thought in Schelling and the Hegelian philosophy. But Edwards comes to the subject afresh, as if it had never been broached before. One cannot help feeling that in this sphere of devout speculation on the hidden mystery and destiny of the creation, he might have been the peer of his predecessors or followers had he only been free to indulge the bent of his poetic-creative genius. But while Edwards is free, so far as the presumptions of traditional theology are concerned, yet the demands of a practical theology are always uppermost in his mind. If at times he appears to forget himself and soars in philosophic contemplation, or seems as if he would lose himself and revel in the open mystery of God, he soon returns to his direct purpose, which is to give a final blow to the remotest cause of the Arminian heresy. Until he had done this, his work was not complete.

All other questions had been leading up to the determination of the final object for which God made the world. Back to this issue were to be traced the fundamental differences which divided the two religious schools. But in one respect these schools were agreed, dominated as they were by the spirit of the eighteenth century, in regarding happiness as the end of existence. Edwards defines God as a supremely happy Being, in the most absolute and highest sense possible, so that God is free from everything that is contrary to happiness, — so that in strict propriety of speech there is no such thing as pain, or grief, or trouble in Him.[1] In all that God does, He has reference to His own happiness. The Arminians, on the other hand, made the happiness of the creation the ultimate end of God, representing Him even as if indifferent to His own interests or dignity in order to secure the happiness of the creature. This tendency to think of happiness as the primary issue lowers the tone of the discussion. Before theology could recover from the degradation into which it fell in the last century, an ethical purpose must be conceived as having supremest sway in the divine existence, and in consequence permeating the universe of created things.

[1] Cf. *Freedom of the Will*, § 9, ch. 4.

Edwards did not deny that God had some reference, in the final end of the creation, to the happiness of the creature; but it must be an indirect and subordinate end, not the ultimate or crowning purpose. It is one part of his aim to reconcile this subordinate reference to the creature with the more important principle that God's supreme end in all things is Himself alone. Of this Edwards was convinced above all, that God had made the world for His own glory. This had been the dearest conviction of his life from the time of his youth onward. Only let God be supremely happy, let Him be lovely in all His glorious beauty, and it did not matter so much about the world of created things. But it was also part of Edwards' belief that God gave it to some of His creatures to share with Him in His felicity. It was therefore necessary to show that God's purpose in bestowing happiness upon these could be reconciled with His supreme devotion to Himself.

Two points stand out with great clearness in Edwards' discussion of his theme; they may be taken as axioms in his mind, so unhesitatingly does he assume them. The first is, that God cannot love anything other than Himself. He is so great, He comprises in Himself so preponderating an amount of being, that what is left is hardly worth considering. Or, to use Edwards' words, the whole system of created beings, if put in comparison with the Creator, "would be found as the light dust of the balance (which is taken no notice of by him that weighs), and as less than nothing and vanity." And in the second place, so far as God has any love for the creation, it is because He Himself is diffused therein. The fulness of His own essence has overflowed into an outer world, and that which He loves in created beings is His essence imparted to them. In seeking the creature, God does not go out of Himself, but rather seeks Himself. If God may be said to have any pleasure in the happy state of the creature, it is because and in so far as He Himself exists by emanation in the creature. That which is communicated to the creature, which makes him an object of God's complacency or love, is something divine, something of God. God thus becomes all in all with reference to the felicity of His chosen ones. He continues to pour His own divine essence into them, in proportion to their capacity to receive it, until in the final consummation they shall become, as it were, swallowed up in God.[1]

Such is Edwards' solution of the question, how God can love Himself supremely and exclusively and yet include the creature in His love. To reach this result he appears as denying any degree of self-dependent existence to the creation. He has, indeed, met the Arminian position, but in so doing has sacrificed all that is not God. Some other inferences are also apparent. If this treatise represented his final judgment, the idea of creation as an origination *de nihilo*, the received doctrine

[1] Vol. ii. pp. 210, 211.

of the church, could hardly find a legitimate place in his system. He does not reject it, but he constantly substitutes emanation for creation, as if its full equivalent. Throughout this treatise "emanation" is the word about which the thought revolves. The book has a Gnostic or Neo-Platonic atmosphere. The old phrases, such as the overflow of the divine fulness, diffusion of the divine essence, emanation from God compared with the light and heat which go forth from the sun, — these constitute the verbal signs of Edwards' thought. It is possible that he might have avoided them had he known their earlier association. But they represent truly the tendency of his mind; they stand for principles which had been lying for years beneath his practical theology. The distinction between an elect and non-elect humanity, to which the Gnostics also gave great prominence, forced him into a similar philosophical exposition of the ground on which the distinction rested. There were various ways in which the Gnostics represented the final disposition of the non-elect portion of the race. But they are one with Edwards in regarding the elect as containing in varying degrees an infusion of the divine essence which makes their salvation possible.

There is also another marked resemblance between Edwards' thought and the Gnostic theosophies. He is not only asking the same questions under similar circumstances and with substantial agreement in the answer, but he also denies that the divine love goes forth to every part of the creation. In the most emphatic manner does he assert, and reiterate the assertion, that the creation exists only for the elect portion of humanity.[1] The end of the lower creation is man, and the end of mankind is the elect, and the end of the elect is God. But he would not willingly reject the expression, however he may empty it of reality, that God loves the world. The expression is a true one, but only when we consider the creation as a system or as a whole. If we cease to consider the interests of the individual man, evidence can be found for the divine benevolence in the scheme of the universe. Or, to quote again the words of the younger Edwards, commenting on his father's achievement in this argument as another victory over the Arminians: "The declarative glory of God is the creation taken, not *distributively*, but *collectively*, as a *system* raised to a high degree of happiness."[2]

As to the question, whether the creation was an eternal necessity in the nature of the divine Being, the thought of Edwards vacillates. He argues that it is fitting and desirable that the divine activity should be manifested, and that without a creation the divine attributes would have had no exercise. The power which is sufficient for such great things, unless there had been a creation, must have been dormant and useless.[3] It is also a good thing in itself that God's glory should be

[1] Cf. *End in Creation*, pp. 211, 224, 245.
[2] *Works*, vol. i. p. 481. [3] *End of Creation*, vol. ii. p. 204.

known and rejoiced in by a glorious society of created beings. As he thinks of the church of the redeemed, he is almost tempted to feel as if it were necessary to the completion of the divine happiness, as though God would be something less than God without it. The creation may in some sense be regarded as the multiplication of the divine Being, just as the fulness of good that is in the fountain increases into the river, or as the light flows forth in abundant streams from the sun. But if expressions like these point toward creation as a necessity in God which would almost justify the doctrine of an eternal creation, yet there are other passages in which the opposite is plainly asserted. God's happiness and glory before the creation are represented as capable of receiving no addition, as if He knew Himself and rejoiced in Himself without the exercise of His powers in a continuous creation. One would have supposed that a Deity whose powers, as Edwards asserts, "lay dormant and useless as to any effect" until the creation, must at least have been an imperfect Deity, if indeed He could be conceived as having existence at all. But in this treatise on God's Last End in the Creation, no effort is made to overcome the contradiction. The deeper questions which concern the nature of being, or of personality or consciousness, are left untouched. But we hasten to add that Edwards confesses himself not entirely satisfied with his statements and conclusions. Such an admission is so rare in his writings that it arrests attention as worthy of special remark. More than once he alludes to the difficulty of the subject, the mystery which enshrouds it, the inadequacy of language to express such exalted realities. He still believes in endeavoring to discover what the voice of reason teaches upon these things; but revelation is the surest guide, and to what Scripture teaches he devotes the remainder of the treatise.

As we follow him here, it is apparent that he is still within the circle of his own reason and cannot go beyond it. He lays down the principles on which he proposes to interpret Scripture, but these principles he has first derived from reason. The result is that Scripture adds nothing to the argument: it offers only a large and varied field of illustration. He is more particularly impressed with the familiar phrase so common in the Old Testament, that God's providence in the world is manifested for His name's sake. To the study of this phrase — the *name of God* as the end of the divine activity — he devotes two sections of his treatise. But he does not get beyond the theology of the Old Testament in studying the mystery of the divine name. God's name's sake is simply His own sake, and His name is identical with His glory. There is a moment, however, when he seems to stand on the eve of a great transition. He remarks: "I might observe that the phrase *the glory of God* is sometimes manifestly used to signify the second person in the Trinity. But it is not necessary at this time to consider that matter." The point whose consideration might have relieved him from his perplexity he passes over as irrelevant. He passes over the momentous fact that while it is God's name's sake in the Old Testament, it is the name of Christ that gives significance to the new dispensation. It is strange that he should not have recalled in this connection how the prayers of the Christian church in every age had been offered in the name of Christ, till the formula had almost come to be regarded as an essential ending to all petitions. So prominent has been the name of Christ during the Christian ages that, unless there be some eternal organic unity of Christ with God which rests in the very nature of the divine Being, it would seem as if God had been robbed of His glory by One whose special mission it was to proclaim and honor Him, whose meat and drink it was to do the will of Him that sent Him.

In passing over all that the name of Christ implies as not essential to his argument, Edwards rejected the aid which would have saved him from confusion and failure. In the doctrine of the Trinity lay the resolution of the problem he was considering. If the doctrine means anything at all, it must mean everything when discussing the last end of God in the creation. It is of Christ that St. Paul remarks that *for* Him are all things, as well as *by* Him, and that *in* Him all things consist. Because Edwards did not recognize the bearings of this doctrine, he is driven to conceive the motive of God in the end of things as a selfish one. In this treatise, as in his Nature of True Virtue, the apparent effect is to glorify an infinite and celestial selfishness. It is true that God seeks His own glory, and is Himself the final end of His creation. But this truth must in some way be counterbalanced by the equally essential truth that God also exists for another, and in existing for another, and seeking the glory of another, most truly exists for self and realizes His own peculiar glory. It has been admirably remarked, as a summary of the question at issue, that the divine nature demands, in the eye of thought, either an eternal Christ or an eternal creation. Otherwise the idea of God becomes impossible. Edwards, one is forced to believe, must have come face to face with the dilemma; but again he is silent where speech was demanded. He had recoiled from deism, as if it were the negation of God. But, if we take this treatise as it stands, he cannot save himself from being wrecked on the opposite shore, — some form of pantheism, which, while seeming to honor the divine name, does so in appearance only, and equally with deism endangers the divine reality. He may have struggled to escape, though he makes no sign, as he approached the dangerous pass, the Scylla and Charybdis of all human speculation on the nature of God.

The speculative treatises at which we have been glancing were written in rapid succession, under the heavy pressure of the cares of life and amid the weakness of declining strength. Until recent years it was by these works alone that Edwards was known as a philosophical theologian. In the opinion of his literary executors, as they may be called, Dr. Samuel Hopkins and the younger Edwards, these works included his final convictions. But we have seen that in this treatise on the Last End of God in the Creation, he had struck some difficulty which he makes no attempt to solve. It is pathetic to find him bemoaning the difficulty and the mystery of his theme. He had flung himself into the infinite abyss confident that a way through the pathless void led up to God. But his later unpublished writings, as we are told, abound in confessions of a sense of the mystery of things. Had his thought, so far as he had completed it, found full expression in these four treatises we have been reviewing, it must be admitted that his work as a speculative thinker had ended in confusion, if not in failure. In all these treatises there is seen the tendency to one common conclusion, — that nothing exists but God: His existence, being infinite, must be equivalent to universal existence. By a downward movement from God, humanity as well as the whole realm of nature are swooped up by the sole activity of the one universal will. But Edwards had not attained a position in which he could rest, securely poised amid the winds and storms that agitate the atmosphere of human thought. He had come to the final question which the mind can ask regarding God and His relation to the world, and was not satisfied with the answer.

As disturbances in the motion of the spheres are said to have suggested the possibility of an undiscovered planet, and even led to the calculation of its size and place, so the perturbations of Edwards' thought point to some supreme object of interest and inquiry, of which no traces are to be found in his collected works, in regard to which his literary executors were silent, and over which his biographer has drawn a deeper veil of obscurity by seeming to give a complete survey of his career. That subject was no other than the Christian doctrine of the Trinity.

VI.

THE DOCTRINE OF THE TRINITY.

For a long time, possibly so far back as the last century, there has existed a suspicion, under whose various forms there was a common substance, that in Edwards' writings there existed a "tentative" element which did not express his final conviction. No student of Edwards' collected works can proceed very far with their examination without feeling that he wrote, at times, more for the purpose of relieving his own mind than for the edification of the reader. In his solitary life, excluded from the company of his equals, and shut out from much of the highest literature, he became accustomed, as it were, to thinking aloud, a feature of his works which does not lend to their elegance of form or to ease in their interpretation. We are also told that he was always writing, thinking with his pen in his hand, stopping by the wayside, or rising at night to record his thoughts. It is not therefore surprising to learn that, voluminous as are his collected works, he should also have left behind him a vast amount of manuscript which, according to the testimony of its curators, surpasses in extent his published writings. That these manuscripts should contain, as is asserted, a "thorough record of his intellectual life," it is easy to believe, as also that there are among them "papers of great interest and value that have never been given to the public."[1]

[1] Rev. Tryon Edwards, D. D., Introduction to *Charity and its Fruits.* Dr. Edwards further remarks: "These manuscripts have also been carefully preserved and kept together; and about three years since (1848) were committed to the editor of this work, as sole permanent trustee, by all the then surviving grandchildren." A writer in the *Independent* for 1853, to whom had been given the privilege of examining the manuscripts, speaks of finding among them a series of sermons on the Beatitudes; a work on Revelation; a Commentary on the whole Bible (904 pages), and a *Harmony of the Old and New Testaments,* which was incomplete. The outward appearance of the manuscripts illustrated the scarcity of paper and the necessity of economizing it. "He used to make rough blank-books out of odds and ends, backs of letters, scraps of notes sent in from the congregation; and there is one long parallelogram of a book made entirely out of strips from the margin of the old London *Daily Gazetteer* of 1743. There is another most curious manuscript, made out of circular scraps of paper, 147 leaves, being in the shape of half moons, intermingled with the patterns of caps and such other like remnants of housewifery." — Cf. *Living Age,* vol. xxxvi. p. 181.

In 1854 the Rev. A. B. Grosart, a Scottish divine and the accomplished editor of various publications, crossed the Atlantic for the purpose of assisting toward a complete and worthy edition of Edwards' works. The way for him having been prepared by correspondence, immediate access was given him to all the manuscripts of Edwards. He found the labor of examining them, as he remarks, " an onerous but very pleasant one," and was rewarded by the discovery of " papers of rare biographical interest and value." The treasure of the whole proved to be a Treatise on Grace, " carefully finished and prepared for the press." Mr. Grosart determined to take out of the country many of Edwards' manuscripts, including some of his letters, and in regard to these he remarks, " I possess already priceless and hitherto unknown materials for a worthy biography." From these materials in his possession he selected enough to form a volume of two hundred and nine large octavo pages. Although he did not deem himself at liberty to publish anything, there seemed " no valid objection " to printing. " In response to many frequent and urgent requests," this volume of selections was printed at Edinburgh for private circulation, and the edition was limited to three hundred copies.[1]

[1] *Selections from the Unpublished Writings of Jonathan Edwards, of America.* Edited, from the original MSS., with *facsimiles* and an Introduction, by the Rev. Alexander B. Grosart. Kinross. Three hundred copies. Printed for private circulation,

But there were other papers also of rare value, among the manuscripts of Edwards, to which Mr. Grosart makes no allusion. It was in the year 1851 that the late Dr. Bushnell called attention to a dissertation on the Trinity which Edwards was reported to have written. "I very much desired in my exposition of the Trinity to present some illustrations from a manuscript dissertation of President Edwards on that subject. Only a few months ago I first heard of the existence of such a manuscript. It was described to me as an '*à priori* argument for the Trinity, the contents of which would excite a good deal of surprise' if communicated to the public. The privilege of access to the manuscripts is denied to me, on the ground, as I understand, of the nature of the contents."[1] That Dr. Bushnell must have had authority for his statement is evident on the face of the above quotation. In an article on Edwards, contributed a few years later (about 1855) to Herzog's Real-Encyclopädie, by the late Prof. C.

1865. The remarks of Mr. Grosart above quoted are from his introduction to this volume. In addition to the "Treatise on Grace" (pp. 19-56), this volume contains "Annotations on Passages of Holy Scripture from President Edwards' Interleaved Bible" (pp. 59-179); "Directions for Judging of Persons' Experience" (pp. 183-185); and "Sermons" (pp. 189-209). Among the Sermons is the full outline of one preached to the Indians at Stockbridge in 1753, on the text, "All Scripture is given by inspiration of God," etc. A copy of this work is in the library of Harvard University. There are said to be but two copies in the country.

[1] Bushnell, *Christ in Theology*, p. vi.

E. Stowe, allusion is made to this dissertation on the Trinity, as though the writer had himself perused it, and formed his own judgment of its character. "Among the manuscripts of Edwards," he remarks, "there is one on the Trinity which is prepared with great care, and is marked by power and boldness and great independence of thought."[1]

The call of Dr. Bushnell for the publication of the dissertation on the Trinity met with no response. But whether it was owing to his call or to other causes, a fresh interest was excited in Edwards' writings. In 1852 Dr. Tryon Edwards edited from the manuscripts a work of some five hundred pages entitled Charity and its Fruits.[2]

---

[1] "Unter seinen handschriftlichen Werken ist ein sorgfältig ausgearbeitetes über die Lehre von der Trinität, das mit grosser Selbstständigkeit des Denkens, Kühnheit und Kraft der Gedanken abgefasst ist."— Herzog, *Real-Encyclopädie*, art. "Edwards."

[2] *Charity and its Fruits; or Christian Love as manifested in the Heart and Life.* By Jonathan Edwards, sometime Pastor of the church at Northampton, Mass., and President of the College of New Jersey. Edited from the original manuscripts, with an Introduction, by Tryon Edwards. New York, 1852. This work consists of a series of sermons delivered at Northampton in 1738, and presents Edwards in his most delightful aspects as a preacher. The volume possesses historical importance, and is also indirectly related to Edwards' views on the Trinity. In the second lecture is contained the important principle, which Edwards afterwards incorporated into his *Distinguishing Marks of a Work of the Spirit of God*, that the ordinary operations of God's Spirit are higher than His extraordinary gifts, such as inspiration and miracles. The fifteenth lecture is closely related to the *Treatise on Grace*, which is yet to be noticed. It is entitled "The Holy Spirit forever to be communicated to the saints in charity or love."

A new edition of Edwards' works was also projected in Scotland, to consist of about fourteen volumes. This edition was expected to remedy the fault of previous editions which had departed in some places from the text, and to contain also the more important treatises existing in manuscript. It was with reference to this project, which never was realized, that Mr. Grosart had visited this country.

In 1880 Dr. Oliver Wendell Holmes repeated the call for the " withheld " or " suppressed " dissertation on the Trinity. The suspicion in regard to its contents, at which Dr. Bushnell had hinted, had now become more definite. " The writer (Dr. Holmes) is informed on unquestionable authority that there is or was in existence a manuscript of Edwards, in which his views appear to have undergone a great change in the direction of Arianism or Sabellianism."[1] The editor of the Hartford Courant reiterated the call for publication, describing the size of the unpublished manuscript, repeating the rumor that it contained a departure from Edwards' published views on the Trinity, and adding other rumors to the effect that it contained a modification of his teaching on original sin, even approaching so far as Pelagianism. This last call brought forth a response in the shape of a small treatise entitled Observations concerning the Scripture Œconomy of the Trinity and Covenant

[1] *International Review*, July, 1880.

of Redemption.[1] The history of the manuscript is given, and the reasons why it had not been published before, among which there is seen no ground for serious hesitation on account of its alleged defection from orthodoxy. The work shows anything but a Sabellian or Arian tendency: it is rather Tritheistic, with its formal and as it were algebraic method of presenting the subject. The disappointment felt on its appearance must have been in proportion to the interest which its announcement had created. It was a relief, then, to learn that this was not the dissertation to which Dr. Bushnell had referred, and of which Professor Stowe had remarked that it was worked out with great care, and was marked by power and boldness and great independence of thought. In 1881 there appeared in the Bibliotheca Sacra two remarkable articles from one who spoke with undoubted authority.[2] These articles, for the time being, put an end to the discussion. From them

---

[1] *Observations concerning the Scripture Œconomy of the Trinity and Covenant of Redemption.* By Jonathan Edwards. With an Introduction and Appendix by Egbert C. Smyth. New York: Charles Scribner's Sons. 1880. The notes which Professor Smyth has added have great value in elucidating the text, as well as for the history of theology in New England. He has also given additional extracts, hitherto unknown, from Edwards' MSS., one of them, in particular, of the highest importance. Cf. pp. 92-97.

[2] Professor Edwards A. Park, D. D., *Bib. Sac.*, January and April, 1881. To these articles I am greatly indebted, and could not have written this chapter without them. They contain a masterly exposition of Edwards' doctrine of the Trinity.

it may be inferred that Edwards wrote a dissertation on the Trinity which justified the comments of Professor Stowe. But the manuscript has since been mislaid, and so late as 1881 had not been found. It had been read, however, several years before these articles appeared, by their writer, who had also taken notes of some parts of the argument. No one is better fitted than Professor Park to form a true judgment regarding the missing manuscript, or to report correctly as to its substantial contents. It was divided, we are told, into two parts. The first part corresponded in substance with the Observations concerning the Scripture Œconomy of the Trinity, published in 1880; the second part corresponded in substance with the third section of the Treatise on Grace, which was printed in Edinburgh, in 1865. In addition to this information, fresh material from Edwards' manuscripts is also furnished in the above-mentioned articles in the Bibliotheca Sacra, which possesses the highest value, throwing a light upon the workings of his mind, without which it would have been impossible to understand or to do justice to the labors of his later years. To these suggestive hints from his manuscripts, to the Observations on the Trinity, and to the Treatise on Grace, we now turn in the order enumerated. The doctrine of the Trinity has played so large a part in the history of religious thought in New England, that Edwards' contribution to the subject must be regarded as still possessing great significance, even though it has been unknown until recent years, and the best part of his thought is still secluded in a volume printed for private circulation, or buried in the missing manuscript.[1]

Toward the close of his life, and within perhaps four or five years of his death, Edwards became acquainted with one of the most remarkable theological works of the last century, — The Philosophical Principles of Natural and Revealed Religion, unfolded in Geometrical Order by the Chevalier Ramsay, author of the Travels of Cyrus. Glasgow, 1747.[2] From a notice which Edwards saw of

[1] Were it not for Professor Park's conjecture that the missing essay was written somewhere between 1752 and 1754, it might have been inferred from "internal evidence" that it was written after the *Nature of True Virtue* and *The Last End of God in the Creation*; i. e. some two years later (1756). The suggestion is here hazarded that, because these two dissertations needed to be adjusted to the thought contained in the missing essay, or in the *Treatise on Grace*, Edwards kept them back from the press and proceeded with his work on *Original Sin*, which was going through the press at the time of his death. No date is assigned for the *Observations on the Trinity*, or the *Treatise on Grace*. It may be assumed that they were written after 1752. It is to be noted that Edwards does not allude to any of these treatises above named, in his letter to the Trustees of Princeton College, in which he describes the books he is then projecting (1757). But he makes the significant remark, "I have also many other things in hand, in some of which I have made great progress, which I will not trouble you with an account of. *Some of these things*, if divine providence favor, *I should be willing to attempt a publication of*." — Dwight, *Life of Edwards*, p. 570.

[2] Andrew Michael Ramsay, commonly called the Chevalier Ramsay, was born in Ayr, Scotland, 1686. After studying at Edinburgh and St. Andrews he went abroad, residing mainly in France, where he died 1743. Among other positions which he held was

the work in the Monthly Review, he became aware of its significance and was desirous to purchase it. The book may have been in his possession by 1754. Its author must have been a man closely resembling Edwards in the type of his mind, — a speculative thinker aiming at a system of absolute Christian thought. But if the Chevalier Ramsay had been familiar with Edwards' books he could not have more directly opposed Edwards' methods and conclusions. His Philosophical Principles combats the theories of Berkeley and Malebranche, as tending directly toward Pantheism, which he regarded as an immoral fatalism as well as a practical atheism. Predestination, also, and the denial of freedom of the will, he condemned, tracing them to the principle that Deity was the sole efficient cause, — a principle which, as he sought to show, led back ultimately to Spinoza's doctrine of the one substance, with its two attributes of thought and extension.

Edwards does not seem to have been influenced at all by these denunciations of his favorite doctrine. But while these two minds were at the antipodes of speculation on these profound issues, they had also much in common, and at one point

that of tutor to the children of the Pretender, called James III.; and it has been thought that the doctorate conferred on him by Oxford was partly owing to his Jacobite relations His *Philosophical Principles* is hardly orthodox from the Roman Catholic stand-point, as it urges a final restoration of all souls to God. A copy of it is in the library of Harvard College, which is rich in the theological literature of the last century.

their thought tended to coalesce in a common conviction. Both had been going through a similar theological experience, in that they had recoiled from the deism of the eighteenth century, which relegated God to some remote spot outside of His creation. The Scotchman, however, had first fallen into deism, accepting its postulate of Deity as singleness of essence, and reducing religion to a reverence for and the practice of virtue. All religions, as he then thought, contained these simple ideas, but were also full of false theories and evil superstitions, with a complicated ritual which obscured the essential truth. Ramsay did not long remain in this position. Under the influence of Poiret, he encountered the fascination of French mysticism, which led him in 1710 to seek an interview with Fénelon. The story of his conversion to Roman Catholicism is told in his Life of Fénelon,[1] by whom he was convinced that there was no middle ground between deism and the Catholic faith. After his conversion, as he pursued his great inquiry regarding the nature of God, he discerned that the pantheism in which thoughtful minds were taking refuge from an impossible deism was also but a makeshift, and like deism resulted in a loss of the consciousness of the living God. It was at this point that he met Edwards, who had also arrived by a process of his own at conclusions which are closely related to Spinoza's doctrine of the one substance.

[1] *Life of François de Salignac de la Mothe Fénelon*, London, 1723, pp. 189–247.

The issue which Ramsay had confronted, and which Edwards must also have seen, even if at a distance, was no passing mood in human thought. It involves the same essential condition in which the early fathers of the Christian church had found themselves when they felt the necessity of reconciling the truth in Stoic pantheism with Jewish monotheism. If the idea of God as infinite personality was lost in Stoicism, which conceived of Deity as universally diffused, permeating the universe as all-pervading breath, equally difficult was it to find satisfaction in the deistic conception of the Jew. A Deity idle or dormant, silently reposing in Himself until he comes forth for the creation, must be a being without relationships, and therefore without consciousness. It was here that Platonism came to the rescue of embarrassed thinkers, with its idea of a Logos which bridged the gulf between pantheism and deism. Or, as transmuted by Christian thought, the true Logos was the Christ, the Son eternally generated from the Father, God's second self, in whom He saw Himself reflected, between whom and Himself there existed from eternity the activity of divine communication and love. The doctrine of eternal distinctions within the divine essence satisfied the necessity of early Christian thought, as it sought some adequate conception of God.

The following sentence from Ramsay's book had first arrested the attention of Edwards: — "The Infinite Spirit, by a necessary, immanent, eternal activity, produces in Himself His consubstantial image, equal to Himself in all His perfections, self-origination only excepted; and from both proceed a distinct, self-conscious, intelligent, active principle of love, coequal to the Father and the Son, called the Holy Ghost. This is the true definition of God in His eternal solitude, or according to His absolute essence distinct from created nature." This passage Edwards had copied from a notice in the Monthly Review, before he was yet in possession of Ramsay's work. When he had secured the book, he copied out other passages which bear upon this leading thought. Among them are the following sentences:—

"Such inactive powers as lie dormant during a whole eternity in God, are absolutely incompatible with the perfection of the divine nature, which must be infinitely, eternally, and essentially active. . . . Since God cannot be eternally active from without, He must be eternally active from within. . . . An absolutely infinite mind supposes an absolutely infinite object or idea known. . . . Hence this generation of the Logos or of God's consubstantial idea is sufficient to complete the perfection of the divine understanding. . . . Thus it is certain that, antecedent to all communicative goodness to anything external, God is good in Himself. . . . He does not, therefore, want to create innumerable myriads of finite objects to assert His essential beneficence and equity; since he produces within Himself from all eternity an infinite object that exhausts, so to speak, all His capacity of loving, beatifying and doing justice. The Deists Socinians, and Unitarians, who deny the doctrine of the

Trinity, cannot explain how God is essentially good and just, antecedently to, and independently of, the creation of finite things; for God cannot be eminently good and just where there is no object of His beneficence and equity. . . . To complete the idea of perfect felicity there must be an object loving as well as an object loved. . . . There is a far greater felicity in loving and in being loved than in loving simply. It is the mutual harmony and correspondence of two distinct beings or persons that makes the completion of love and felicity. Hence God could not have been infinitely and eternally loved if there had not been from all eternity some being distinct from Himself and equal to Himself that loves Him infinitely. The eternal, infinite, and immutable LOVE which proceeds from the idea God has of Himself is not a simple attribute, mode, or perfection of the divine mind; but a living, active, consubstantial, intelligent being or agent. . . . We may represent the divine essence under these three notions, — as an infinitely active mind that conceives; or as an infinite idea that is the object of this conception; or as an infinite love that proceeds from this idea. . . . There are three; there can be but three; and all that we can conceive of the Infinite mind may be reduced to these three: infinite LIFE, LIGHT, and LOVE. . . . These three distinctions in the Deity are neither three independent minds, . . . nor three attributes of the same substance, . . . but three coeternal, consubstantial, coördinate persons, coequal in all things, self-origination only excepted. . . . All those who are ignorant of the doctrine of the Trinity, of the generation of the Logos, of the procession of the Eternal Spirit, and of the everlasting commerce among the sacred three, look upon God's still eternity as a state of inaction or indolence."

Exactly how much Edwards may have meant by copying into his note-book passages like these from Ramsay, it is not easy to determine. At least he was interested in the thought they contained; to a certain extent it must have been new to him. How far its influence may be traced in his later writings remains to be considered. The Observations on the Scriptural Œconomy of the Trinity shows that a profound change was passing over the mind of its author in regard to the nature of the divine existence. Although, as has been remarked, this work created a sense of disappointment when it appeared, yet the disappointment is only an evidence how thought has moved since Edwards' day. Had it been published in his lifetime it might have involved him in another controversy, and that with his own household of faith. A passage like the following shows him to be aware that he is making an innovation on views which were widely prevalent: "It appears to be unreasonable to suppose, as some do, that the Sonship of the second person of the Trinity consists only in the relation He bears to the Father in His mediatorial character."[1] Edwards was contending for the Trinity as grounded in the nature of things, or in the necessity of God's

---

[1] *Observations*, etc., p. 56. The opinion which Edwards was controverting was advanced by Dr. Thomas Ridgeley in 1731. In 1792 Dr. Samuel Hopkins speaks of it "as gaining ground and spreading of late." Cf. Prof. E. C. Smyth, Appendix to *Observations*, etc., p. 91, for a list of references bearing on this point. But Edwards was also controverting his own earlier view. Cf. the passages where he alludes to the Trinity, *ante*, p. 99.

being. Although he could not have been acquainted with the process of historical theology, yet the working of his mind was leading him into the same path through the mazes of thought, which Origen and Athanasius had also followed. The way in which he was travelling was by no means a familiar one in the Calvinistic churches, and by many it was regarded with distrust or mislike. The method of Calvin had been for the most part prevalent, which waived aside the doctrine of the eternal generation of the Son as unnecessary or unprofitable, or even as "an absurd fiction."[1] Such a method as Calvin's might answer the practical needs of the church, so long as thought lay dormant, or tradition and Scripture possessed an unquestioned authority. In the eighteenth century, when the appeal was carried to the reason, the divinity of Christ was endangered by the silence of those who refused to follow the voice of reason as it pointed toward Christ as the eternal Son, without whose coequal and coeternal presence with the Father even the thought of God was becoming impossible. To maintain the divinity of Christ, as

[1] "I do not undertake," says Calvin, "to satisfy those who delight in speculative views. . . . Studying the edification of the church, I have thought it better not to touch on various topics which could have yielded little profit, while they must have needlessly burdened and fatigued the reader. For instance, what avails it to discuss, as Lombard does at length, Whether or not the Father always generates? This idea of continual generation becomes an absurd fiction from the moment it is seen that from eternity there were three persons in one God."— Calvin, *Institutes*, book i. ch. 13.

was then the custom, solely on the ground that it was essential to His making an adequate atonement for sin, was to involve the rejection of His divinity if such a theory of atonement should become obnoxious. If the Spirit of God, as popularly conceived, was but the divine energy applying the benefits of Christ's atonement, there would be no necessity for His existence as a coequal factor or distinction in the divine essence, when some different and higher view of human nature should have arisen in place of the doctrine of original sin. Such was the process by which, in the mind of the last century, the doctrine of the Trinity was undermined. Not to ground the distinctions in the divine essence by some immanent, eternal necessity was to make easy the denial of what has been called the ontological Trinity, and then the rejection of the economical Trinity was not difficult or far away.

This little treatise of Edwards, then, is far from being unimportant or commonplace. It adds to our estimate of his work as a theologian. He was stemming the theological tide instead of yielding to it. He was asserting a doctrine of the Trinity which implied its eternal necessity in the nature of God, even had there been no fall, no need of an atonement for human redemption. Had his thought been fully developed, it must have led him to the recognition of Christ as sustaining an organic relation to the world of outward nature. As Christ is the creative wisdom of God in whom

God saw Himself reflected, so the beauty and the glory of Christ is visible in the world of created things. The following exquisite passage deserves no apology for being reproduced at length. It does not belong to the Observations, but has been recently recovered from Edwards' manuscripts:—

"We have shown that the Son of God created the world for this very end, to communicate Himself in an image of His own excellency. He communicates Himself properly only to spirits, and they only are capable of being proper images of His excellency, for they only are properly *beings*, as we have shown. Yet He communicates a sort of a shadow or glimpse of His excellencies to bodies which, as we have shown, are but the shadows of beings and not real beings. He who, by His immediate influence, gives being every moment, and by His spirit actuates the world, because He inclines to communicate Himself and His excellencies, doth doubtless communicate His excellency to bodies, as far as there is any consent or analogy. And the beauty of face and sweet airs in men are not always the effect of the corresponding excellencies of mind; yet the beauties of nature are really emanations or shadows of the excellency of the Son of God.

"So that, when we are delighted with flowery meadows and gentle breezes of wind, we may consider that we see only the emanations of the sweet benevolence of Jesus Christ. When we behold the fragrant rose and lily, we see His love and purity. So the green trees and fields, and singing of birds, are the emanations of His infinite joy and benignity. The easiness and naturalness of trees and vines are shadows of His beauty and loveliness. The crystal rivers and murmuring streams are the footsteps of His favor, grace, and beauty. When we behold the light and brightness of the sun, the golden edges of an evening cloud, or the beauteous bow, we behold the adumbrations of His glory and goodness; and in the blue sky, of his mildness and gentleness. There are also many things wherein we may behold His awful majesty: in the sun in his strength, in comets, in thunder, in the hovering thunder-clouds, in ragged rocks and the brows of mountains. That beauteous light with which the world is filled in a clear day is a lively shadow of His spotless holiness, and happiness and delight in communicating Himself. And doubtless this is a reason that Christ is compared so often to those things, and called by their names, as the Sun of Righteousness, the morning-star, the rose of Sharon, and lily of the valley, the apple-tree among trees of the wood, a bundle of myrrh, a roe, or a young hart. By this we may discover the beauty of many of those metaphors and similes which to an *unphilosophical person do seem so uncouth.*

"In like manner, when we behold the beauty of man's body in its perfection, we still see like emanations of Christ's divine perfections, although they do not always flow from the mental excellencies of the person that has them. But we see the most proper image of the beauty of Christ when we see beauty in the human soul." [1]

[1] *Observations*, etc., Appendix, pp. 94-97. When this passage was written there is no means of determining without further appeal to the manuscripts. I should like to think that it belonged to Edwards' later years, and was nearly contemporaneous with his writings on the Trinity. But it may have belonged to his youth, and have been written not long after the *Notes on the Mind.* For similar expressions of thought regarding the relation of Christ to the creation, the reader may be referred to Dorner, *Person of*

This beautiful passage, which illustrates the poetic temperament of Edwards, has also its theological significance. He was reproducing the Christ of the early church, who is organically related to nature and to man, — the manifestation of the wisdom of God. But he was resuming also, though he may not have known it, the discussion of the Trinity at the point where it was dropped in ancient controversies, developing the doctrine after a manner of his own which deserves the closest attention. His Treatise on Grace, however uninteresting its title, contains perhaps his most important contribution to theological progress. Of this work Mr. Grosart, its Scotch editor, has remarked: " I shall be surprised if this treatise do not at once take rank with its kindred one on the Religious Affections. There is in it, I think, the massive argumentation of his great work on the Will, but there is in addition a fineness of spiritual insight, a holy fervor, not untinged with the pathetic frenzy of the English Mystics, as of Peter Sterry and Archbishop Leighton, and, especially toward the close, a rapturous exultation 'in the excellency and loveliness' of God ; a *glow* in iteration of the wonder, and beauty, and blessedness of Divine Love; and a splendor of assertion of the claims, so to speak, of the Holy Spirit, which it would be difficult to overestimate." The distinctive purpose

---

Christ, Eng. trans., vols. i. and ii. Cf., also, Twesten, *Vorlesungen*, vol. ii. pp. 199, ff., for an admirable statement of how the second person in the Trinity is organically related to the external world.

of this unknown work, printed only for a limited circulation, will not be exaggerated when placed in comparison with two other treatises, like it small in extent, but vast in their influence, — works which have created epochs in Christian thought and experience, — Athanasius on the Incarnation of the Word, and Anselm's *Cur Deus Homo*. The work of Athanasius reveals the import of the Nicene theology as centring in the Word made flesh, while Anselm formulated the conception of an atonement which became the controlling idea in Latin Christendom. Edwards brings out, as it had not been done before in the whole history of theology, the doctrine of the Holy Spirit — as related on the one hand to the inner mystery of the divine nature, and on the other to the spiritual life of man.

Among the characteristics of the Treatise on Grace, one of the foremost to arrest attention is the abandonment of the ethical principle laid down in the Nature of True Virtue. Edwards had there asserted in his most positive manner that virtue primarily consists in love to being in general; in the propensity, as he calls it, in the impulsion or gravitation, as it were, of the infinitely smaller fragments of being to the infinitely larger mass of being. Or, as he had there said: " True virtue primarily consists, not in love to any particular Beings because of their virtue or beauty, nor in gratitude because they love us, but in a propensity and union of heart to Being simply considered."[1] But in the Treatise on Grace he writes: "The main ground of true love to God is the excellency of His own nature." These two kinds of love Edwards had designated as the "love of benevolence" and the "love of complacence." In his dissertation on Virtue he placed love of benevolence first, as the primary ground of virtue, to which the love of complacence was secondary or subordinate. He now asserts: "Of these two, a love of complacence is first, and is the foundation of the other; *i. e.* if by a love of complacence be meant a relishing, a sweetness in the qualifications of the beloved, and a being pleased and delighted in his excellency. This in the order of nature is before benevolence, because it is the foundation and reason of it. A person must first relish that wherein the amiableness of nature consists, before he can wish well to him on account of that loveliness."[2] This passage is bracketed, as it stands in the manuscript, — an indication, it may be, that Edwards was aware of the contradiction, or wished to give the subject fuller consideration. But not to speculate on his purpose in bracketing the passage, or as to what would have been his final conclusion, it is more important to observe the openness of his mind at an age when most men have fixed their conclusions beyond the possibility of change. He seems to be exemplifying here the resolution of his youth, that he will be impartial

---

[1] *Nature of True Virtue*, vol. ii. p. 264.
[2] Grosart, *Selections*, etc., p. 47.

in hearing and receiving what is rational, how long soever he may have been used to another method of thinking. As to how this extraordinary contradiction is to be accounted for, only a word of suggestion can be offered. The necessities of the controversy against the Arminians, the desire to find a basis for virtue which would include the natural man, the non-elect as well as the elect, forced him to take one view; when he wrote apart from this necessity, he was irresistibly impelled toward the other. The contradiction reaches down to the depths of Edwards' theology. It conceals an intimation that the distinction between elect and non-elect was not defensible in the last analysis of his thought, without some sacrifice of essential truth, which he was unwilling to make. The probability is that on this point we must leave Edwards in his self-contradiction, as his only method of maintaining his fundamental tenet.

It is a leading feature of the Treatise on Grace that it identifies grace with the indwelling God in the soul. As one reads Edwards' glowing words on this subject, the mind travels back through sacramental theologies to the time when the "doctrines of grace," as they are called, were first formulated in the Latin church of the fifth century. In the earlier and higher thought of the fathers before the time of Augustine, a personal Christ or the indwelling divine wisdom had been the formula which represented the power of God unto salvation. But when an "impersonal grace" was substituted for the personal life of God in the soul, sacramental agencies were placed foremost as the channels through which an occult spiritual influence was imparted. "Grace" remained a word undefined, despite the various meanings assigned to it, through the Middle Ages and on through the Reformation age. The word "grace" plays a large part in Edwards' theology. But it was impossible that he should be content without attempting its definition. In his conception of grace he has made another important contribution to the advancement of theology which is not included among the so-called "improvements" in which the younger Edwards[1] has summarized his father's work. To Edwards belongs the honor of reasserting the indwelling and personal life of God in the soul, in place of the substitutes which men had devised. His own words on this point, contained in his unpublished Treatise on Grace, are too emphatic and impressive to be omitted : —

"The doctrine of a gracious nature being by the immediate influence of the Spirit, is not only taught in the Scriptures, but is irrefragable to Reason. Indeed, there seems to be a strong disposition in men to disbelieve and oppose the doctrine of immediate influence of the Spirit of God in the hearts of men, or to diminish and make it as small and remote a matter as possible, and put it as far out of sight as may be. Whereas, it seems to me, true virtue and holiness would naturally

[1] Remarks on the Improvements made in Theology, by President Edwards, *Works*, vol. i. pp. 481-492.

excite a prejudice (if I may so say) in favor of such a doctrine; and that the soul, when in the most excellent frame and the most lively exercise of virtue, — love to God and delight in Him, — would naturally and unavoidably think of God as kindly communicating Himself to him, and holding communion with him, as though he did, as it were, see God smiling on him, giving to him, and conversing with him; and that if he did not so think of God, but on the contrary should conceive that there was no immediate communication between God and him, it would tend greatly to quell his holy motions of soul, and be an exceeding damage to his pleasure.

"No good reason can be given why men should have such an inward disposition to deny any immediate communication between God and the creature, or to make as little of it as possible. 'T is a strange disposition that men have to thrust God out of the world, or to put Him as far out of sight as they can, and to have in no respect immediately and sensibly to do with Him. Therefore so many schemes have been drawn to exclude or extenuate, or remove at a great distance, any influence of the Divine Being in the hearts of men, such as the scheme of the Pelagians, the Socinians, etc. And therefore these doctrines are so much ridiculed that ascribe much to the immediate influence of the Spirit, and called enthusiasm, fanaticism, whimsey, and distraction; but no mortal can tell for what."[1]

It is another feature of the Treatise on Grace that it supplements the deficiencies pointed out in the Last End of God in the Creation. The conception of Deity there presented was closely akin

[1] Grosart, *Selections*, etc., p. 40.

to the Sabellian monad, who dwelt in silence and inactivity until He came forth for the creation. But the doctrine of eternal distinctions within the divine essence, of a spiritual fellowship from all eternity between the Father and the Son whose mutual bond is the Holy Spirit, is now presented in such an eloquent way, with such deep conviction, as to leave no doubt that it formed an essential element in Edwards' thought. That it does not, however, appear in his earlier works, has already been noticed. He was silent, as has been shown,[1] when he should have spoken, as in his sermon on Justification, where he declines to define too closely the organic relationship of the believer with Christ. But the omission is now remedied. "Herein lies the mystery of the vital union that is between Christ and the soul of a believer, which orthodox divines speak so much of, — that is, His Spirit is actually united to the faculties of their souls. . . . And thus it is that the saints are said to live, yet not they, but Christ, lives in them. The very promise of spiritual life in their souls is no other than the spirit of Christ Himself. So that they live by His life as much as the members of the body live by the life of the Lord, and as much as the branches live by the life of the root and stock. 'Because I live ye shall live also.' We are dead, but our life is hid with Christ in God."[2]

It is characteristic still further of the Treatise

---

[1] Cf. *ante*, pp. 97, ff.
[2] Grosart, *Selections*, p. 54.

on Grace, that it aims to win a place for the Holy Spirit, not only in the economy of redemption but also in the nature of Godhead, which shall be coequal with that of the Father and the Son. In the Miltonic descriptions of the councils in heaven, where God the Father is represented as deliberating or making covenant with the Son in regard to the deliverance of man, the Divine Spirit finds no equal footing of honor and dignity. So, also, in the ancient church, the work of the Spirit had been left undefined at the Nicene Council, nor did the ensuing discussion of the subject possess the same general or enduring interest as the controversy over the equality of the Son with the Father.[1] And those who still approach this exalted theme can more readily see the force of the reasoning which demands an Eternal Son, while they experience difficulty in formulating the position which the Spirit holds in the mystery of the Godhead or in the redemption of man. The two largest divisions of the Catholic Church are still and have long been separated by a subtle, it seems to some an almost incomprehensible, distinction in regard to the procession of the Holy Spirit. Edwards was conscious that on this subject his mind was moving in advance of the popular thought: "If we suppose no more than used to be supposed about the Holy

---

[1] "The doctrine of the Holy Ghost," says Dr. Schaff, "was not in any respect so accurately developed in this period as the doctrine concerning Christ, and it shows many gaps." — *Hist. of the Chris. Ch.*, vol. iii. p. 666. The remark might be extended to cover the later periods of Christian history.

Ghost, the honor of the Holy Ghost in the work of Redemption is not equal in any sense to the Father's and the Son's."[1]

How, then, did he meet the difficulty? The answer may be given in a brief analysis of the Treatise on Grace. In the first place, grace is made identical with charity or divine love. This love is not merely exerted toward men, but rather primarily and mainly toward God. Love is the essence of Christianity. When love shall be free from all mixtures which accompany or disfigure its earthly state, it will stand forth in its exaltation as the charity which never faileth. Love is so essential that all religion is but hypocrisy and a vain show without it. From it and comprehended in it are all good dispositions and duties. The love to God is not distinct from the love to man; they are one and the same principle flowing forth toward different objects. But how shall this divine love be defined, seeing that "things of this nature are not properly capable of a definition, they are better felt than defined"? But the love which has God for its object may be described, if not defined: it is the soul's relish of the supreme excellency of the Divine nature, inclining the heart to God as the chief good. The saving grace in the soul, which radically and summarily consists in divine love, " comes into existence in the soul by the power of God in the influences of the Holy Spirit, the Third Person in the Blessed Trinity." But the Scripture

[1] Grosart, *Selections*, p. 51.

speaks of this holy and divine love in the soul as not only from the Spirit, but as being in itself spiritual. It is not called spiritual because it has its seat in the spirit of man as contrasted with his body. It is called spiritual because of its relation to the Spirit of God.

At this point Edwards makes the transition which brings him rapidly to the climax of his thought. That love within the soul which constitutes saving grace is not merely a result wrought by the influence of the Spirit, it is not merely an attribute of the divine character, but it is an infinite personality; it is in itself nothing less than the very essence of the Spirit of God. Of the Holy Spirit it must be affirmed that in some peculiar sense He is love, even as it cannot be predicated of the Father and the Son. It is true that the Godhead, or the entire Divine essence, is said to be love. *God is love, and he that dwelleth in love dwelleth in God and God in him;* and yet it is added, *Hereby we know that we dwell in Him because He hath given us of His Spirit.* Edwards is careful to insist that the basis of his position is a Scriptural one. "In an inquiry of this nature, I would go no further than I think the Scripture plainly goes before me. The Word of God certainly should be our rule in matters so much above reason and our own notions." And this appears to him to be the teaching of Scripture, that love is the Holy Spirit and the Holy Spirit is love. Love is not an attribute of God, but it is God, — an infinite and vital energy which is most truly conceived as personal. Because it indwells in man, it makes him the temple of the Holy Ghost. "Scripture leads us to this conclusion, though it be infinitely above us to conceive how it should be." Just as wisdom or Λόγος is spoken of as the Son of God, after the same manner is love called the Spirit of God. It is said of the Word or Wisdom of God: "Then was I with Him as one brought up with Him, and I was daily His delight, rejoicing alway before Him." Or again, in the Prologue of the Fourth Gospel: "In the beginning was the Logos (or Word), and the Logos was with God, and Logos was God." Just as the fathers in the ancient church had asserted of reason, however or wherever it might be manifested, that it was no human quality casually exerted, but evidence of the indwelling of the divine reason which is God, so Edwards now speaks of the Spirit. It is the common mode of speech to say that God is love. It indicates some profound change in the basis of thought when the expression is reversed and it is said that love is God. But to such a mode of thinking Edwards had come. And now the qualifications of his earlier writings tend to disappear as he expounds his conviction that Love, in some peculiar sense, is an infinite person. Life, and Light, and Love, — these are God. It makes the spiritual nature of man throb as with the pulsations of eternity to know that the action of God upon the soul is no impartation of power from without, but the presence of the divinity within. In this process the highest place is assigned to the personal indwelling Spirit. When it is said that the Father and the Son love and delight in each other, so that there is perfect and intimate union between them, it must be understood that the bond of this felicity is the Holy Spirit.

"The Holy Spirit does in some ineffable and inconceivable manner proceed and is breathed forth from the Father and the Son, by the Divine essence being wholly poured and flowing out in that infinitely intense, holy, and pure love and delight that continually and unchangeably breathe forth from the Father and the Son, primarily toward each other and secondarily toward the creature, and so flowing forth in a different subsistence or person in a manner to us utterly inexplicable and inconceivable, and that this is that person poured forth into the hearts of angels and saints. Hence it is to be accounted for that, though we often read in Scripture of the Father loving the Son and the Son loving the Father, yet we never once read either of the Father or the Son loving the Holy Spirit and the Spirit loving either of them. It is because the Holy Spirit is the Divine Love, the love of the Father and the Son. Hence also it is to be accounted for, that we very often read of the love both of the Father and the Son to men, and particularly their love to the saints; but we never read of the Holy Ghost loving them, for the Holy Ghost is that love of God and Christ that is breathed forth primarily toward each other, and flows out secondarily toward the creature. . . . He is the Deity wholly breathed forth in infinite, substantial, intelligent love, . . . and so standing forth a distinct personal subsistence." [1]

Three inferences are deduced by Edwards from his exposition of the nature and office of the Holy Spirit. In the first place, he believed that he had vindicated the coequality of the Spirit with the Father and the Son, as against a prevailing theological tendency which subordinated or obscured His true function. But now, wonderful as is the love of God manifested by the Father in that He so loved the world as to send His Son, wonderful as is the love of the Son in that He so loved the world as to give Himself, yet these manifestations of divine love are followed by a third and higher display of love, for the Holy Spirit is the Love itself of the Father and the Son. "So that, however wonderful the love of the Father and the Son appear to be, so much the more glory belongs to the Holy Spirit in whom subsists that wonderful and excellent love."

In the second place, it is now seen what is meant by man's becoming a partaker of the Divine nature. Phrases like this as they occur in Scripture, or similar expressions of his own, abound in Edwards' writings. But they are generally accompanied with qualifications, such as "as if" or "as it were," — indications that Edwards hesitated about committing himself in language which might seem to imply the identification of the human with the divine. But as the need of these qualifications has

[1] Grosart, *Selections*, etc., p. 47.

disappeared in consequence of the ethical conception of the Spirit as the inmost essence of God, so Edwards' language tends toward positive, unqualified assertion. The Holy Spirit is the fulness of the Godhead, the *summum* of all good. "Because this Spirit which is the fulness of God consists in the love of God and Christ, therefore we by knowing the love of Christ are said to be filled with all the fulness of God." When we are told that the saints are made partakers of the Divine nature, we are to understand that "they are not only partakers of a nature that may in some sense be called divine because it is conformed to the nature of God, but the very Deity does in some sense dwell in them." They partake of the holiness wherewith God is holy. Hence the reality of the language of Christ appears when He prays that the "Love wherewith Thou hast loved Me may be in them and I in them."

And in the third place, Edwards disputes the customary language which speaks of a principle or habit of grace. He does not like such language: it seems in some respects to carry with it a wrong idea, because it does not, as it were, personalize the divine love in ever-fresh and creative divine activity. To speak of a habit of grace is to reduce grace to an attribute or quality, or to make it a consequence of some previous divine action. And so once more the Berkeleyan principle, in the extreme form in which Edwards held it, reappears in perhaps its strongest expression : —

"The giving one gracious discovery or act of grace, or a thousand, has no proper natural tendency to cause an abiding habit of grace for the future, nor any otherwise than by divine constitution and covenant. But all succeeding acts of grace must be as immediately, and to all intents and purposes, as much from the immediate acting of the Spirit of God upon the soul as the first; and if God should take away His spirit out of the soul, all habits and acts of grace would of themselves cease, as light ceases in a room when the candle is carried out. And no man has a habit of grace dwelling in him any otherwise than as he has the Holy Spirit dwelling in him in His temple, and acting in union with his natural faculties, after the manner of a vital principle. So that, when they act grace, 't is, in the language of the apostle, 'not they but Christ living in them.' "[1]

The substance of the missing essay, as we are assured on the best authority, is given in these two treatises, — Observations on the Trinity, and the Treatise on Grace. We are therefore in a position to judge whether Edwards' thought contained a departure from received views in the Puritan churches, as also how it stands related to the larger thought of the church in every age. That there is a departure, and a significant one, needs no further demonstration. The missing essay plainly justifies the comment already quoted, that it was worked out with great care, and was marked by great boldness and independence of thought. No student of Edwards' works can help noticing the

[1] Grosart, p. 55.

difference in his tone in these treatises under review as compared with his other works. It seems like listening to an interlude in his thought, or as if he had wandered for a moment in distant and unfamiliar fields, and were in danger of forgetting his old haunts, of not returning again to the principles by which his name is known in theology. It need scarcely be said that his view of the Trinity is not Arian or Sabellian, nor does it show any leaning to Pelagianism. He was reproducing to a certain extent what is known as the Nicene or Athanasian theology, whose affiliations, if they had been followed out to their legitimate conclusions, would have led him far away from the tenets of Augustine or Calvin. Dr. Bushnell was not far from the truth when he spoke of the missing essay as containing an *à priori* argument for the doctrine of the Trinity. The stages in the history of the doctrine of the Trinity have been briefly and accurately summarized as, in the early church, a doctrine of reason; in the Middle Ages a mystery, in the eighteenth century a meaningless or irrational dogma; and again, in the nineteenth century, a doctrine of the reason, a truth essential to the nature of God. In an age when there existed a widespread tendency to reject the doctrine as irrational, and when those who held it betrayed the influence of their environment by avoiding thought upon the subject as dangerous, or taking refuge in Scripture as the only sure foundation for its support, Edwards appears as anticipating that feature of modern theology which finds in the doctrine of the Trinity the essence of the Christian faith, as well as the formula for the interpretation of Christian experience.

But if Edwards appears as tending toward the Nicene theology, or even as carrying its development to a higher result in the doctrine of the Holy Ghost, till his statement approximates the Hegelian principle of the life of the Spirit, yet one essential aspect of that theology he not only failed to grasp, but, it may be, he sternly and to the very last rejected. We read in his Treatise on Grace how the Spirit, which is the mutual love of the Father and the Son, takes up His abode in human souls, and how this love is no mere attribute or quality infused from without, but a divine personality within. Why could he not also have maintained, as ancient fathers had done, as Justin Martyr had so eloquently taught, that the Logos or Divine Reason also indwelt in humanity, so that mankind was constituted in Christ, and shared with Him in the consubstantial image of the Father? If love may indwell as a personal force in the soul, why not also the Divine Reason, — the light that lighteth every man that cometh into the world? What is there in man with which the Spirit may fitly associate if it be not this potential image of the Son? Upon what can the Spirit fasten in humanity unless it be this divine principle in the soul, which, deeper and stronger than the evil in every man, binds the soul to Christ as its organic head? It was not that Edwards failed to see this truth, that he did not receive it. As we turn over again the discolored pages of that ancient periodical, the Monthly Review, for the year 1750–51, in which he first met the Christian philosophy of Ramsay, we seem to be brought into closer contact with Edwards' mind. There were passages, over which we may imagine him as bending in serious contemplation, which yet he does not seem to have copied into his note-book. There is one in particular which reads as follows: —

"The consubstantial Logos united Himself also from the beginning to a finite nature composed of soul and body, that so he might converse with created intelligences in a sensible manner; be their conductor and guide, their model and high priest; lead them into the central depth of the Divinity, and from thence into all the immense region of nature; show them by turns the beauties of the original and the pictures; and teach them the homage finite beings owe to the Infinite."

In that exquisite quotation from Edwards' manuscript given above,[1] where he speaks of outward nature reflecting the beauty of Christ, he comes very near speaking of humanity as if it also reflected the same glorious beauty. But when he reaches the point where we await this confession, he turns aside, unwilling to admit that man as man has any relationship with the Son of God, unless it may be in the lower beauty and grace of the human body. Outward nature may reflect Christ's

[1] Cf. *ante*, p. 355.

glory, but as yet humanity does not. Or, in his own language: "From hence it is evident that man is in a fallen state, and that he has scarcely anything of those sweet graces which are an image of those which are in Christ. For no doubt, seeing that other creatures have an image of them, according to their capacity, so also the rational and intelligent part of the world once had according to theirs."

And so from the consideration of this high theme of the Christian Trinity Edwards turned away to his exposition of the doctrine of original sin. It has already been suggested [1] that he contemplated such a work as a supplement to his Freedom of the Will. He may have been only following out an earlier purpose, when he turned from the mystery of the divine nature to the process by which humanity had been deprived of its birthright. But the transition may have also another significance. It looks as if he were not altogether satisfied with any of these later dissertations, — on Virtue, the End of the Creation, on Grace, or the Trinity. He may have retained them for revision, or in order to recast their shape, before giving them to the world. He may also have felt that the development of his later thought regarding the nature of God, if fully carried out, would lead to results incompatible with those doctrines to whose advocacy he had devoted his life; or that he was standing on safer grounds when dealing

[1] Cf. *ante*, pp. 298, 299.

with humanity in its ruined state than when exploring the inner mystery of the being of God. However it may be, there were grave deficiencies in his dissertations on Virtue and on the End of the Creation, and the same remark applies to his exposition of the Trinity. His thought upon this subject cannot have been a mere episode in his mental history, — there is too much in his earlier writings which points in this direction. But his treatment of the doctrine of the Trinity, great as is its beauty and value in some respects, still remains incomplete. He does not emphasize the Eternal Sonship of Christ, nor does this truth find anywhere in his works an adequate exposition. His thought revolved around God in His sovereignty, or the Holy Spirit who sanctifieth all the people of God. In the Sonship of Christ is involved humanity with its interests and destiny. But as humanity in itself and as a whole possessed no importance in his eyes, so Christ, who is its head, fills no conspicuous place in his theology. The truth of the Incarnation was weakened, if not neutralized, by the tenets of original sin and predestination.

CONCLUSION.

EDWARDS' short residence at Stockbridge is in beautiful contrast with the fever and tumult which marked the last years at Northampton. He speaks of himself as finding " both pleasure and profit" in the performance of tasks congenial to his mind. His worldly affairs were also falling again into comfortable order after the troubles and damage which his removal had cost him. But while he was absorbed in his work, he seems as if oblivious to the flight of years. He was a living illustration of the words, with which no one could have been more familiar, "Of making many books there is no end, and much study is a weariness of the flesh." His life had been one of prolonged and intense exertion, of that kind also which drains the strength of the vital faculties. He ought to have had many years yet before him. His father, his mother, his grandparents, had lived to an advanced old age. But he had inherited a delicate, nervous constitution, unequal to the strain to which it had been subjected. Several times he had been brought low with illness, which had interrupted his work. But notwithstanding these warnings that his health had begun to decline, he continued to write his books, and the more he wrote "the more and wider the field opened before him." In his secluded home he was almost buried to the world. The great movement of life, with its "rushing strain and stir of existence, the immense and magic spell of human affairs," was shut out from his view. But had it swept by his very door, it would have had no charm to him. From his youth he had sacrificed the life that now is, in the conviction that the life which is most real is to come hereafter.

> "He threw on God
> (He loves the burthen)
> God's task to make the heavenly period
> Perfect the earthen."

He had yielded himself to the search for God as the only reality: and while he was still eagerly following the search,—

> "This high man,
> With a great thing to pursue,
> Dies ere he knows it."

In the last year of his life he received a call to become the president of Princeton College. The call was unexpected, and must have reached him at the same time as the tidings of the death of President Burr. He had now attained the age of fifty-three, being the elder of his son-in-law by only thirteen years. In a very interesting letter to the trustees, he opened his mind freely in regard to his fitness for the position. Among the obstacles in his way, he mentions the difficulty of finding a purchaser for his estate at Stockbridge, the expense of removing his numerous family, the burden which the proper support of such an office would entail. He also enters into particulars regarding his constitution, remarking that it is a peculiarly unhappy one; that he is troubled by "a low tide of spirits, often occasioning a kind of childish weakness and contemptibleness of speech and behavior, with a disagreeable dulness, much unfitting me for conversation, but more especially for the government of a college." He admits a deficiency in some branches of learning, as in the higher mathemathics and the Greek classics. Nor would he care to spend his time in teaching languages, unless it be Hebrew, in order to improve himself while instructing others.

But the chief cause which induced hesitation and even reluctance in accepting the extended honor was his devotion to his studies, his unwillingness to put himself where he should be incapable of pursuing them, as would be the case if he were to undertake the office of president as Mr. Burr had conceived and fulfilled it. Among the projects before him, there were still points of dispute with the Arminians which he wished to consider. But the thing which interested him most was a "great work" which it lay on his heart and mind to write, — a History of Redemption. It was to be "a body of divinity in an entire new method, being thrown into the form of a history." It was to begin and end with eternity, all great events and epochs in time being viewed *sub specie eternitatis*. The three worlds — heaven, earth, and hell — were to be the scenes of this grand drama. It was to include also the topics of theology, as living factors each in its own place, but so that " every divine doctrine will appear to the greatest advantage, in the brightest light, in the most striking manner, showing the admirable contexture and harmony of the whole." [1] It was to combine poetry and history, philosophy and theology, the features of the Divine Comedy, or the Paradise Lost and Regained, with those of Augustine's City of God. There is no evidence that this was more than a splendid dream which excited Edwards' imagination. He lacked the necessary learning for such a task. More than any other which he had undertaken, did it call for requisites not at his command. We know, however, what its leading characteristic would have been had he lived to complete it. Unlike Gibbon's great picture, there would have been no effort to trace the operation of second causes. The human element, the mysterious currents and counter-currents in human history, the great works which men have done, — all this would have been passed over as unworthy of attention. History would have appeared as alive with a divine force, — the impulse of an immediate divine presence. Everything would have centred in the accomplishment of redemption, the mystery which angels desire to look into. There would

[1] Dwight, *Life of Edwards*, p. 570.

have been no sharp distinction between the creative act and a divine providence following in its wake. God's providence would be only another name for a continuous creation. As all things were *from* God, so all things tend *to* God in their conclusion and final issue.[1]

The call to Princeton was accepted, notwithstanding an unfeigned reluctance on Edwards' part to abandon a retirement so fruitful in results, so full of promise for the future. A council was called, according to the custom of the Congregational churches, which, having listened to a presentation of the case, decided that it was his duty to take the presidency of the college. When this decision was announced, it is said that Edwards fell into tears, a thing unusual for him in the presence of others. Leaving his family behind him, he set out for Princeton in the month of January, 1758. There he was awaited by his daughter Esther, in the freshness of her great sorrow, and by another daughter, Lucy, who remained unmarried. Hardly had he reached his destination when he learned of the death of his aged father. For several successive Sundays he preached in the college hall, but the

---

[1] Cf. *History of Redemption*, pp. 556. This treatise of Edwards is composed of a series of sermons preached in 1739. It may be taken as the first rough draft of his projected work, and as indicating his method. It was first published in Edinburgh, 1777. It has been one of the most widely read of Edwards' writings, as if it had taken the place with his readers which his *magnum opus* was intended to fill. It adds little, however, to Edwards' thought beyond what has been already given.

only work which he undertook as president was to give out "questions in divinity" to the senior class. When the students came to meet him with their answers, he is said to have impressed them all with satisfaction and with wonder. As a preacher also he appeared full of interest and power, as he had done in the early years of his ministry.

At the time when Edwards reached Princeton the community were in a state of alarm over the spread of the small-pox in the village and its vicinity. As Edwards had not had the disease, the situation seemed to justify in his case the preventive treatment known as inoculation, in the hope of preserving a life so dear and valuable. The objections to the practice had grown weaker in the course of years; it was also said to have been attended with good results under the skilful direction of the physicians at Princeton. Edwards himself proposed its trial, and the corporation of the college consented. He was inoculated on the 13th of February, and so successfully that for a while it was believed that the danger in his case was over. But the hope was a delusive one, and the end was near. As he lay dying, aware that his time was short, his thoughts reverted to the children who were to be fatherless, and more particularly to the absent wife in the distant home at Stockbridge. "Tell her," he said to his daughter, who took down his words, "that the uncommon union which has so long subsisted between us has been of such a nature as I trust is spiritual, and therefore will continue forever." After this, when he seemed insensible and those around him were already lamenting his departure, he spoke once more: "Trust in God and ye need not fear." His death took place on the 22d of March, 1758, in the fifty-fifth year of his age. Only sixteen days afterwards his daughter Esther followed him out of the world. Nor did Mrs. Edwards long survive. In September of the same year, she died at Philadelphia, where she had gone by way of Princeton to assume the charge of her infant grandchildren. In the graveyard at Princeton they rest together who were lovely and pleasant in their lives, and in their deaths were not divided.

The letters which passed among the sorrowing members of the family, beginning with the death of Mr. Burr, are still preserved. They are filled with utterances of resignation to the will of God, but beneath these expressions of religious faith there is seen the intensity of human feeling and of deep, unspeakable anguish. The devotion of human souls to each other is there, though veiled beneath a deep reserve. They had been schooled to an almost Stoical repression of the natural emotions. They had dissevered their ideal from earth as too vast and exalted to be realized in this lower sphere. Their eyes were fastened upon a revelation of heaven to the world. Even when he was a boy working out the theory of the outward world as ideal or immaterial, Edwards had noted, as if with a feeling of triumph, that such a doctrine did not disturb the conception of heaven as the place where God resides. Later in life he again expressed himself in similar fashion : —

"God considered with respect to His essence is everywhere : He fills both heaven and earth. But yet He is said in some respects to be more especially in some places than in others. . . . Heaven is His dwelling-place above all other places in the universe; and all those places in which He was said to dwell of old, were but types of this. Heaven is a part of His creation that God has built for this end, to be the place of His glorious presence; and here He will dwell and gloriously manifest Himself to all eternity.

"All the truly great and good, all the pure and holy and excellent from this world, and it may be from every part of the universe, are constantly tending toward heaven. As the streams tend to the ocean, so all these are tending to the great ocean of infinite purity and bliss." [1]

Over the grave of Edwards the trustees of the college erected a marble monument, with a Latin inscription which speaks of him as second to no mortal man, who as a theologian has scarce had his equal. Other eulogies might be mentioned which seem to vie with each other in expressing the highest admiration which it is lawful to utter. "From the days of Plato," says a writer in the Westminster Review, "there has been no life of more simple and imposing grandeur than that of Jonathan Edwards." "I regard him," said Robert

[1] *Charity and its Fruits*, pp. 467, 474.

Hall, who knew him only by his books, "as the greatest of the sons of men." An eminent Puritan divine, who had seen his face when illumined with the divine communion, remarked that "he was accustomed to look upon him as belonging to some superior race of beings." "I have long esteemed him," said Dr. Chalmers, "as the greatest of theologians, combining in a degree that is quite unexampled the profoundly intellectual with the devotedly spiritual and sacred, and realizing in his own person a most rare yet most beautiful harmony between the simplicity of the Christian pastor on the one hand, and on the other all the strength and prowess of a giant in philosophy."[1] Edwards lived in an age when such impressions could be more easily produced than in our own, when the life was less complex, and the individual could play a larger rôle. Among the great names in America of the last century, the only other which competes in celebrity with his own is that of Benjamin Franklin, who labored for this world as assiduously as Edwards for another world. The memorial window in Edwards' honor in the chapel

[1] In contrast with these testimonies is the judgment of President Stiles, of Yale College, who had a reputation in his day for learning and polite culture, as well as a gift for discerning the foibles of his contemporaries. President Stiles condemned Edwards to oblivion. In his Diary for August 7, 1787, he wrote: "When posterity occasionally comes across his writings in the rubbish of libraries, the rare characters who may read and be pleased with them will be looked upon as singular and whimsical as in these days are admirers of Suarez, Aquinas, or Dion. Areopagita."

of Yale College, where he had studied and taught, contains an inscription revealing the secret of the homage which men have agreed to render, even though differing as widely as heaven from earth about the theology which is identified with his name. "*Ionathan Edwards summi in ecclesia ordinis vates fuit, rerum sacrum philosophus qui sæculorum admirationem movet, Dei cultor mystice amantissimus.*" There was in him something of the seer or prophet who beholds by direct vision what others know only by report. We may apply to him his own words: there was in him "a divine and supernatural light," which is seen but rarely among the generations that come and go. When such a light appears, it does not shine for a moment only or for a few: it casts its beams to a distance, illuminating the ages. He was like a star, says a recent writer, throwing its light afar off, — *ein weithin leuchtendes Gestirn.*

The divine revelation, as it came through him as its vehicle, was associated with much that was untrue. If we can make allowance for the human equation in his teaching, for the reasoning which however solid or true was based upon false premises, if we can look at the negative side of his theology as the local and transitory element of his time, there will then remain an imperishable element which points to the reality of the divine existence, and of the revelation of God to the world, as no external evidence can do. Indeed, it is only by exposing what was false or distorted in his theology that the real man stands forth in the grandeur of his proportions. It is impossible to allude here to his influence upon the later history of religious life and thought in New England. If the sketch which has been given of his work be true, he did not do for the old theology what he attempted or desired. It was his aim to rationalize it, but at every point, under his transcendental touch, it threatened to expand into something very unlike the original. He has had his children according to the letter of his teaching; but those who have also protested most loudly against his errors may be also his children after the spirit. Among these may be counted the late Mr. Maurice, who was at one with Edwards in that which constitutes his essential quality as a prophet, after all that is unworthy has been eliminated from his message. How deeply Maurice recognized his worth may be seen from the following estimate, given in his History of Philosophy : —

"In his own country he retains and always must retain a great power. We should imagine that all American theology and philosophy, whatever changes it may undergo, with whatever foreign elements it may be associated, must be cast in his mould. New Englanders who try to substitute Berkeley, or Butler, or Malebranche, or Cardillac, or Kant, or Hegel for Edwards, or to form their minds upon any of them, must be forcing themselves into an unnatural position, and must suffer from the effort. On the contrary, if they accept the starting-point of their native teacher and seriously consider what is necessary to make that teacher consistent with himself, — what is necessary that the divine foundation upon which he wished to build may not be too weak and narrow for any human or social life to rest upon it, — we should expect great and fruitful results from their inquiries to the land which they must care for most, and therefore to mankind."

The great wrong which Edwards did, which haunts us as an evil dream throughout his writings, was to assert God at the expense of humanity. Where man should be, there is only a fearful void. The protests which he has evoked have proclaimed the divineness of human nature, the actuality of the redemption in Christ for all the world. Only in the intense light which he threw could the necessity for these protests have been so clearly perceived. But those who have made them are more closely related to him in spirit than they are aware or may be willing to admit. It is not too much to say that he is the forerunner of the later New England transcendentalism quite as truly as the author of a modified Calvinism. All who accept the truth, that divine things are known to be divine because humanity is endowed with the gift of direct vision into divinity, are accepting what Edwards proclaimed, what constitutes the positive feature of his theology. There are those who have made the transition from the old Calvinism, through the mediation of this principle, to a larger theology as if by a natural process. Among these typical thinkers were Thomas Erskine, McLeod

Campbell, and Bishop Ewing, in Scotland, or the late Mr. Maurice in England. These and such as these, in whom the God-consciousness is supreme, are the true continuators of the work of Jonathan Edwards.

BIBLIOGRAPHY.

The first edition of Edwards' works was published in Worcester, Mass., in 8 vols., 1809; afterwards republished in 4 vols. It is still in print, the plates being owned, it is said, by Carter Bros., New York. Dr. Dwight's edition was published in New York in 1829, in 10 vols., the first volume being occupied with the life. There is a London edition in 8 vols. by Williams, 1817; vols. 9 and 10 supplementary by Ogle, Edinburgh, 1847. Another London edition in 2 vols., bearing the imprint of Bohn, is still in print, and though cumbrous in form is in many respects excellent. It possesses the only portrait of Edwards which answers to one's idea of the man.

Articles on Edwards may be found in the collections of Allibone, Duyckinck, Griswold, Richardson, and Sprague. The references in Ueberweg's *His. Phil. Am. Tr.*, and Hagenbach's *His. Doc.*, are valuable. The following list embraces some of the more important contributions elucidating the thought of Edwards or bearing witness to its influence.

Atwater, L. H., *Edwards and the New Divinity*, Princ. Rev., 30, 58.

Bancroft, George, Art. in *Appleton's Amer. Cyc.*, 1st ed., also *His. of the U. S.*, vols. iii. and iv.

Campbell, J. McLeod, on *The Nature of the Atonement*.

Chalmers, Thomas, *Christian and Civic Economy of Large Towns*, Works, i. 318-322.

Channing, W. H., *Edwards and the Revivalists*, Chris. Exam., 43, 74.

Edwards, Tryon, *Review of Charity and its Fruits*, New Eng., 10, 222: contains an account of Edwards' MSS.

Fisher, G. P., *Discussions in History and Philosophy*, pp. 227-252, and *His. of the Chris. Ch.*, chap. viii.

Frazer, A. C., *Berkeley* in Blackwood's Philosophical Classics, pp. 138–141, also in edition of Berkeley's Works.

Gillett, E. H., on *Edwards' Dismissal from Northampton*, His. Mag., 11, 333.

Godwin, W., *Inquiry concerning Political Justice*, vol. i. 301. Am. ed. Philadelphia, 1796.

Grosart, A. B., Introd. to *Selections from the Unpublished Writings of Edwards*.

Hall, Robert, *Works*. Bohn ed., p. 284.

Hazard, Roland G., *Review of Edwards on the Will*.

Hodge, Charles, *Bib. Rep.* and *Princeton Rev.*, v. 30, p. 585, claims Edwards for the old theology of the Westminster Confession.

Holmes, O. W., in *Sketches and Reminiscences of the Radical Club*, pp. 362–375, and *Internat. Rev.*, July, 1880.

Hopkins, Samuel, *Memoir of Edwards*, — a work which has the quaint charm of Walton's Lives.

Huxley, T. F., Art. *Edwards*, Encyc. Brit., 9th ed.

Lyon, G., *L'Idéalisme en Angleterre au XVIIIe Siècle*, pp. 406–439.

Mackintosh, J., *Progress of Ethical Philosophy*, Philadelphia, 1834, p. 108.

Magoun, G. F., *Edwards as a Reformer*, Cong. Qu., 11, 259.

Maurice, F. D., *His. of Mod. Phil.*, pp. 469–475.

Miller, Samuel, *Life of Edwards*, vol. viii., Sparks' *Am. Biog.*

Osgood, Samuel, *Studies in Christian Biography*, pp. 348–377.

Park, E. A., *Edwards' Doctrine of the Trinity*, Bib. Sac., Jan. and Apr. 1881; Articles in Bib. Sac. defending Edwards against the claims of Presbyterianism; *The Atonement*, etc.; allusions to in *Memoirs* of Hopkins and Emmons.

Parton, J., *Life of Aaron Burr*.

Porter, Noah, *Edwards' Peculiarity as a Theologian*, New Eng., 18, 737. *Historical Discourse*, on Bp. Berkeley, 1885.

Rogers, Henry, Introduction to Bohn ed. of Edwards' Works.

Smith, H. B., allusions to, in *Faith and Philosophy*; also *His. of the Church*, in *Chronological Tables*.

Smyth, E. C., Appendix to Edwards' *Observations concerning the Trinity*.

Stephen, Leslie, Essay on, in *Hours in a Library*, ii. pp. 44–106.

Stewart, Dugald, *Dissertation on the Progress of Philosophy*, p. 203, ed. 1820.

Stowe, C. E., Art. *Edwards* in Herzog's *Real-Encyclopädie*.

Strong, A. H., on the influence of Edwards on the "New Theology," in *Philosophy and Religion*, p. 167, with other allusions, also, in his *Systematic Theology*.

Tarbox, I. N., *Edwards and the Half-way Covenant*, and *Edwards as a Man*, New Eng., vol. 43.

Taylor, Isaac, Introduction to his ed. of Edwards on *The Will*.

Thompson, J. P., on Edwards' theology, Bib. Sac., 18, 809.

Tracy, J., *His. of the Revival in the Time of Edwards and Whitefield*.

Trumbull, *His. of Conn.*

Tyler, M. C., *His. of Am. Lit.*

Uhden, *The New England Theocracy*, chap. ix.

Woolsey, T., *Historical Discourse*, 1870, at the reunion of the Edwards' family.

INDEX.

ADAM, effects of his fall, 72, 101, 103, 304; lacked freedom, in the sense of power to the contrary, 304; personality of, 305; every man identical with, 308-310.

Alexander, J. W., describes effect of Edwards' preaching, 128, note.

Anselm, Edwards' resemblance to, 81; his doctrine of atonement, 89; on freedom of the will, 301.

Arminianism, Edwards' opposition to, 58, 81, 82, 94, 103, 106, 221, 228, 282, 328; its view of freedom, 111, 282, 301; in the revival, 182; conception of the action of the Holy Spirit, 206 ff; makes the happiness of the creature the end of the creation, 328.

Asceticism, Traces of, in Diary, 32, 33.

Athanasius, his theology, 353, 372; on the Incarnation, 358.

Atonement, the doctrine of, wanting in Mohammedanism, 88; Edwards' conception of, 90-92, 146, 352.

Augustine, his idea of God, 20, 297; abandonment of philosophy, 21; conception of God, 37; celibate ideal of, 44; on predestination, 64; on freedom, 73; connection with monasticism, 163; idea of the church, 269; on real freedom as related to necessity, 301; on grace, 360.

Baptism, Edwards' view of, 265; difference of opinion in regard to, 266, 268.

Beardsley, E. E., on the influence of Berkeleyism at Yale College, 16.

Berkeley, Edwards' coincidence with, 14; whether Edwards had read his writings, 15; relation of, to Johnson, 16; how he differs from Edwards, 17, note; later relation of Edwards to the philosophy of, 60, 61, 110, 308, 309; Edwards' modification of the principle of, 134, 308, 371; combated by Ramsay, 347.

Boston, Edwards' sermon at, on Dependence, 55.

Brainerd, David, first meeting with Edwards, 243; becomes an inmate of Edwards' house, 245; quotation from Edwards on his religious life, 321.

Buddhism, essential principle of, contrasted with Edwards' ruling idea of being, 7.

Burr, Aaron, intercedes for Brainerd, 244; marriage with Esther Edwards, 276; death, 378.

Burr, Aaron, grandson of Edwards, 277.

Bushnell, Dr. Horace, calls attention to Edwards' unpublished essay on the Trinity, 341, 344, 372.

Butler, Bishop, 111, 187.

Calvin, on predestination, 64; denial of human freedom, 73; view of Scripture, 135; his doctrine of the Holy Spirit, 135; his consistency in holding to his denial of the freedom of the will, 294, 295; freedom in necessity, 301; quoted on the Trinity, 353.

Calvinism, contradiction in, 79; old and new schools of, 80; objections urged against, 86; the opposite extreme from Romanism, 114; its doctrine of the Holy Spirit, 135; its idea of God, 291.

Campbell, J. McLeod, indebtedness to Edwards on the Atonement, 91.

Chalmers, Dr. Thomas, his admiration for Edwards, 46, 385; his opinion of the Freedom of the Will, 285.

Chauncy, Charles, opposes the revival, 181, 208, 209.

Christ, relation of believers to, 96-100; tendency to denial of His divinity, 98; relation of, to the creation, 99,

103, 355, 356; the mystical or spiritual, 190, 234; God as existing for, 336.

Church and State, readjustment of their relation called for, 55; Wycliffe's view of their relation, 55; Edwards' attitude on, 56, 254, 269.

Clap, Rev. Mr., Rector of Yale College, 180, 280.

Coleridge, conception of miracle, 66; on the freedom of the will, 300.

Collins, John Anthony, his doctrine of freedom and necessity resembles Edwards' view, 288, note.

Congregationalism, Edwards the father of the modern form of, 270; his strictness on its polity, 271, 272.

Conscience, does not belong in the sphere of the supernatural, 66, 323, 324.

Conversion, hints relating to, in Diary, etc., 35, 36; nature of, in Edwards' case, 37, 38; foundation of Edwards' doctrine of, 134; process of, described, 144; tragic element in, 144, 148; realization of dependence on God, 146; uncertainty of divine love, 148; joyful experience following after the legal phase of, 149; physical accompaniments of, 154, 164, 167; relation of, to morality, 155 ff, 231; signs of, 221-225; results of the acceptance of the idea of, 251, 264, 265.

Cutler, and others, secession of, to Episcopal church, 24.

Deism, Edwards' relation to, 58, 336.

Dwight, S. E., Life of Edwards, 6, note; arrangement of the Notes on the Mind, 11; opinion in regard to Edwards' knowledge of Berkeley, 15, 16; on Mrs. Edwards' portrait, 45.

Edwards, Esther, her marriage to Rev. Aaron Burr, 276, 277; died at Princeton, 383.

Edwards, Jonathan, birth, ancestry, 1; his father, 2; his mother, 2, 3; character as a child, 3; enters Yale College, 4; his manuscript notes, 4; influence of Locke, 5; Notes on the Mind, 5, 282, 288, 314; the theological element predominant, 6; on the nature of excellence, 6; his fundamental principle contrasted with Buddhism, 7; relation of greatness of God to His excellence, 9; genial outlook of his youth, 10, 11; resemblance to Spinoza and Malebranche, 12; transition to philosophic idealism, 13; coincidence in his thought with Berkeley, 1, 4; explanation of this coincidence, 15-20; pushes the doctrine of idealism beyond Berkeley, 18; Spinoza and Augustine, the poles of his thought, 21; early religious impressions, 22; residence at New Haven after graduation, in charge of a Presbyterian church in New York, tutor at Yale, 23; Diary and Resolutions, 24 ff; mystic raptures, 25; moral ideal, 27 ff; spiritual ambition, 30; ascetic tendency, 32; early view of the freedom of the will, 33; sense of sin, not deep in early experience, 34; references to conversion, in Diary, etc., 35; uncertainty as to his own conversion, 36; repugnance to Calvinistic doctrine of sovereignty, 37; the intellectual revolution, 37, 38; ordination at Northampton, 39; personal appearance, 41; methods as a student and preacher, 42, 43; his description of his wife while a young girl, 46; his marriage, 47; domestic life, 48, 49; advantage to, from association with Mr. Stoddard, 51; reverses the principle of Wycliffe regarding church and state, 56, 254; preaches the public lecture in Boston, 56; opposes Arminianism, 58; asserts the divine sovereignty, 59-64; conception of the supernatural, 65, 66; sermon on Supernatural Light, 67, 229; how he modified the earlier Calvinism, 80; defends the doctrine of endless punishment, 82-87; accepts the Anselmic doctrine of atonement, 89; suggests a possible departure from Anselm, 91; his sermon on Justification by Faith, 92-96; refuses to define the *unio mystica*, 97, 100; description of, as a preacher, 104, 105; sermon on the Importance of a knowledge of Divine Faith, 106-108; sermon on Pressing into the Kingdom of God, 109; his method of appealing to the will, 110; his imprecatory sermons, 116; preaches at Enfield, 127-129; continuation of his personal narrative, 130; sense of his own sinfulness, 131; his preaching leads to the first revival at Northampton, 133; Narrative of Surprising Conversions, 138-159; studying the phases of the revival, 143; as a religious director, 149, 151; attaches practical importance to morality, 156; how he regarded the first revival, 161; describes the

Great Awakening at Northampton, 161 ff; Distinguishing Marks of a Work of the Spirit of God, 162; approves of the physical manifestations of the revival, 164, 167, 193, 221; resists impulses and impressions, 170, 203-209; asserts importance of theological culture in the ministry, 175, 211; condemns censoriousness, 174, 216; publishes his Thoughts on the Revival, 183; defends the revival, 184-195; approves the new method of preaching, 188; his method in the case of children, 191; statement of his wife's experience, 198-202; discusses the question of itinerant preachers and lay exhorters, 209-212; asserts necessity of church order, 213; publishes Religious Affections, 218; treats of signs of conversion, 221; in what the reality of the spiritual life consists, 223; publishes Union in Prayer, 232; gives a picture of his time, 238, 239; condemns the prevailing idea of the coming of Antichrist, 240; condemns the Christian Year, 241; desires more frequent celebrations of the Lord's Supper, 242; his meeting with David Brainerd, 243; his dismissal from Northampton, 248-272; effect of his teaching on relation between church and state, 254; opposes the Half-way Covenant, 258, 270; involved in a case of discipline at Northampton, 259; his treatise on the Qualifications of Full Communion, 260, 263, 268; preaches his farewell sermon, 262; controversy on the nature of the church, in reply to Williams, 268, 269; becomes the father of modern Congregationalism, 270; his strictures on its church polity, 271; his removal to Stockbridge, 273; his controversy with Williams, 274; receives an apology from Major Hawley, 275; his relation to the Indians at Stockbridge, 278-281; writes the Freedom of the Will, 281; the treatise makes a literary sensation, 283; marks the culmination of a reaction, 284; testimony of its admirers, 285, 286; possesses historical importance, 287; ambiguity in his use of the word "choice," 288; his agreement with the physical school, 288, 289; assumes the thing to be proved, 289; depends chiefly on the religious argument, 290, 291; the popular inference from Edwards' argument, 292, 293; how he discriminated his position from that of the necessitarians, 293-296; his definition of freedom, 294, 295; how regarded by Calvin, 295; significance of Edwards' distinction in later New England thought, 296; denies that God possesses freedom in the sense of power to the contrary, 297; defects of treatise on the Will, 299; religious aspect of denial of freedom, 301; wrote his treatise on Original Sin, 303, 313; its connection with his work on the Will, 303; denies the self-determining power of the will in the case of Adam, 304; makes God the author of sin, 305; defends the doctrine of original sin by a metaphysical argument on the nature of identity, 308-310; natural deduction from his premises, 310; unethical conception of sin, 311; the fallacy in Edwards' argument, 312; treatise on the Nature of True Virtue, 313-327; reproduces his early speculations on the nature of excellence, 314; reverence for being, as the fundamental ethical principle, 315; defect of this principle, 316, 317; the love of God for his moral excellence, 318; difficulties in the interpretation of his thought, 319, 320; his teaching compared with that of Spinoza, 320, 321; how he differs from Spinoza, 322; virtue consists in the conscious love of God, 323; action of the natural conscience, 324; modern reaction against Edwards' principle of ethics, 326; his treatise on the End of God in the Creation, 327-338; defines God as a supremely happy being, 328; how God's supreme love for Himself is reconciled with His love for the creature, 329, 330; traces of Gnosticism in his thought, 331; the creation exists for the elect, 332; whether the creation is eternal, 333; on the phrase "God's name's sake," 334; neglects significance of the name of Christ, 335; his speculations result in confusion and sense of failure, 337; on the doctrine of the Trinity, 338-376; his peculiarity as a thinker, 338; voluminousness of his manuscripts, 339, 340; call for his unpublished essay on the Trinity, 341-344; reads Ramsay's Philosophical Principles, 347 ff; why he was attracted to Ramsay, 348; his observations on

398   INDEX.

the Scriptural Œconomy of the Trinity, 352–354; approximates the Athanasian statement of the Trinity, 353; the excellency of Christ seen in the creation, 355; his Treatise on Grace, 357–372; Mr. Grosart's estimate of, 357; abandons the ethical principle of Treatise on Virtue, 358, 359; contradiction in his theology, 360; identifies grace with the indwelling Spirit, 360, 361; place and office of the Spirit in the fellowship of the Trinity and in human redemption, 364, 365; the Spirit defined as love, 366–368; coequality of the Spirit with the Father and the Son, 369; participation in the divine nature, 370; disputes the language which speaks of a habit of grace, 371; the missing essay on the Trinity, neither Arian or Sabellian, but Athanasian, 372; defect in Edwards' doctrine of the Trinity, 373–375; decline of his health, 377; call to Princeton, 378; letter to the trustees of the college, 379; proposed to write a History of Redemption, 380; departure for Princeton, 381; his death, 383; testimonies to Edwards as a man and a theologian, 384–386; the imperishable element in his teaching, Maurice's estimate of, 387; the evil element in his theology, 388; his relation to modern theologians, 389.

Edwards, Jonathan, the Younger, compared with his father, 277; summary of "improvements in theology" made by his father, 284, 332, 361; as literary executor of his father, 337.

Edwards, Sarah Pierrepont, her ancestry, beauty, character, etc., 45; description of by her future husband, 46; marriage to Edwards, 47; management of her family, 48, 49; her place in the revival, 197–203; admired by the Indians at Stockbridge, 279; died at Philadelphia, 383.

Edwards, Timothy, sketch of, 1, 2; revivals in his parish, 137; death, 382.

Edwards, Tryon, 339, 342.

Emerson, R. W., Edwards' affinity with, 68; aphorisms of, on evil and punishment, 84, note.

Endless punishment, 77, 78; tendency to denial of, 81; Edwards' mode of defending, 83, 84; annihilation or restoration, etc., no equivalents for, 121; method in preaching, 121–124;

the great majority of men will suffer, 125.

Enfield, Edwards' sermon at, 42, 127, 218.

Episcopal Church, secession to of Cutler, Johnson, and others, 24; how regarded by Edwards, 31; affinity of Mr. Stoddard with, 50; its worship, 241; doctrine of baptism, 268.

Erskine, Dr. John, correspondence with Edwards, 273, 293.

Erskine, Thomas, of Linlathen, 273, 389.

Fisher, Prof. George P., D. D., opinion that Edwards had read Berkeley, 15, 16, note; on the resemblance between Collins and Edwards, 288.

Franklin, Benjamin, 386.

Frazer, A. C., on Edwards' indebtedness to Berkeley, 15.

Gnosticism in Edwards' thought, 331.

God (see Sovereignty), Edwards' consciousness of, 6, 22, 25, 26; excellence of, 8, 314, 318; greatness of, as the ground of His excellence, 9, 315; as the one substance, 12, 21, 60; relation of to the external world, 13, 14, 20, 309; immanence of, 58, 64, 362; providence of, 33, 34; conceived as will, 59; moral government of, 78 ff; justice of, 79, 84, 85, 120, 124, 147.

Goethe, the principle of disinterested virtue, 321.

Grace, identified with divine efficiency, 64; special and common distinguished, 65–75; Edwards' treatise on, 357–372; not impersonal, 360, 361; not a habit, but the continuous influence of the Spirit, 371.

Great Awakening, extent of, 161; Edwards' account of, 162; abuses of, 163, 169, 170, 177, 188, 203 ff; opposition to, 181; Edwards' defence of, 164, 184; physical accompaniments of, 154, 164, 167, 193–196; Mrs. Edwards' place in, 197–203; decline of, 218, 234; summary of the results of, 249–256.

Grosart, Rev. A. B., results of examination of Edwards' manuscripts, 340, 341; estimate of Edwards' Treatise on Grace, 357.

Half-way Covenant, weakened the church, 55; Edwards' dislike to, 230, 257; original purpose of, 55, 257, 266; rejection of, 270.

Hall, Rev. Robert, criticism of Ed-

wards' ethical principle, 316; estimate of Edwards' character, 385.
Harvard College, Timothy Edwards, graduate of, 1; pronounces against the revival, 181; library of, 347.
Hazard, Rowland G., comment on Edwards' Freedom of the Will, 286.
Heaven, as a locality, 384.
Hobbes, Thomas, his doctrine of necessity, 288.
Holmes, Dr. O. W., calls for Edwards' Essay on the Trinity, 343.
Holy Spirit, importance assigned to, in Calvinistic churches, 135; immediate influence of, 152, 177, 204 ff, 224, 360, 361; as causing physical manifestations, 167, 193; does not inspire impulses and impressions, 203–209; identified with grace, 361, 362, 371; defined as love, 365; co-equality of, with the Father and the Son, 369.
Hooker, Thomas, 45.
Hopkins, Dr. Samuel, on the attractiveness of Mrs. Edwards, 45; uncertain of his conversion, 231; opposition to slavery, 250; inferences from Edwards' doctrine of Virtue, 320, 321; Edwards' literary executor, 337; on the Trinity, 352, note.
Hume, David, law of association, 6; on causation, 288, 289.
Hutchinson, History of Massachusetts, quoted on the importance of the elders, 39; belief that the moral decline in the churches was exaggerated, 54.

Impulses and impressions, 171, 203.
Incarnation, subordinated to Atonement, 89, 99; dependent on divine sovereignty, 100; significance of, 317, 318.
Indians, The, their opinion of Mr. Stoddard, 40; in Stockbridge, 278; Edwards' relations to, 279.
Inspiration, as direct insight, 12, 70, 71; the gift of, inferior to saving grace, 172, 173, 205.
Irving, Edward, 174.
Itinerant preachers, 179, 209–211.

Johnson, Rev. Samuel, D. D., acquaintance with Berkeley, relation to Edwards, 16.
Justification by faith, Edwards' modification of, 93.

Kames, Lord, his interpretation of Edwards on the Will, 293, 295.

Lecky, W. E. H., comment on Edwards' treatise on Original Sin, 312.
Locke, John, influence on Edwards, 5; his principle that ideas are derived from sensation, 13; his conception of substance, 13; Edwards' dependence on, 61.
Lord's Supper, The, regarded as a converting ordinance, 50, 51, 257, 258; Edwards desires its weekly celebration, 242; Edwards' opposition to the practice of admitting unconverted persons to, 258, 259, 263, 267.
Luther, religious experience of, compared with that of Edwards, 24, 34; his doctrine of justification, 95; dislike of the Zwickau prophets, 178; conception of freedom, 301.
Lyon, Georges, suggestion that Edwards may be indebted to Malebranche, 17; he suggests the possibility of a later date for Notes on the Mind, 17; *Idéalisme*, 225, note.

Mackintosh, Sir James, 285.
Malebranche, Edwards' approximation to, 12; suggestion that Edwards had read, 17.
Mather, Dr. Increase, in controversy with Rev. Solomon Stoddard, 258.
Maurice, Rev. F. D., quoted, 315, 387, 389.
Methodism, indebted to Puritanism, 136; how it differed from Puritanism, 212.
Mill, J. S., on causation, 6, note; on necessity, 289.
Milton, John, 76, 219, 364.
Miracles, Edwards' conception of, 65, 66, 70, 229.
Mohammedanism, its conception of God's sovereignty, 88.
Mysticism, marks of, 25; combination with dialects, 81.

Nature, communion with God through, 132; reflecting the beauty and glory of Christ, 355, 356.
New England, ascetic element in the people of, 32; conversion as known in its early history, 36; change in the constitution of its churches, 56; intellectual element in religion of, 106; conscious self-direction of the will, in its religious life, 112.
Norris, John, Theory of an ideal world, 17, note.
Northampton, settlement of, 39; character of the people of, 40; importance of the church of, 41; connection with Boston, 43; church of,

congratulated, 57; excitement over Arminianism, 82; revival in 1735, 133; Edwards' description of the people of, 138, 139; why the revival may have begun there, 140; deterioration in the revival, 179; peculiar case of discipline at, 259; action of the town at the time of Edwards' dismissal, 261; movement to establish there another church, 273.

Original Sin, its enormity, 73, 74; interpreted as total depravity, 85, note; as extending to children, 74; Edwards' treatise on, 298, 299, 302; God the author of, 305; the doctrine of, defended by the metaphysical argument of the nature of identity, 308-310.

Pantheism, forms of, 119; heretical expressions of, condemned, 224; danger of, in Edwards' thought, 336; Ramsay's opposition to, 348; contrasted with deism, 349.

Park, Dr. Edwards A., 344 note; on Edwards' Essay on the Trinity, 345, 346.

Plato, Edwards' agreement with his idea of God, 12, 37; conception of knowledge, 106; influence of, in early church, 349.

Porter, Professor Noah, D. D., explains Edwards' relation to Berkeley, 15, note.

Prayer, subjective doctrine of, 236.

Predestination, 62-64; effects upon, of the belief in conversion, 251.

Presbyterianism, revival of the spirit of, 136; discipline of, 182; compared with Methodism, 212; Edwards on its form of church government, 271.

Puritanism (see Calvinism), the atmosphere of Edwards' youth, 6, 22; Edwards' acceptance of, 38; severity of, 45; ideal of a minister's wife, 47; in relation to the Lord's Supper, 50, 242; experiment of the theocracy, religious decline, 53, 254, 256; its creed endangered, 55; necessity of reaffirming the principle of, in order to a reform of its discipline, 56; its doctrine of divine sovereignty, 79; conditions of church membership, 135; weakened by the results of the Great Awakening, 182, 209; its parochial organization, 209, 210; its sensitiveness in regard to modes of worship, 241; its doctrine of relation between church and state, 253 ff; rejection of the sacramental principle, 263; Edwards' relation to the early New England type of, 269, 270.

Quakerism, Edwards' prejudice against, 70; Puritan dread of, 178, 267; how Edwards differs from as to external rites, 242; relation to slavery, 250.

Ramsay, Chevalier, his Philosophical Principles, 346-351; quotations from, 350, 351.

Religious Affections, Edwards' treatise on, 218-232; quotation from, on sorrow after conversion, 35; intimates Edwards' dislike to Half-way Covenant, 258.

Responsibility, 62, 293.

Revelation, Edwards' early idea of as immediate, 12; considered as light, 68.

Revival at Northampton, 133-136; previous movements of a similar kind, 137; how the revival began, 140; effects of, 142; successive stages of, 144 ff; physical manifestations of, 154; taking the covenant, 156; results in large admissions to the church, 158; subsidence of, 159, abnormal tendency in, 159.

Royce, J., Religion of Philosophy, 88, note.

Sandeman, asserts the principle of inactivity, 115.

Saybrook Platform, connection with of Mrs. Edwards' father, 45; effort to enforce the principles of, 182.

Schleiermacher, his sermons on dependence, 57; idea of the miraculous, 66.

Scotland, Edwards' influence in, 91, 134, 162; memorial from, 232, 233; Edwards' correspondents in, 271, 273; reception of his Freedom of the Will in, 293.

Scripture, study of, 29, 43, 108; Calvin's view of, 135.

Sin (see Original Sin), no pervading sense of, in early experience, 34; extent and enormity of, 73; relation of, to punishment, 85; origin of, 87, 88; unpardonable, 113; unethical conception of, 311.

Smyth, Prof. E. C., 344, 352, note.

Sovereignty of God, Edwards' early repugnance to, 37; ignored by Arminianism, 58; Edwards' assertion of, 59, 60, 297; relation of, to God's moral government, 79, 81, 87;

connection with Justification by Faith, 96; how it affected Edwards' preaching, 115; in Edwards' later experience, 131; in the religious experience of the revival, 149; contradiction of, in Freedom of the Will, by attributing necessity to God, 297.

Spinoza, resemblance to Edwards, 12, 21, 37, 57, 317, 348; the *Ethica* of, 320–322.

Stiles, Dr. Ezra, his estimate of Edwards as a tutor at Yale, 23; opinion of Edwards' writings, 385.

Stoddard, Solomon, Timothy Edwards married a daughter of, 2; virtues of, reflected in the daughter, 3; character of, 39, 40; his death, 50; his theology, etc., 51; revivals in his time, 137; condition of Northampton after death of, 139; his modification of the Half-way Covenant, 257, 263.

Stoicism, 349, 383.

Stowe, Prof. C. E., 342.

Taylor, Isaac, 285.

Taylor, Dr. John, Examination of the Doctrine of Original Sin, 306, 311.

Tillotson, Archbishop, 98.

Tracy, J., Description of the Great Awakening, 161, 181.

Transcendentalism, in Edwards' thought, 68.

Trinity, the doctrine of, 338; Edwards' first statement of, 10; subordinated to the atonement, 89, 99; tendency to the denial of, 81, 98; Edwards' essay on, 341 ff; Ramsay's statement of, 350, 351; necessity of eternal distinctions in the Godhead, 352–354; fellowship of the Father and the Son in the Spirit, 363, 368.

Tyler, M. C., on Edwards' relation to Berkeley, 15.

Virtue, Nature of, early theory of, 6–11; treatise on, 313–327; contradiction in Edwards' views of, 358, 359.

Wedgwood, Miss, on Wesley's indebtedness to Edwards, 134, note; on Wesley's methods, 171.

Wesley, Charles, 171.

Wesley, John, reads Edwards' Narrative, etc., 134, note; belief in regard to impressions, 171; edits Edwards' Thoughts on the Revival, 203; sanction of lay preaching, 212; rejected the distinction between elect and non-elect, 251.

Westminster Confession, Edwards willing to subscribe the substance of, 271; his departure from, in regard to Adam's freedom, 304.

Whitefield, his sermons, 42; description of Edwards' household, 49; belief in impulses and impressions, 170, 171, note; introduces confusion into New England churches, 180, note, 210.

Will, The, Edwards' earlier view of, 33; God conceived as, 59; denial of the freedom of, 62, 73, 110, 111; freedom of, in God, 62, 297; as addressed by Edwards in preaching, 109; conscious self-direction of, 112; Edwards' conception of freedom of, 111, 294, 295, 303; consequences of the denial of the freedom of, 73, 112, 116, 117, 294, 295; no unconscious growth of, 148; Edwards' treatise on, 281–301.

Williams, Rev. Solomon, replies to Edwards' Qualifications, 264; Edwards' rejoinder to, 268, 279, 280.

Witchcraft delusion, impossible a generation earlier or later, 53.

Wycliffe, on church and state, 56, 256.

Yale College, inchoate condition of, 4; Berkeley's philosophy in, 16; relation of to the revival, 181; refuses degree to Brainerd, 243–245; memorial window to Edwards in chapel of, 386.

The Jonathan Edwards Center at Yale University

http://edwards.yale.edu

The mission of the Jonathan Edwards Center and The Works of Jonathan Edwards Online is to produce a comprehensive online archive of Edwards's writings and publications that will serve the needs of researchers and readers of Edwards, to support inquiry into his life, writings, and legacy by providing resources and assistance, and to encourage critical appraisal of the historical importance and contemporary relevance of America's premier theologian.

Contact us at:

http://edwards.yale.edu

Jonathan Edwards Center at Yale University
409 Prospect Street
New Haven, CT 06511

Tel: 203.432.5340
Email: edwards@yale.edu

www.ingramcontent.com/pod-product-compliance
Lightning Source LLC
Chambersburg PA
CBHW071436300426
44114CB00013B/1461